Praise for *Wealth Woman* . . .

"The history of the Klondike, even today, is nearly always told as a tourist-friendly myth about brave pioneers, stoic Indians, and gold nuggets as big as your fist. The author casts this tired and clichéd paradigm aside in favor of a nuanced account that includes the perspectives of indigenous peoples (while never romanticizing them). An excellent example of the New Western History that seeks to recover previously marginalized voices of women, among other groups."

—Ross Coen, author *of Fu-go: The Curious History of Japan's Balloon Bomb Attack on America* and *Breaking Ice for Arctic Oil*

"In the spirit of Howard Zinn's classic, *A People's History of the United States*, this book teaches and inspires, and no doubt will challenge historians and general readers alike to rethink their heroes. The writing is well-researched, strong, and so lyrical that I read many paragraphs a second time for the sheer pleasure of it."

—Kim Heacox, author of *Jimmy Bluefeather* and *The Only Kayak*

"Deb Vanasse's incredible research and poignant writing reveal the complex story behind the tragedy and the glory of Kate Carmack's life. Her vivid scenes of Tagish Indian life before, during, and after the discovery at Bonanza Creek offer an important contribution to the history of the Klondike discovery and its impact on the North."

—Claire Rudolf Murphy, author of *Gold Rush Women*

"This story is well-known by descendants of Kate Carmack who have passed it on orally in the Yukon Territory for more than a century. Deb Vanasse adds new dimensions from written records that document Kate's experiences in the years following the Klondike gold rush."

—Julie Cruikshank, author of *The Social Life of Stories* and *Life Lived Like a Story*, in collaboration with Angela Sidney, Kitty Smith, & Annie Neal

"With this deeply researched and richly imagined biography, Deb Vanasse draws one of the Klondike's most essential yet elusive characters from the wings and restores her to her rightful place."

—Frances Backhouse, author of *Women of the Klondike* and *Children of the Klondike*

WEALTH WOMAN

WEALTH WOMAN

Kate Carmack and the Klondike Race for Gold

DEB VANASSE

UNIVERSITY OF ALASKA PRESS
Fairbanks

Published by
University of Alaska Press
P.O. Box 756240
Fairbanks, AK 99775-6240

Electronic cover by Cyrusfiction
Print cover by UA Press
Interior design by Publishers' Design and Production Services

Front cover photo: Kate Carmack. (Yukon Archives, James Albert Johnson fonds, 82/341, #21)

Library of Congress Cataloging-in-Publication Data

Names: Vanasse, Deb.
Title: Wealth Woman : Kate Carmack and the Klondike race for gold / by Deb
Vanasse.
Description: Fairbanks, Alaska : University of Alaska Press, 2016. | Includes
bibliographical references and index.
Identifiers: LCCN 2015022637 | ISBN 9781602232778 (paper : acid-free paper)
Subjects: LCSH: Carmack, Kate, approximately 1862-1920. | Klondike River
Valley (Yukon)—Gold discoveries. | Alaska—Gold discoveries. | Frontier
and pioneer life—Yukon—Klondike River Valley. | Women
pioneers—Yukon—Klondike River Valley—Biography. | Tagish
Indians—Yukon—Klondike River Valley—Biography. | Klondike River Valley
(Yukon)—Biography. | Carmack, Kate, approximately
1862–1920—Travel—Pacific Coast (U.S.)
Classification: LCC F1095.K5 V365 2016 | DDC 971.9/102092—dc23
LC record available at http://lccn.loc.gov/2015022637

Support for this publication was provided by the Terris and Katrina Moore Endowment.

To the Carcross-Tagish First Nation

CONTENTS

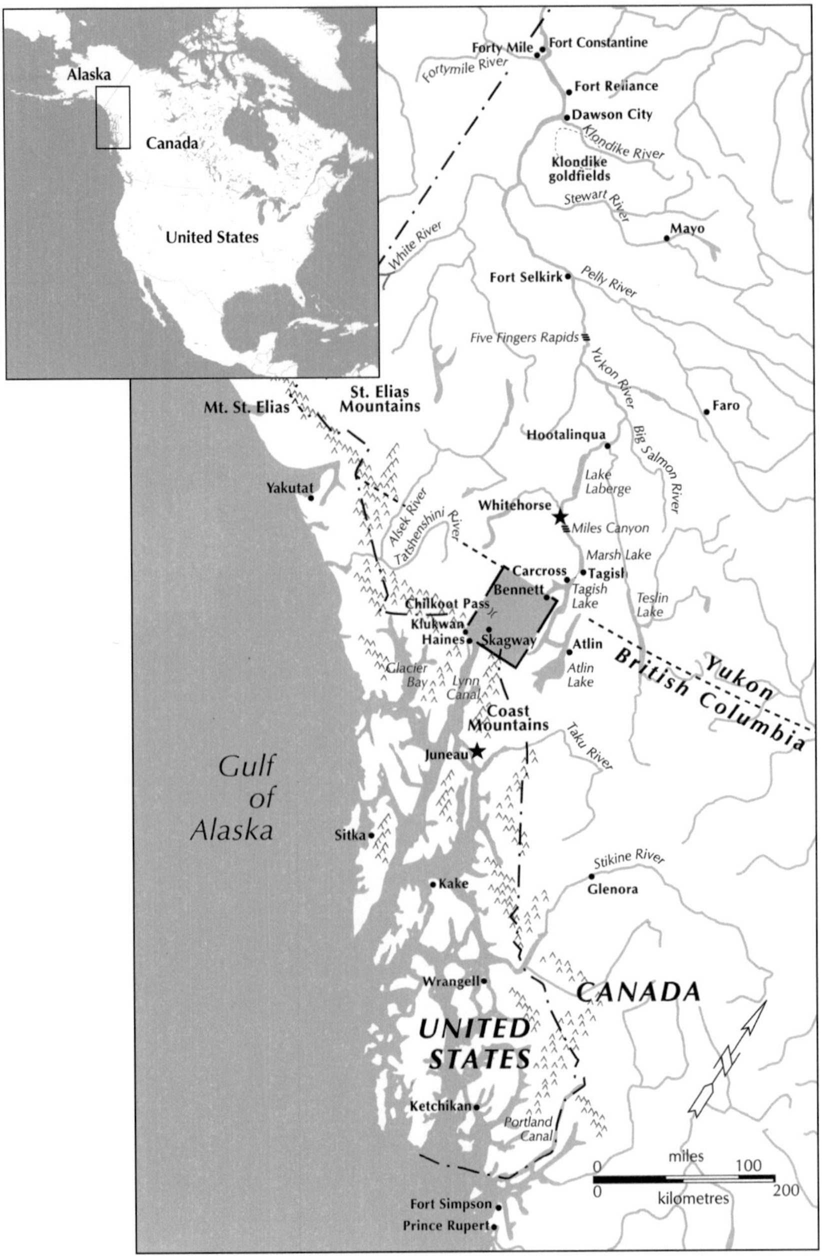

Regions within Alaska, British Columbia, and Yukon Territory where Kate lived at various times in her life. The shaded area between Skagway and Bennett represents the vicinity of the Chilkoot Trail (see detail, page 26). From *Chilkoot Trail: Heritage Route to the Klondike*, David Neufeld and Frank Norris, 2005, Lost Moose Publishing (an imprint of Harbour Publishing), www. harbourpublishing.com. Used with permission of publisher. Edited by UA Press.

PREFACE

It was on a steep and arduous trek along the Chilkoot Trail, a living museum littered with gumboots and rust-coated tools and collapsible boats cast off by gold-seekers who'd grown weary of their loads, that I first became interested in the Native women of the gold rush era who'd packed for hire over the summit—a feat I could scarcely imagine, given my fear of heights and my struggles with a lightweight, ergonomically designed pack.

That fascination quickly narrowed to an interest in one woman in particular, Kate Carmack, who was wife, sister, and aunt to the men who made the initial big find at Bonanza Creek. As it turned out, the Chilkoot Trail was the least of the hurdles Kate negotiated. The great irony of her life—that she inadvertently helped trigger a stampede that forever changed the lives of her people—was one I was especially drawn to, having lived in remote Native Alaskan villages in the immediate aftermath of a more contemporary stampede, the rush to exploit crude oil discovered on Alaska's North Slope.

Initially, I was also intrigued by Kate's story as a classic tale of a woman wronged—in life, when her husband abandoned her and cheated her out of her share of their wealth, and in death, when George Carmack's biographer James Albert Johnson did such a good job of redeeming his subject's reputation by maligning his Native wife that one editor wrote, ". . . after reading about Kate, who could blame a man for shedding her."[1]

But no story is so simple. An exceptional and complex woman, Kate was neither angel nor demon. Well into my research, I realized that her life's story was not that of victim but of survivor, a woman who ultimately reclaimed her sense of self. Yet her perspective—and indeed the perspective of all Native people—has been overlooked time and again in the plethora of books that have been written on the Klondike experience, popular accounts of the gold rush that emphasize the values and accomplishments of outsiders. With the first headlines that screamed "Gold! Gold! Gold!" the rush to the Klondike quickly became the stuff of myth. It was the Wild West all over again, the cowboy hero (typically white, male) recast as prospector, a rugged individual who, given the right mix of determination and luck, prevailed against the challenges of a harsh, untamed wilderness previously occupied only by "savages."

In one form or another, nearly every popular account of the Klondike experience perpetuates this myth: the earliest guidebooks to the North, some ghostwritten by authors who'd never traveled there; the widely read stories of Jack London, who spent only a few months in the Yukon; and the popular poetry of Robert Service, who arrived in the Klondike several years after the rush was over. Even esteemed gold rush chroniclers such as Canadian author Pierre Berton, who pledged to tell the "unvarnished story" of the Klondike, have relied on witnesses whose views were skewed by their immersion within a dominant culture that celebrates conquest and individual achievement.[2]

From a Western perspective, the act of discovery is the crux of Kate's story. But within her own personal culture, the right ways of behaving with regard to the known world mattered more than who found the gold. It is from that perspective that I aim to convey not only what happened during the Klondike discovery and its aftermath but also what occurred during other seminal points in Kate's life: her early interactions with outsiders; the loss of her Tlingit husband and child; the death of her brother-in-law in a skirmish over rights to the Chilkoot Trail; and her second marriage and subsequent years of wandering with her husband, George Carmack. By revealing new details about her life, I challenge readers to consider the iconic events of the gold rush from an entirely different vantage point, one belonging to those who were there first: the indigenous people of Alaska and the Yukon.

There were many reasons *not* to write this book. Perhaps most obvious, I was not born Tagish-Tlingit, and no amount of research can change the fact that I come to Kate's story as an outsider. Had not her life already been so utterly misappropriated in the popular press, beginning with newspaper accounts from her era and continuing into our current age (James Albert Johnson's *George Carmack* and Howard Blum's *The Floor of Heaven* are among the books that discredit her), I would have left Kate's biography to be written by an author from within her own culture. As it stands, I hope the source material I've gathered will inspire someone from Kate's background to offer an insider's perspective on her life.

Our understanding of history is always subjective. Those who also read James Albert Johnson's biography of George Carmack will note many discrepancies between how he and I depict some of the same events. As Lael Morgan noted in the Whitecap edition of his book, "Johnson's job was to give us Carmack's view and a good view of Carmack." In doing so, he portrayed Kate in a less than favorable light, and he held back primary source material in which Carmack's own words reveal his character flaws.

I fault Johnson for none of that. He wrote with a different purpose, in a different era, without access to many of the sources I've consulted; most notably, he relied on the George T. Snow/ George Carmack collaboration without realizing how much of it had been fabricated by Snow. And without Johnson's foresight in purchasing the papers of Judge James Wickersham from a used bookstore in Seattle in 1957, I could never have pieced together Kate's story.

During years of research, I experienced firsthand the reasons why the voices of Native women have remained mostly silent in the historical record: Unable to read and write, Kate left no journals, no diaries, and no written accounts of her life beyond letters penned by others on her behalf. It is only through a fortuitous combination of correspondence, legal proceedings, ethnographic study, and the generosity of Kate's relatives that her story can now be told.

In particular, without the information shared by two of Kate's nieces, Angela Sidney and Mrs. Billy Smith (now deceased), as well as elders Annie Auston and Ida Calmagene, it would have been much more difficult to challenge the prevailing historical accounts of Kate's life. Also helpful to my research were archival holdings in Yukon Territory, Alaska, Washington State, and California, as well as Catharine McClellan's ethnographic study *My Old People Say* and Thomas Thornton's *Ethnographic Overview and Assessment*, commissioned by the Klondike Gold Rush National Historical Park.

In the course of my work, I consulted with dozens of living descendants, including those related to Kate and also the descendants of those who knew her. I also visited the places where Kate lived and traveled: Tagish Lake, Lake Marsh, Lake Bennett, the Chilkoot Trail, the Haines-Tlákw.aan (Klukwan) coastal region of Alaska, the Forty Mile district, Fort Selkirk, Dawson City, Bonanza Creek, the Yukon River, Seattle's Pioneer Square district, San Francisco, and San Benito County, California, where I used old township maps to locate the ranch where Kate spent two winters.

Because my background is in the humanities, I took a broader approach to this book than either a historian or an anthropologist might. I'm also a novelist, and I must admit to a temptation to fictionalize Kate's story—it would certainly have been easier than sifting through sands for facts that others had overlooked. But when so many misperceptions had already been circulated, I couldn't see intentionally making up more stories about my subject.

Instead, I set out to write a thoroughly researched and documented narrative that would draw readers into Kate's world. From contemporary sources, I gathered grounding details: the weather on particular days, the hazards along particular parts of the Yukon River, descriptions of the Deisheetaan clan house. Newspaper accounts and letters written on Kate's behalf purport to convey what she felt and thought at certain junctures in her life, but several of these sources are suspect, given the motives—some well-intentioned, others self-serving—of those who penned them. Wherever I suggest how Kate thought and felt at particular moments, I've drawn what I believe to be the most likely conclusions based on the circumstances, discerning as best I could the reliability of the source materials that have survived her.

Even when a person of history has left written records of her life, a biographer's work involves some interpretation of who that person was; others may, of course, reach different conclusions from the same set of facts, facts being more subject to interpretation than we like to think. Even the basic question of Kate's cultural affiliation can be disputed: Was she Tagish? Tagish-Tlingit? Or, given recent assertions that there is no actual difference between Tagish and Tlingit, is it incorrect to use the term "Tagish" at all?

According to the Yukon Native Language Centre, Tagish is one of eight aboriginal languages spoken in what is now the Yukon Territory; of these, one is Tlingit and the rest, including Tagish, are categorized as Athabascan (this term is spelled in various ways, including "Athabaskan"). Tagish was spoken in the small, loosely defined region where Kate spent most of her life, near the source of the Yukon River, on the inland side of the Coastal Mountains that traverse one border between Alaska and Canada.

As anthropologist Julie Cruikshank notes in her introduction to *Life Lived Like a Story*, the various bands of indigenous people who reside in what is now Yukon Territory never formed distinctly bounded social units. Like other Tagish speakers of their time, Kate and her family also spoke Tlingit, which was in the process of replacing Tagish as the more culturally dominant language.[3]

Nevertheless, in her work with Cruikshank, Kate's niece Angela Sidney and other elders of her generation were very clear in self-identifying as Tagish. As Sidney and others told it—and as Tlingit sources of the period affirm—the Tlingit people began moving inland when the fur trade accelerated in the 1800s, with marriage alliances between Tlingit women and Tagish men helping to strengthen these trading relationships. Part of what makes Kate's story so fascinating is that by virtue of her birth and upbringing, she was adept at adjusting to cultural differences; for people of her region, such skills were vital. But there is no evidence that she ever referred to herself as Tlingit. To avoid anachronism, I've opted to set aside current Tagish-Tlingit debates and refer to Kate only as Tagish, the same affiliation claimed by the Carcross-Tagish First Nations today.

My goal has been to illuminate a life, and, in doing so, to encourage fresh perspectives on what we think we know. A few particulars concerning my approach: No dialogue is invented. Wherever possible, I've avoided using *sic*, preferring to retain original wording, mistakes and all, from primary sources. A greater difficulty was deciding how to handle the overtly racist and sexist language and tone of many of these sources. Because such attitudes framed the "new normal" for indigenous people in the post-contact era, I've chosen to let these quotes stand as evidence of the vast differences between how Kate was perceived by others and how she perceived herself.

When referring to first peoples of Alaska and the Yukon, I've named the individual band or tribe wherever possible, using the terms *Native, indigenous,* and *aboriginal* when the reference is broader, and the term *Indian* when the reference is narrow enough to exclude other Native groups (such as Yup'ik or Aleut). *Indian* is, of course, a deeply vexed term, a misnomer assigned by outsiders, one that acquired pejorative overtones, particularly in decades past. In Canada, *First Nations* is the modern-day substitute for *Indian*. In the United States, *Native American* is the substitute term, though objections to its use have been raised, resulting in this notation in *The Chicago Manual of Style*: "Many among those who trace their roots to the aboriginal peoples of the America prefer *American Indians* to *Native Americans*, and in certain historical works *Indians* may be more appropriate."[4]

Mindful of these perspectives, I've used the terms *Native American, Alaska Native,* and *First Nations* wherever the context is modern. But for references during Kate's lifetime, I've referred to her as she herself would have, as either Tagish or Indian, designators that are conveniently neither wholly American nor wholly Canadian; for most of her life, Kate moved freely between these two nations.

As outsiders came to Alaska and the Yukon, they assigned new names to people and places that already had perfectly good ones. In this book, I've switched from using the indigenous names of people and places to the names assigned by outsiders whenever, as best I could determine, those involved in the narrative began to use the newly assigned names. Thus, Kate is referred to as Shaaw Tláa until her marriage to George Carmack, after which she became known as Kate.

For the Tagish, Tlingit, and Hwëch'in spellings used in this book, I've consulted resources provided by the Yukon Native Language Centre and the Sealaska Heritage Institute. For pronunciation assistance with Tagish and Tlingit names and terms, I urge readers to access the online language resources of these organizations, especially the audio recordings that allow sounds to be heard rather than puzzled out through charts that assume some linguistic understanding. For Tlingit, the Tlingit Alphabet audiovisual guide at www.sealaska.org is an excellent starting point.

Tagish is not taught in schools, and of the few speakers who remain today, the knowledge is passive: the language is understood but not spoken.[5] And while active efforts to preserve the Tlingit language have resulted in a recently updated orthography, Tagish spellings remain less uniform. Among the valuable resources available through the Yukon Native Language Centre (www.ynlc.ca) are audio recordings featuring one of the best (and sadly, one of the last) Native speakers of Tagish, Lucy Wren.

It should be noted that Tagish and Tlingit renderings of certain words differ. Most notably for this text, Kate's original name, Shaaw Tláa, is translated by her niece, Angela Sidney, as meaning "Mouldy Mother," while in Tlingit it means "Ancient Mother," "Old Mother," or "Mother of the Ancients."

One final but important note: All stories and songs belong to the clans; in a very real sense, these are their wealth. Those referenced in this book have been published previously, as noted in the citations, and my intent has been to summarize rather than retell them.

In the spirit of reciprocity, which is foundational within Tagish-Tlingit culture, a portion of the proceeds from the sales of this book are donated to the Skookum Jim Friendship Centre, a nonprofit organization that depends in part on revenues generated by the trust fund set up by Kate's brother Keish (Skookum Jim) to advance the well-being of First Nations people in the Yukon.

CHAPTER ONE

Gold I Bring

The *Roanoke* is loaded with gold. Bags, cans, boxes, and crates cram its lower deck, jammed with a whopping ten tons of the precious metal panned and sluiced by lucky devils in the northern wilderness. Only a year ago, few had heard of the patch of low mountains and dense northern spruce now known as the Klondike. But these days, like an incantation of magic, the very word *Klondike* invokes abundance, the vindication of the American dream and the triumph of the individual in its most measurable manifestation: wealth.[1]

Nine days after setting out from the dreary and once sleepy port of St. Michael near the wide, muddy mouth of the Yukon River, the *Roanoke* chugs toward the dock of the North American Transport Company in Seattle, a city that enjoys a symbiotic relationship with the Klondike and its magic, the city having built the magic and the magic having built the city.

Four hundred fifty-eight passengers crowd the ship's decks, eager for land. Sunshine seeps past clouds to light the throng gathered to welcome them and their gold: women in cinched-waist dresses and high, narrow hats; men in suits and suspenders, bowlers and derbies and straw tops. Everyone wants to see who has gotten rich in the Klondike and who has returned empty-handed. In the Gilded Age of Horatio Alger and unbridled capitalism,

Americans are exhorted to industry, thrift, and temperance. No one can quite reconcile the idea of gold so easy and plentiful that you need none of these virtues to claim it. The idea is as unsettling as it is enticing, and on this day in 1898, there is no small amount of envy as the *Roanoke* steams for shore, especially when it comes to the scruffy common folk on her decks, the *nouveaux* made *riches* by gold.

A particular challenge to American precepts on money, virtue, and class is the lone Indian woman on board the *Roanoke*, first called Shaaw Tláa, now called Kate Carmack. On her wrists and fingers, she wears gold, thin bands that belie her new and extraordinary wealth. With a firm, dark-eyed gaze, she meets life head-on, grounded in the knowledge of who she is and from where she has come. Her features are soft, graceful; her resolve, unwavering. Possessed of a ready smile, she is resilient, resourceful, and strong—headstrong, even, with a temper. Determined and accomplished, she has already adapted in remarkable ways to circumstances beyond any she could ever have imagined, but the challenges ahead will prove even more formidable.

Kate Carmack's distinction—her claim to fame, as it were, though to her such a concept is foreign—is that she is thought to be the richest Indian woman in the world; since the extinction of the sixteenth-century colony for which the *Roanoke* is named, she is better situated with what passes for wealth than nearly any indigenous person of the United States or Canada has ever been. As of yet, she knows nothing of those who've gone before her and failed, Indians such as Sitting Bull and Crazy Horse and Quanah Parker, who have only recently been consigned to a scrubbed-out existence on lands no one else wants.

The crowd gathered on this one Seattle dock exceeds twice again the entire population of Kate's Tagish Indian band, of whom she knows each by name. Like all Indians of Alaska and the Yukon, the Tagish clans travel in yearly rounds, hunting caribou and Dall sheep, gathering berries, harvesting salmon, and trapping beaver and muskrat. Thanks to the gatekeeping of their Tlingit neighbors, they have been among the last aboriginal people on the continent to confront head-on the object-driven culture of the West. They occupy the final frontier, some might say, although the US Census Bureau in 1890 declared the American frontier more or less closed, and at any rate, when your ideas about land have more to do with proper use than with tightly defined boundaries, the whole idea of a frontier becomes pointless.[2] Adapting is among the actions that have traditionally sustained Kate's people, but there's a tipping point between adaptation and assimilation that they've yet to fully test.

Her first language centers on verbs, her integrity tied to how well she protects, relates, negotiates, and adapts. In the form of luck, destiny comes to her; she does not seek it out. In Kate's essence, her *yaahei*, which is Shaaw Tláa and not Kate, it is the journey that matters, not the end. The route is a circle, traversed with way-finding that demands close attention and behaviors that honor defined relationships.

In contrast, nineteenth-century Americans are a people of objects, their language driven by nouns. In their way of thinking, destiny requires pursuit; it is no coincidence that in their language, the words *destiny* and *destination* share the same root. They travel in lines, from point to point, toward tangible goals. They explore, they assert, they acquire. Among their most thrilling and coveted prizes is gold, of which Kate Carmack has quite a lot.

Kate's voyage had begun nineteen days earlier, when she left Dawson City, a boomtown at the junction of the Klondike and Yukon Rivers, in what is popularly known to Americans as Alaska but is in fact the newly formed Yukon Territory of Canada. Despite her fortune in gold, she has until now occupied with her husband and daughter a small, tidy cabin built of hand-hewn logs on one of the family's Bonanza Creek claims, claims that by one estimate will yield $2.5 million in gold.[3] Within her modest home, she has sewn fur mittens and baked bread to sell to neighboring miners, though she draws the line at taking in laundry.

Two weeks before she began her journey, a huge white tent went up across the river from Dawson, belonging to a woman who could hardly have been more different than Kate. In this four-hundred-pound tent, New York heiress Mary E. Hitchcock can host seventy-five dinner guests, serving them tinned oysters, asparagus, and lobsters, and ice cream made from the freezer she has brought to the wilderness. She can entertain her new friends with her gramophone and her movie projector and her portable bowling alley, not to mention her flock of pigeons, her parrot, her canaries, and a Great Dane.[4]

Penned between practicing on her zither and mandolin, Mary Hitchcock kept a detailed journal of the route Kate has traveled (though in reverse), by steamer and sternwheeler[5] through the Pacific to the Bering Sea and up the Yukon River to Dawson. Steaming from the mainland toward the mouth of the Yukon with traveling companion Edith Van Buren, grand-niece of President Martin Van Buren, Mary Hitchcock was struck by the profound silence as their ship navigated a field of ice floes. A stretch of wet, windy days at the dreary Alaskan port of St. Michael tried her patience as they waited for the water in the Yukon to rise to accommodate the sternwheeler. It vexed her to learn that she would not, as promised, be among the first passengers to put off in Dawson that year.

Once they finally got on the river, Mary Hitchcock disembarked whenever the boat stopped, which was often, sternwheelers having large appetites for wood. Fighting off gnats and mosquitoes and horseflies, she gathered wild roses, mulberries, currants, and raspberries, as well as groundsel, which delighted her canaries. Where she could, she photographed Indians who turned out along the river, though she refused to descend into the traditional community houses to photograph their dancing, for fear of the vermin, and she became indignant when a group of Indian women covered their heads with shawls and demanded a sitting fee. Though she misperceived the tundra as prairie with great potential for agricultural development, she admired the mountains and rapids and gorges as her boat approached Dawson.[6]

This is the country that Kate has left behind, though unlike Mary Hitchcock, she is unable to record her impressions of it, because she cannot read or write. But in the age of Yellow

Journalism, American reporters are already poised to spread the legends that will spring up about her. Random photos of Indian women will circulate, the owners claiming to have captured Kate's image. In order to find her way, she will purportedly leave hatchet marks in the fancy woodwork of the Seattle Hotel.[7] With her husband, she will toss gold coins from the hotel's top floor, causing mayhem among pedestrians who scramble for easy money.[8]

And when George abandons her at a California ranch 2,500 miles from her home, Kate will discover the extent to which she has been made to embody a longstanding metaphor that simultaneously casts Indian women in the role of exotic princess and dangerous savage.[9] As such, she will be expected to defy her own people in a self-imposed banishment that aligns her with the dominant culture but that ends, more often than not, in premature death.[10]

The *Roanoke* is among sixty new boats and barges that serve the gold fields, plowing across the North Pacific and charging up and down the Yukon at such an alarming rate that it's a wonder they don't collide. Sternwheelers from two rival carriers now race, quite literally, to and from the Klondike; the one that delivered Kate down the Yukon to the Roanoke set a new record as it zipped in six days from Dawson City to St. Michael. Aboard the *Roanoke*, the vessel's owner is beaming, though his mood darkens when he's reminded of two gold heists that have plagued this voyage, the victim of one of these thefts being Kate's brother Keish, known as Skookum Jim Mason; at some point during their journey, $4,000 of his gold was replaced with lead shot.

Even with this loss, the family partnership that consists of Kate and Jim plus their nephews Káa Goox (also called Charlie) and Kootseen (called Patsy) and Kate's husband George Carmack still have a quarter million dollars in gold stashed in the lower reaches of the *Roanoke*, and this is only a portion of the fortune they're wresting from the frozen earth.[11] The son of a California farmer, Kate's husband claims credit for having discovered the gold that set off the Klondike madness. So do her brother and

On the upper deck of the Roanoke, before departing St. Michael. Behind Graphie (seated) is her father, George Carmack. To his right is Kate, and to her right is Charlie. To George's left is Jim, and to his left is Patsy. (Dawson City Museum, 1999.11.9)

nephew; there's even talk that Kate played a role in plucking the first nuggets from the creek.

As the *Roanoke* was about to set sail for Seattle, Kate and her family posed for a photo on deck. Though he should be at the peak of his game, George appears in this photo more bedraggled than the rest, his suit coat rumpled and his tie loose at the collar. He's not yet forty, but he suffers from rheumatism, which Kate treats with traditional medicines, coltsfoot and devil's club. A drifter who tried his hand at shepherding, which he hated, and the military, from which he went AWOL at age twenty-two, George Carmack appeared in the Yukon at a fortuitous time. Though he now claims gold as his destiny, in truth he wandered the North for years with no real destination. After a dozen years as husband to Kate, he has finally written to his sister to tell her he's married. His wife, he says in his letter, is Irish.[12]

"Lying George," as fellow prospectors call him, is known for telling a stretcher now and again. Interviewed in his *Roanoke* stateroom, he complained he'd never seen the true story of the Klondike discovery in print.[13] Before he's through, he'll fabricate multiple versions of this "true story." He brags to the reporter that he plans to take Kate and Charlie and Jim to the big 1899 expedition in Paris. But in fact, when he writes his life story, he'll leave Kate out completely. It will be as if she never existed.

In the photo taken from the *Roanoke* before its departure, Kate appears beautiful by any standard, posing assuredly behind a crate of gold, dressed in a dark frock with lace collar and sleeves, a shawl draped over her shoulders. While not the height of fashion, her flat-topped hat is graced with a length of fancy ribbon. Though in one hand she clutches a white handkerchief—has she been crying?—her lips turn in a slight smile. The only woman on deck, she stands out among dozens of stern-faced men, including her nephew Charlie, who slouches at her side, hands stuffed in the pockets of his three-piece suit. In front of Kate sits her five-year-old daughter, Graphie Grace, too young to recall a life without gold. Wearing a heavy dress and a lace-collared cape, Graphie scowls, perhaps having already spied the high-topped button boots she'll demand her father purchase right off another child's feet, to replace the Indian moccasins made by her mother.[14]

In this photo, no one touches Kate's husband, but a fellow miner rests his hand on the shoulder of her brother Keish. Known also as Skookum, or "Strong" Jim, he strikes a handsome, confident pose in his suit, his derby hat tipped stylishly to the side, one hand in his pocket, the other on his hip, displaying a gold ring. Jim is acclaimed for his prowess and strength—in a single load, he once packed 165 pounds of bacon over the Chilkoot Trail, dubbed the meanest thirty-three miles in history.[15] Another time he went hand to claw with a bear. Two years before striking it rich in the Klondike, an encounter with the fleeting Wealth Woman of Tagish legend bestowed Jim with luck, which he now shares with

Kate's husband, whom he befriended even before they became brothers-in-law, a relationship that to the Tagish is deeply infused with obligations.[16] Even though one of George's "stretchers" was that Indians could not file Discovery claims, Jim has stuck by him as the family digs gold from the gravels of Bonanza Creek.[17]

Standing so close to Jim that their arms overlap is Kootseen, whom George has dubbed with the unfortunate name of "Patsy"—all of Kate's family has been renamed like this, at random, by George or other white people who've found their given names too difficult. Among the Tagish, uncles take special responsibility for nephews, rearing them almost as fathers would; for years, Patsy and Charlie have traveled with Jim. Like his uncle, Patsy sports a smart three-piece suit, but he's young and slight, and his hands clasped at his waist betray his unease, as if he alone knows what's ahead.

In truth, Seattle is hardly the best place to make your first acquaintance with urban America in the waning years of the nineteenth century. Inspired by the gold rush, swindlers and speculators are everywhere. In this booming city, you can buy everything imaginable, and then some, to ease your way in the Arctic: patented Blizzard Resister Suits, Klondike underwear, Klondike hosiery, Klondike gloves. You can purchase frost extraction devices and insect-proof masks—pound for pound, the Klondike is rumored to be almost as heavy with mosquitoes as it is with gold.[18] Would-be millionaires can also equip themselves with automated gold pans and steam-powered sleds, crystallized eggs (some turn out to be nothing but cornmeal), scurvy cures, collapsible boats, Klondike bicycles, and slot machines that operate on gold nuggets instead of coins—all of it, save perhaps the scurvy cure, utterly worthless upon arrival in the North. Yet already $60 million has been spent in the race for gold.[19]

The Klondike feeds the longings of an adolescent nation in the throes of nineteenth-century capitalism. Industrialism has funneled wealth to the likes of Rockefeller, Carnegie, and Morgan in quantities unimaginable to the average American, so that there are only two classes, according to Populist Jerry Simpson: the robbers and the robbed.[20] Following the Panic of 1893, factories closed, unemployment skyrocketed, and foreclosures were rampant. Depositors stormed banks, demanding their money in gold. At first the US Treasury drew on reserves to satisfy them, but the nation's burgeoning deficit and European distrust of the American dollar created such a downward spiral in confidence that by early 1895, the US government was about to run out of gold, a crisis that would have caused the nation to default on its debt.

Only by brokering a deal in which the US Treasury sold bonds in exchange for gold from a syndicate led by banker J.P. Morgan was President Grover Cleveland able to avert an international run on American banks that might have turned the 1893 Panic into an all-out depression. Naturally, Morgan made a hefty profit on the transaction, though the exact amount was never disclosed.[21] Still the recession deepened. Cleveland's reputation was ruined. Populist presidential candidate William Jennings Bryan ran on the silver platform, eschewing the gold standard as the tool used by greedy bankers to manipulate the money supply. "You shall not crucify mankind upon a cross of gold!" Bryan proclaimed.

Six weeks after this pronouncement, George Carmack or one of his Tagish relatives—depending on whose version you believe—discovered the nuggets that precipitated a rush that flooded worldwide markets with gold, renewing confidence and setting off a boom in transportation and industry to accommodate the would-be millionaires headed north that dampened the furor over gold versus silver. Thanks to an enthusiastic advertising campaign launched by Erastus Brainerd, a former journalist who rivals P.T. Barnum for showmanship, nearly all the traffic in the Seattle harbor now points toward the Klondike.

Nearly all the traffic, that is, except the *Roanoke*, about to deliver Kate to the throng. Can wealth be the destiny of an obscure Indian woman, transported from a place that, for better or worse, is gaining fame as the resurrected (and last) frontier? Everything in the nineteenth-century American soul screams against it. But for Kate Carmack, née Shaaw Tláa, destiny is hardly the point. You act as you must, trusting in the combined sum of your actions to keep you whole. You hope against hope that out of the mad rush for Klondike gold will come a legacy of triumph—not of wealth, but of spirit.

An exceptional and complex woman, Kate will prove herself neither angel nor demon. Her perspective—and indeed the perspective of all Native people—will be overlooked time and again in the plethora of books that will be written about the Klondike, popular accounts of the gold rush that emphasize the values and accomplishments of outsiders. But when pieced together decades after her death, her life's story will demonstrate the many ways in which a singular quest for wealth played out for those who were there first, the indigenous people of Alaska and the Yukon.

CHAPTER TWO

They're Coming Now

VARIOUSLY DEFINED AS PLACE, process, relationship, and experience, the frontier has embodied, for better and worse, much of the American and Canadian experience.[1] Notwithstanding the US Census Bureau's statement about the frontier having become a thing of the past, the Far North where Shaaw Tláa would grow into womanhood was quietly becoming known, even before the Klondike discovery, as a new frontier, long inhabited but only recently transgressed.

Until her family discovered gold, Shaaw Tláa's experience with what others called the frontier—a term she herself would not have used—would involve encounters with persons who had ventured north with a variety of interests and intents: missionaries, naturalists, military men, traders, and prospectors. The perceptions of those who traveled to Alaska and the Yukon (indeed, the perceptions that framed much of American and Canadian history through the end of the nineteenth century) were colored by ways of thinking that have entered into intellectual discourse as *isms*—colonialism, imperialism, expansionism—forces that shaped the ways in which Shaaw Tláa was perceived by nearly every outsider who met her, and many more who would only learn of her secondhand.

During her lifetime, one had to look back only a generation or two for very real examples of what it might mean for an outsider to encounter an Indian along the frontier.[2] Bloody battles, massacres, attacks—these clashes with aboriginal bands and nations had been the very real fallout of westward expansion in the United States and Canada. Despite the completion of the Transcontinental Railroad in 1869 and the influx of cattlemen that resulted in the mass slaughter of buffalo, bloodshed from Indian wars had continued well into the 1870s, involving the Comanche and Sioux in particular but also other Plains tribes who through their skills in battle had managed to thwart and even turn back some of the incursions into their traditional lands.

Hostiles, savages, marauders—these terms and more were transferred wholesale to people of the many distinct indigenous cultures of the North. Outsiders assessed Natives like Shaaw Tláa according to their perceived trustworthiness, meaning how inclined they were to accept intrusion without a fight and how reliably they conformed to the expectations of newcomers. Within this context, indigenous peoples and the new arrivals made accommodations to one other for what they perceived—often wrongly—as advantage.

Isolated by economic and geographic circumstances during her childhood, Shaaw Tláa knew little of what happened when cultures collided. Her sense of self was rooted in her *haa shagóon*, her story, reaching back to mythical time, when Crow first threw sand to make the world and then carved thick poplar bark, breathing into it to make the first humans.[3] She was of the Dakl'aweidí, the Killer Whale nation. Because the Tagish were matrilineal, she was known as the daughter of Gus'dutéen, who was the daughter of Húnx̱u.aat, whose people came from Tahltan, the flat place now called Telegraph Creek. Led by two old men, Shaaw Tláa's ancestors had traveled under a glacier to the mouth of the Shtax'héen River, now called the Stikine, to a place now called Wrangell, where they camped on a pebbly beach from which they got their name, Dakl'aweidí. From that beach, some journeyed along the coast and then up the Chilkat River and over Bear Creek Pass to where they made the village of Tagish. Their song "Shove It out Now" was sung in remembrance of the time when they pushed their boat out under the glacier.[4]

Shaaw Tláa was a middle child of eight born to Gus'dutéen and Kaachgaawáa, a crow of the Deisheetaan, or beaver clan. The name *Shaaw Tláa* was, and continues to be, passed from person to person within the Dakl'aweidí. Its meaning, "moldy mother," might strike outsiders as odd, but there is among Tagish legends one of Shaatláax̱, or Moldy Head, whose mother knew precisely how to save him after he had been turned into a fish.[5]

The date of Shaaw Tláa's birth is uncertain—on census and other records, the year is given as 1865, 1859, and 1857. The birth year inscribed on her tombstone, erected long after her death, is 1857, but based on the events of her life, Shaaw Tláa was more likely born between 1862 and 1867.[6] At any rate, chronicling her birth wouldn't have been especially important to her family. Better to remember when the caribou had come through the previous year and to know when they might come through the next.

Precisely where she was born is equally difficult to determine. Like all Yukon Indians, her family moved with the seasons, mostly within a small area surrounding four long lakes that spread like a pinwheel, lakes now called Tagish, Bennett, Nares, and Marsh. Lines drawn to distinguish the traditional lands of the Tagish clans from neighboring bands are mostly arbitrary. In practical terms, there was much mixing of languages and families across these imagined boundaries, and there was no sense of land ownership in the way that Western cultures perceive it. Rather, each group concerned themselves with stewardship over the lands they traveled, the boreal forests that spread across much of the Yukon and Alaska, dense with trees that thrive in glacier-scraped soils—birch, aspen, cottonwood, lodge pole pine, larch, subalpine fir, and white spruce. In the places where all but the top layer of soil stays frozen year round, spindly black spruce tilt drunkenly across the boggy landscape.[7]

When Shaaw Tláa was young—on August 7, 1869, to be precise—the sun disappeared. The response of her family to this celestial event stands in stark contrast to what happened a short journey away, on the coastal side of the mountains, where the Tlingit Indians—many related in one way or another to Shaaw Tláa—viewed the eclipse in the company of strangers, white men who were mostly a mystery to the Tagish clans, in no small part because the Tlingit preferred it that way.[8]

The full solar eclipse of 1869 occurred during *K̲uk'eet,* the month of new snow on the mountains, the time for storing up salmon and picking berries and hunting mountain goats. At the time, the entire Tagish band, with its own distinct language, consisted of less than a hundred people represented by two clans, the Dakl'aweidí and the Deisheetaan. During *K̲uk'eet,* Shaaw Tláa's family put up salmon caught with fish traps and nets at the north end of Marsh Lake, near the headwaters of the Yukon River, which meanders northwest through the present-day city of Whitehorse, where it broadens into a silty but navigable waterway through which hordes of fish migrate.[9]

To those who don't know this region, the Yukon landscape feels not only vast but inhospitable in this part of the North, swarming with relentless mosquitoes in summer and mind-numbing with dark and cold in winter. Not so for Shaaw Tláa, raised from birth with a deep understanding of the land. Besides putting up fish, her family also scoured the surrounding woodlands, gathering plants used for food and medicine—bearberry, wild chamomile, goldenrod, fireweed, horsetail, coldsfoot, lungwort, Labrador tea, yarrow, and wild sage.

On the day of the solar eclipse, Shaaw Tláa was doing more or less as she pleased, as all Tagish children did, perhaps playing with dolls made from bits of fur and wood or swinging while her brothers and sisters and cousins walked in a circle around her, singing songs, or building a playhouse of rocks and brush, where boys and girls played during warm weather—the girls demonstrating even in play the power Tagish and Tlingit women wielded within the home.[10]

To look after her were not only her parents but also her relatives in both clans, although Shaaw Tláa had to be mindful of who was whom among her extended family, as certain relationships demanded an extra level of respect, lest she inadvertently start a feud that could only be resolved with an expensive, face-saving potlatch. Warm praise let her know she was loved, even as certain grown-ups—her joking relations—caused her to look away with their relentless teasing.[11] If her behavior got out of hand, the pronouncement that an owl was coming to take her away was enough to quiet her.

Early on, Shaaw Tláa learned to avoid saying anything bad about moldy fish or speak harshly about bears. Aside from dogs, which were kept for transportation though they were also associated with evil,[12] living creatures were to be treated with respect, even by children. When she ate bone or blood soup, she avoided looking into the bowl, or the *yek* of the animal that had been killed might see her.[13] So she would not grow up to be lazy, she made sure not to keep stones in her pockets. And she knew better than to play with baby birds—that would bring on bad weather.

Yet on that day in August, nothing done by her or any other child could account for the sun's disappearance. As a shadow began to cross over the brilliant orb, an unnatural darkness spread across the forest, followed by an uncanny silence. Even the dogs that were used for packing and pulling winter sledges quit their yapping and howling. Without doubt, Shaaw Tláa was afraid. But there were proper behaviors for even the most extraordinary of circumstances, and the Tagish adults knew precisely how to respond.

As the sun shrank beneath the moon's shadow, Shaaw Tláa's mother and aunts and cousins hung their best furs, button blankets, and other valuables outside on lines. They tied gopher snares to their walking sticks and waved them at the disappearing disc, as if to snare it. Some shook blankets at it. Together, they sang, urging the sun to come back for all the pretty things they'd set out.[14]

Still the light receded, until only a bright, narrow, sharply-defined sliver commanded the sky. Then its final edge disappeared, and all went dark.

On the far side of the Coastal Mountains, Shaaw Tláa's Tlingit relatives experienced the eclipse in the company of outsiders, a group of white men that included William Seward, making his first visit to Alaska after successfully wrangling the US Congress into its purchase two years prior. It was from such outsiders that Tlingit traders, well-positioned as middlemen, had isolated their Tagish relatives. But in the aftermath of the eclipse—perhaps even because of it—the Chikat Tlingit chief Kohklux would make a crucial decision that opened direct access, albeit limited, between the outsiders and the Interior groups that included Shaaw Tláa and her family.[15]

On the morning of the eclipse, near the Tlingit village of Tlákw.aan, a small group of white men gathered around a set of scientific instruments: a Hipp chronograph, mounted to a Frodsham break-circuit chronograph; a variety of thermometers and barometers; and a large Fraunhofer telescope, protected by a tent-fly from the breeze that blew lightly from the southeast.[16] As the moon's shadow slid away and a line of light slid over the snow-covered peaks, rose-colored flames spilled from the sun's corona, as viewed through the telescope. "The solemn feeling with which the growing darkness, the bold dark mountains, the rush of the swift-flowing river, and the wild surroundings had affected everyone gave way to bursts of admiration at this magnificent glory in the heavens," wrote George Davidson, the man at the eyepiece.[17]

When daylight returned, Kohklux and his clansmen came out from their homes, demanding to know what role their guests had played in the sun's sudden sickness. Initial explanations failed to satisfy the chief. Regal, high-strung, and recognized among white men as both a warrior and a diplomat, Kohklux exuded a commanding if high-strung presence; he stood nearly six feet tall with a broad, high chest, his good looks marred only by a prominent scar on his cheek, incurred in one of the many tribal disputes that complicated his leadership duties, one in which he had found himself staring down a revolver pointed directly at his face.[18] Though the gunshot tore through his cheek and shattered his teeth, Kohklux had spit the bullet from his mouth and handed it to his assailant, saying simply, "You cannot hurt me."[19]

The perplexing influence of the white men and their instruments on the normally reliable sun set the tone for a meeting that took place later that day between Kohklux and the Great Tyee—the boss man, in Chinook trading jargon—former US Secretary of State William H. Seward. Having been hailed as the best spot in the world to view the eclipse, the Tlingit village was a key stop on Seward's tour of the new US territory, which was still being mocked as "Seward's Icebox." An outspoken man of firm convictions, Seward's face, like Kohklux's, featured a prominent scar, his from the gash of a knife wielded by a conspirator in the plot to assassinate President Lincoln.

Kohklux feted Seward and his companions with fresh fish and wild meats cooked over open fires in one of three lodges in which the wealth of the Tlingit was displayed: piles of blankets painstakingly woven from mountain goat hair, totems fashioned from fragrant red cedar, handcrafted wooden boxes, and elaborate carvings, one of which filled an entire wall. For this wealth, Kohklux and other Tlingit leaders, including the Chilkoot Tlingit to the south, depended greatly on their trade advantage with inland groups like the Tagish, a position they protected fiercely. Inadvertently, the Tlingit middlemen also spared Shaaw Tláa's people—for the moment—much of the havoc that resulted from direct contact with outsiders, including disease, alcohol, and violence.

After the feast, Kohklux gathered a large number of his clan around the central fire and lay before the men who had commandeered the sun a test of their power, initiating a dialogue that illustrated the sorts of cultural accommodations that would eventually become integral to Shaaw Tláa's way of life. The Tlingit of Sitka, site of the capital of Russian America, had several years earlier killed three men of Kohklux's clan. Kohklux wanted to know what the Great Tyee, William Seward, planned to do about it.

Ever the diplomat, Seward proposed that since the killings had occurred prior the US purchase of Alaska, the matter should be taken up with the Russians. "We did appeal to the Emperor of Russia," said Kohklux, via interpreter. "But he gave us no redress. Perhaps he was too poor. We know he was, because he had to sell his land to the Great Tyee."[20]

By Tlingit as well as Tagish reckoning, scores were settled with actions, so Kohklux asked Seward's permission to kill three Sitka Indians for each Chilkat life lost. No killing, Seward replied unequivocally. "We know that the Boston Men are averse to any killing, except by their own soldiers," Kohklux said. "So we have sometimes consented to take pay in blankets."[21]

With this concession, Seward negotiated a settlement: four blankets to be given over by the US government for each Indian life lost, though the total was tripled once Kohklux pointed out that the three Chilkat killed were the sons of chiefs.[22] The successful negotiations, not to mention the return of the sun, were cause for celebration. Kohklux changed from leggings to a suit of black broadcloth and joined a flotilla of brightly colored canoes that delivered him along with his subchiefs and warriors and their wives to the Great Tyee's boat. As they feasted once more, Kohklux asked again that the white men explain how they'd managed to make the sun vanish and reappear. At the conclusion of an impromptu astronomy lesson in which an apple and orange stood in for the sun and the moon, it fell to Kohklux to make a final diplomatic response.

"The chiefs have understood much, though not all, that the Great Tyee has told them," Kohklux said. "They understand him as saying that the eclipse was produced by the Great Spirit and not by man. Since he says so, they will believe it. They have noticed, however, that the Great Spirit generally does whatever the Boston Men want him to."[23]

In the aftermath of the eclipse and the subsequent negotiations and feast, Kohklux revealed to one of his guests, surveyor and astronomer George Davidson, the various passages to the Interior secreted and guarded by the Tlingit. Having never before put pencil to paper, the Chilkat chief and his wives spent two full days sketching maps that detailed every footpath, camp, settlement, and food cache between their village and the ill-fated

Fort Selkirk, a Yukon trading post raided twelve years earlier by Kohklux and some of his men in protest of what they perceived as the Hudson Bay Company's encroachment on their trading territory.[24]

That Kohklux perceived some advantage in accommodating the outsiders on his own terms was no secret; he later sported a tattoo that read "Seward."[25] But while he and the Chilkat Tlingit maintained control of their trading routes, the Kohklux map was a concession akin to the cracking of a door, one that before the century ended would swing wide to accommodate the rush for gold.

Following the eclipse, discharged soldier William Henderson stayed on with Kohklux, who promised to take him into the Interior in search of gold and other minerals; according to Henderson, Kohklux was as enthused about these prospects as the outsiders. For reasons unknown, Henderson never returned. The hazards of the North were many—avalanches, treacherous rivers, extreme weather, even death by retribution, the assumption being that all white people were of the same clan and therefore might be held to account for one another's wrongs.[26]

In 1875, while Shaaw Tláa was still living with her parents, a second prospector trekked inland to Marsh Lake, where her family harvested salmon in the summer. Guided by the L'ukaax̱.ádi Tlingit, this miner returned to the coast with claims of having found gold, though he failed to reveal any details.[27]

Initially, Shaaw Tláa's people suspected the white men had come from the clouds. At the beginning of time, a barrier had fallen from heaven, separating the ordinary world from a winter world where everything was white: animals, landscape, and people. Tired of the eternal cold, animals in the white world recruited the bloodsucker to poke a hole through the barrier. Wolverine widened the gap so the animals could slide from one world to the next. With their magical powers, shamans could also pass from the ordinary world to the white one, returning with prophecies and instructions for living. By virtue of their skin color, the first white people were thought to have slipped through this hole.

A Tagish story-song refines this understanding. While traveling to gather meat for his grandmother, a boy is sidetracked by a rainbow. As he stands beneath it, he hears a voice without seeing the speaker, a voice that tells him to eat from a sack dropped from the sky. Returning to his grandmother, the boy eats the strange food and sleeps in a bed raised up from the floor. "I'm going to be a white man," he says. "They're coming now."[28]

And come they would. Pretty things hung on lines and gopher snares tied to sticks had convinced the sun to return, but no such tricks would persuade the outsiders to do anything other than precisely what they pleased. One of the first to come was Frederick Schwatka, who in 1883 passed through the Tagish lake country where Shaaw Tláa grew up.

Not a trader but a US military explorer, Schwatka began his journey on something of a covert mission, the American military having failed to get permission from the Canadians to mount an expedition through their territory. Two years after the trek, Schwatka's observations—frank, derisive, and opinionated—were written up in what would become one of the most influential books about Alaska and the Yukon during its day; following the Klondike discovery, Schwatka's account of his journey would be used as a bible of sorts by stampeders making their way through unfamiliar territory in search of gold.[29]

Of more direct consequence to Shaaw Tláa, Schwatka's observations are rife with the sorts of judgments she would face throughout her life. As Schwatka traveled through the traditional lands of the Tagish clans, he renamed every landmark while making snide observations about the people who lived there. The Tagish cottonwood canoes offered for his use at Lindeman Lake he called "the most dilapidated looking craft that ever were seen." At Todezáané (later renamed Caribou Crossing, or Carcross), he noted "a dejected camp of two Tahk-heesh families" and the "very ancient reindeer ham hanging in front of their brush tent." When the "gum canoe" towed behind Schwatka's sixteen-by-thirty-two-foot raft disappeared from the expedition's camp at nearby Lake Nares, he blamed these Tagish families for stealing it, though he acknowledged that he could not be too critical, since the canoe was one of two he himself had swiped from Lindeman Lake.[30]

In a rude assessment that even a young Tagish child knew better than to make, Schwatka deemed the dried fish hung to dry at Marsh Lake as "ranking somewhere between Limburger cheese and walrus hide." He was also bemused by the refusal of a Tagish boy to trade a pair of shell earrings acquired in trade with the coastal Tlingit, not even for Schwatka's absurd offer of a double-barreled shotgun, a thousand rounds of ammunition, a gold watch, a camp stove, and two sacks of flour. Overall, based on these minimal encounters while floating through the territory traditionally occupied by the Tagish clans, Schwatka pronounced Shaaw Tláa's people "one of the most dejected races of people on the face of the earth," although he did concede that compared to the "more arrogant Chilkats," the Tagish "seemed much more like Eskimos in their rude hospitality and docility of nature."[31]

It's tempting to shuttle away such cursory and condemning assessments; from a modern perspective, they hardly bear reprinting. Other outsiders, including journalist Edward Glave, who preceded Schwatka by two years in a journey through a nearby part of the Yukon, made more reasoned and respectful reports concerning the land and the people. But to ignore Schwatka and the ways in which he both embodied and influenced perspectives on what would be called the new frontier of the North, the places and peoples of which most Americans and Canadians otherwise knew very little, would be to miss the very real difficulties Shaaw Tláa would face when her life took the dramatic turn that made her Kate Carmack.

CHAPTER THREE

FAIR TRADE

WHILE A GOOD PART OF THE NINETEENTH CENTURY was marked by heated debates in the newly industrialized United States over whether a time-honored metal like gold should back currency or whether real value came from the production of actual goods and services, the Tagish and Tlingit eschewed currency altogether, trading within their own complex but well-defined system. For as long as anyone could remember, the Tagish had exchanged caribou hides, moose hides, furs, float copper, flint, goat wool, birch bows, lichen dyes, and moccasins for abalone, smoked cockles, dried clams, cedar boxes, dried salmon, dried seaweed, seal oil, and eulachon oil from the coast.[1]

Because they controlled the mountain passes between the Interior and the coast, it was the Tlingit who initiated the trading, which occurred during the more restful phases of the yearly subsistence cycle: *K'óox Dísi*, the early spring Moon of Marten Trapping, when men would deliver furs to trading posts; the midsummer *Tlexa Aatx̱aan Dísi*, or Smoking Salmon Moon; and midwinter, during the *T'aawák Dísi*, or Goose Moon, when the mountain snow packs were blown hard and the avalanche danger was small, making crossings less hazardous.[2]

But in the decades leading up to Shaaw Tláa's birth, the nature of these long-established trading relationships was beginning to shift dramatically, the stakes heightened by the demand from primarily Russian and British traders for furs—especially the thick, warm pelts of otter and marten and mink that populated the inland waters of Alaska and the Yukon. To the north of where Shaaw Tláa grew up, the Hudson Bay Company (HBC) maintained river-based trading routes, but their efforts to push southward had been thwarted by Kohklux and his 1852 raid on Fort Selkirk.

Decades would pass before traders rebuilt Fort Selkirk. In the meantime, the Tlingit included Western goods such as calico, tobacco, and guns as they bartered for furs with the Indians of the Yukon. But though they trapped furs to acquire such goods, the Tagish clans lacked the wealth of the Tlingit, who enjoyed easy and abundant harvests from the oceans. For the Tagish people, subsistence in the boreal forest was a greater challenge, one that required them to stay on the move. Wealth wasn't measured in carvings or trinkets or gold but by what you kept in your head, the story-songs you passed down to your children, stories that told you how to live and behave and even how to die.

Through well-established trading rituals, Shaaw Tláa's best prospects for marriage—expected of every Tagish adult—would be from among her father's Tlingit trading partners, with trade between her father's clan and the clans of the coast approaching its zenith by the time she began wearing old clothes in anticipation of her first menstrual period. Though young, she was prepared to marry. From her mother, she had learned to gather plants for food—soapberries, cranberries, blueberries, stoneberries, wild celery, rhubarb, mossberry, Labrador tea, and bear root. She had also learned sewing, a craft in which she soon became proficient. As she grew, story-songs were her reward for doing extra chores—like all Tagish children, she was eager to be entrusted with the stories of her people.[3] By the time she was ten, she was telling stories herself before a small audience of grown-ups, although as she approached puberty, she was increasingly expected to stay in the background while assuming an increased level of responsibility within her family and community.[4]

Her behavior during this critical time would shape the course of her life, bringing either good luck or bad, and it could even affect the fortunes of her relatives. The moment her menstruation began, she had to stay right where she was, even if she was outside in the bitter cold. Older women, including her mother, would see that a brush shelter was built around her. There she would observe the rules and taboos that tempered the power of her menstrual blood.

After donning a hood stitched by her mother, she would reject food for the first few days of her seclusion; by letting someone else eat, she would be sure not to go hungry in the future. Once she could safely eat again, she still had to shun fresh meat for fear of her new power disturbing a lingering animal spirit. So her lips wouldn't touch water, she drank through a straw fashioned from a swan's bone. She kept busy with sewing, but she was not allowed to do any cutting. To ensure she would always be light on her feet, she blew on the down from a swan. To make sure her teeth stayed strong even after she turned old, she rubbed her teeth with white rocks. But she had to be careful. If it not used properly, spirit power could have unintended consequences.[5]

When she emerged from seclusion, Shaaw Tláa prepared to marry Kult'ús, of the Chilkoot Tlingit, son of her father's trading partner, a clan chief who was also Shaaw Tláa's maternal uncle. Traveling with his father, Kult'ús came from Lḵoot, the Place of Abundance of Food,[6] south of Tlákw.aan, following the trail that came to be known as the Chilkoot, which began at Taiya Inlet, accessible by canoe as long as one knew the places to wait out the powerful tides and winds that characterized this part of the ocean, known later as the Lynn Canal. From there, Shaaw Tláa's future husband traveled two days on foot over the Chilkoot Pass, a hazardous journey during which lives were sometimes lost. While in the mountains, bathing and washing were forbidden, as these actions might precipitate melting snow and avalanches.

On the far side of the Coast Mountains, at Lake Bennett, the Chilkoot traders boarded skin canoes and floated downriver to Marsh Lake, where Shaaw Tláa's family had their fish camp. As

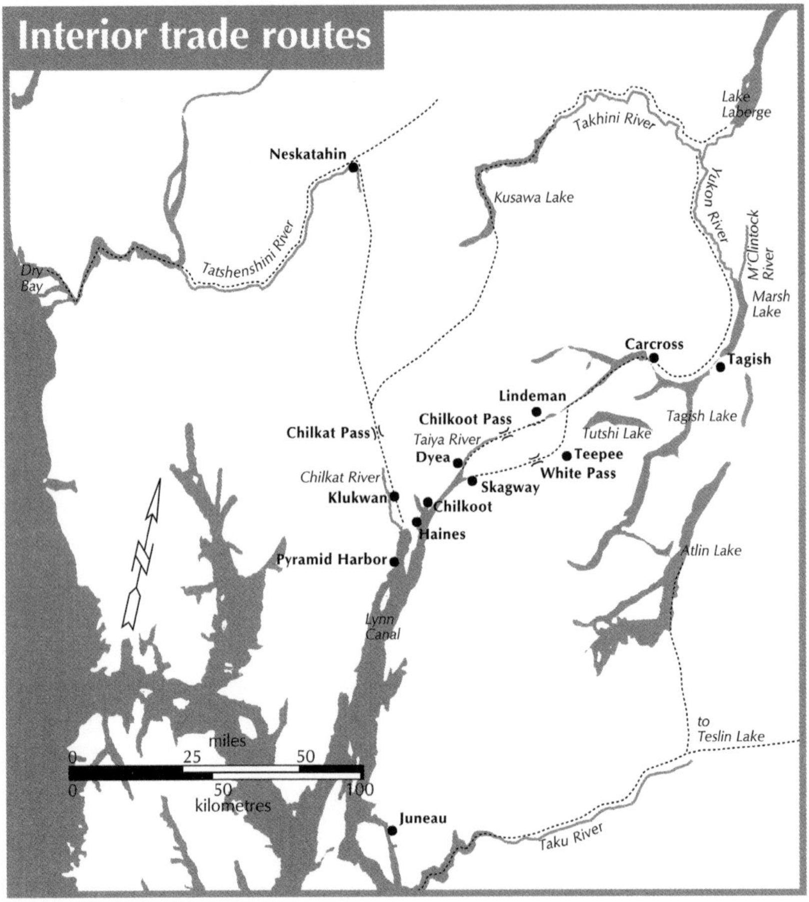

Traditional trade routes of the Chilkat Tlingit, via the Chilkat Pass, and the Chilkoot Tlingit, via the Chilkoot Pass. From *Chilkoot Trail: Heritage Route to the Klondike*, David Neufeld and Frank Norris, 2005, Lost Moose Publishing (an imprint of Harbour Publishing), www.harbourpublishing.com. Used with permission of publisher. Edited by UA Press.

they approached, the Chilkoot fired at a large tree to signal their arrival, then lined up at the edge of the settlement. The Tagish men lined up opposite them, each facing his trading partner. After opening with a drum dance and a song, Shaaw Tláa's father welcomed his guests, and after reiterating his promise to come at this time, the Chilkoot leader took the drum so that his men could perform their own song.

As much about relationships as it was about the exchange of goods, Tagish-Chilkoot trade was carried out in a formal manner that ensured each of the partners walked away feeling both generous and satisfied.[7] After the welcome, the visiting leader handed over all of his packs (except his personal belongings) to Shaaw Tláa's father, who set these aside without looking inside them. While Shaaw Tláa and her sisters prepared a meal, their parents shared tobacco brought by the Chilkoot traders. After eating, the guests offered more food from their packs, exotic items like sugar and tea. Entertainment followed—perhaps a moose-skin blanket toss or a broad jump contest. As the festivities wound down, Shaaw Tláa and her cousin Kult'ús would have slipped into the woods for their own fun, an extension of the trading ritual known as "pairing off."

At some point in the early 1880s, Shaaw Tláa and Kult'ús were officially married in a transaction initiated by the groom's parents, who discussed with Shaaw Tláa's mother and father her skills in sewing and putting up food. Finding her satisfactory, Kult'ús' parents paid the bride price in skins, furs, and beads to her mother, who accepted these gifts after consulting with the elders to make sure they agreed that Kult'ús was a good hunter and worker; with their extensive knowledge of how everyone was related, the elders could make sure no mistakes in clan affiliations would be made with the marriage.

Once the decision was made, Shaaw Tláa's parents hosted a feast at which the elders gave the couple advice about how they should treat one another. At first, the newlyweds lived with her parents, so Kult'ús could prove his skills as a hunter and provider. In marriages that were not so much for love as to firm up a trading alliance, or when the bride's family was of a higher social standing than the groom's, the couple might live permanently with her parents.[8] In Shaaw Tláa's case, her Tlingit husband's family had more wealth than hers, and her family had already established its trading alliance with them, so after her first year of marriage she moved with her husband to the coast to live in a Chilkoot village, as several of her siblings had already done: one of her older brothers had gone off to the coast with a Tlingit wife and an older sister had left with her Tlingit husband.

But Shaaw Tláa's brother and sister both died, struck down by one of the diseases that plagued people on the coast, owing to the direct contact of the Tlingit with outsiders—smallpox, measles, whooping cough, tuberculosis. According to custom, Shaaw Tláa's sister Aagé was sent to marry the Tlingit husband of her dead sister. But before she reached the coast, he too had died, so when Aagé arrived in Lk̲oot, she instead became the third wife of his brother, L'unáat, second chief of the Chilkoot Tlingit, a man who would play a prominent role in the dealings between his people and outsiders who wanted to use the Chilkoot Trail in order to get to the Yukon, where they hoped to make their fortunes in gold.[9]

When Shaaw Tláa left for the coast with her new husband, only two of her sisters remained with their mother. Though leave-taking is never easy, hers was necessary to help insure strong networks and alliances among the Crow and Wolf moieties on both sides of the mountains.[10] On a clear, sunny day, the work of picking her way up and over the Chilkoot Summit, a pass the Tagish called *Kwatese* and the Tlingit called *A Shakée*, has its own rewards—sweeping views from the top, and on the coastal side of the slope, the lush, green temperate rain forest, where cool, moist air settles like dew on the skin and thick spruce boughs hang over the crashing Taiya River, the sun playing through the leaves, shifting patches of light over a forest floor thick with spruce needles. Compared to the boreal forest of the Interior, these dark coastal woods feel decadent and—perhaps to a newcomer like Shaaw Tláa—also frightening.

But Shaaw Tláa was her mother's daughter, strong and well-trained. She had paid attention to the songs and stories in the clan house. She had followed the rules of her seclusion. Perhaps she had rubbed a little too long with white stones on her teeth, but she had a beautiful smile. She sewed in fine stitches that would please her new mother-in-law, and she would learn to gather seaweed and shellfish left by the tides. Most of all, in their coupling, she and Kult'ús would make a child, and that would please everyone.

Shaaw Tláa's new home, Lk̲oot, later called Chilkoot, was poised on the shore of a lake near a deep, steep-banked fjord along the eastern arm of Chilkat Inlet, the chilly waters of Northern Pacific gray-green with run-off[11] from glacial rivers that tumble out of snow-capped mountains rising straight up from the ocean shores. Thick green hemlock, spruce, and cedar darken forest floors watered by plentiful rains and snows dropped from clouds as they rise over the mountains. In the summer, the Chilkoot men used large rocks as platforms for spearing the sockeye salmon that spawn in the short but productive Chilkoot River. Drawn by the salmon, eagles swoop from water to sky in air that smells of fish, mud, and cold. The seashells Shaaw Tláa gathered along the gravel beaches of the inlet may not have been as plentiful as blueberries on a sunny hillside of the Interior, but as trading items they had great value.

While her life had been indirectly affected by the trading ships that plied the northern Pacific—she wore mostly Western-style clothes, for instance, instead of traditional skin garments—it was on the coast that Shaaw Tláa would experience firsthand the mutual adaptations made by her Tlingit relatives to the ways of outsiders who came and went in their big sailing ships. Even as she adjusted to a new landscape, she entered into new cultural terrain similar to what has been identified by historian Richard White as the "middle ground," where creative misunderstandings between members of indigenous cultures and representatives of state-based societies generated new practices, rituals, and beliefs comprised of elements drawn from each group.[12]

At Chilkoot, Shaaw Tláa and Kult'ús occupied one of eight hand-hewn log structures, each housing ten to thirty people, among them her sister Aagé and her husband, L'unáat. As rising chief of the L'ukaax̱.ádi,[13] L'unáat had his hands full. Despite an abundance of food and substantial wealth, there was trouble on the coast, and plenty of it—diseases that the Indian doctors could not squelch; occasional alcohol-fueled skirmishes with the people of Tlákw.aan, the Chilkat village up the inlet from Chilkoot; and dealings with the new Presbyterian missionaries. The missionaries had come in part at L'unáat's request, and while they seemed kind enough, they bumbled when it came to knowing how to behave—their insistence that the dead should be buried, not burned, had brought to the Chilkoot in 1882 one of the worst winters in recent memory, resulting in even more disease and more death.

The first white woman encountered by Shaaw Tláa would have been thin-faced, wide-eyed Carrie Willard, who with her husband founded the Presbyterian Mission across the inlet from Chilkoot, at the place that would become Haines, Alaska. Born in Pennsylvania in 1853, Willard was an unusual child, so preoccupied with the "labors and trials" of procuring souls for God's kingdom that as a young girl, she organized a missionary society among her playmates.[14] When at age eleven she fell so ill that her family feared she would die, Carrie was said to have waited with longing to be taken up with Christ. Only with her parents' assurance that she had God's work to do here on earth did she find the will to recover.

Her health remained delicate, making it all the more shocking that upon her marriage to missionary Eugene S. Willard in 1879, the couple departed in haste for Alaska. In 1881, the Willards settled in what they hoped would be the neutral location of Deishu, the End of the Trail place, located between the villages of the sometimes fractious Chilkat and Chilkoot Tlingit, a place that would become both geographical and cultural middle ground.

Depending on the state of their rocky relationship with the newcomers, L'unáat and his wives, including Aagé, sometimes lived near the mission and sometimes withdrew to their former village. Kult'ús and Shaaw Tláa likely did the same. The Indians were curious about the missionaries; at times, Carrie reported they would peer through the windows of the mission house to watch the goings-on inside. For her part, Carrie was impressed by the beauty of the coastal rainforest, likening it to the tropics with its monstrous leaves, shady waters, and mossy trees.

Gathering his people in the dark, cavernous Whale House in which Chilkat wealth was stored—carvings and blankets and vessels of oil—the Tlingit chief Kohklux made Carrie Willard an honorary member of his clan, the Kaagwaantaan, crested as the Cinnamon Bears.[15] By the light of the crackling fire that burned in the center of the clan house, Carrie perceived the faces of her new clanspeople as lit up with love for her.[16] She in turn demonstrated her admiration for the Tlingit by describing them as "a superior race to the plain-Indian."[17]

But admiration is fickle, and if there was genuine affection between Carrie Willard and the Tlingit she viewed as her charges, there was also suspicion and mistrust. Among the local customs that most vexed Carrie was the puberty seclusion of girls. Appalled that girls were shut away for months and sometimes years in preparation for womanhood, she longed to establish a mission home that would receive children from their parents and raise them in the ways of the church. She and her husband frowned also on potlatches, the multiday feasts in which missionaries believed the hosts redistributed far too much of their wealth to their guests.

To counter beliefs in witchcraft and superstition, Carrie brought groups of Indians into her home to show them her sewing machine and clock. "If some dirt got into the fine wheels of a watch," she asked, "did they think that all the medicine-men in Chilcat could charm it into running-order without removing that obstruction?"[18] So it was with the human body, she tried to explain. Only the medicine of the missionaries, coupled with prayer, could make them well.

The Chilkat and Chilkoot began to bring her the sick, of which there were many, in hopes that through logic or faith—it didn't matter which—their loved ones would be cured of the diseases that had beset them in waves since their first contact with outsiders. For Carrie, much was at stake with each life that hung in the balance. Though the white men's medicine saved some, others were lost, and with each of those deaths the credibility of the missionaries was diminished.

Inadvertently, Shaaw Tláa's Tagish relatives also got the Willards in trouble. Like the few other white people who knew of the Tagish, Carrie called them the Sticks, lumping them together with all inland people, such as the Tahltan, who could be reached via the Stikine River.[19]

The advent of the missionaries was one more change heaped on many that were testing the established rules of conduct between the Tlingit and the Tagish. In a break with protocol, one of Shaaw Tláa's people was bold enough to bring a squirrel robe over the Chilkoot Pass to sell directly to Carrie Willard's husband for a substantially lower price than he would have paid had he bought it through one of the Tlingit middlemen—the mark-up on such items could be as high as 2,000 percent. "You can scarcely imagine the hornet's nest that was stirred up," wrote Carrie Willard. "The people were ready to mob us."[20]

The morning after the offensive transaction, several Tlingit leaders gathered at the mission house, with Aagé's husband, L'unáat, as their spokesperson. "The Sticks are our money," he said, according to Willard's account of the meeting. "We and our fathers before us have gotten rich from them. They are only wild: they are not men, and now you have told them these things and taken away our riches."[21]

Mr. Willard scolded L'unáat, warning that he was heaping up wrath that would return to him on the Judgment Day. To this, Shaaw Tláa's brother-in-law took offense; he was a man of prestige within his clan, and his father and grandfather were men of wealth. The missionaries had brought nothing of value, he said; they had only taken. In anger, L'unáat moved his family back to Chilkoot village. Neither Shaaw Tláa's sister Aagé nor L'unáat's other two wives—polygamy was another sore point with the Willards—would show their faces in church again.[22]

The trouble between the Willards and the Tlingit was compounded when a child died in the village. In a victory for the missionaries, his mother decided to forego the customary burning of the body, which was done in order to free the spirit so it would not return to haunt the living. Instead, the grieving mother consented to have the boy buried, as the Willards had been urging. Following the burial came a horrible winter of blinding storms and snow so deep that only the peaks of the outhouse roofs could be seen. Unable to reach their storehouses, everyone was desperate for food. In an admission that her violation of proper behavior had brought both bad weather and famine, the mother of the dead child finally relented—a great fire was built on the beach, and the child's body was dug up and burned.[23]

Still there came another round of sickness. The Willards' baby screamed and went into spasms. Welts formed on her back. Though Carrie called for her husband to stoke the fires and heat water for the baby, he was felled by a headache so severe that he could only roll on the floor in agony. As he grew delirious, Carrie packed both him and Baby, as she called their child, in scalding packs. Somehow, they pulled through.[24]

Others were not so fortunate, including Shaaw Tláa, when the sickness came to her family.

CHAPTER FOUR

FREE TO ALL WHITE MEN

As waterfalls splashed melted snow from the mountains, the *Kahaakw.ish* moon brought an end to the long northern winter. Sandpipers scurried over the tide-exposed shores of the northern Lynn Canal. In the forests, the warbling of the pine grosbeak, the white-winged crossbill, and the red finch were punctuated by the caw of the raven, the screech of the Steller's jay, and the tapping of the woodpecker.

As they did at the end of each winter, Shaaw Tláa and the women of Lk̲oot searched the receding snowline for spring roots.[1] When the seals delivered their pups, the gulls laid their eggs, and the black seaweed ripened, hordes of *saak*—hooligan, or eulachon, also called candlefish—crowded the mouths of the Chilkat and Chilkoot rivers, where careening gulls and eagles shrieked over the bounty of fish.[2] Under normal circumstances, this was a joyous time on the coast, when all but the very old and the very young abandoned their dark winter shelters to camp in the open air at the edge of the ocean in order to harvest the plump, plentiful fish that benefited both health and wealth, the hooligan and its oil being prized for trade with the Tagish and other inland tribes.[3] Burned whole, the small fish gave light during the dark winter months. Rendered, hooligan oil was good medicine, a commodity so valuable that the trading routes over the mountains from the coast to the Interior were known as "grease trails."

Standing in the prows of their canoes, Tlingit husbands and fathers and uncles pushed their poles into the ocean waters, then hoisted them up to display hooligan speared on nails that stuck out from the wooden paddles. In no time, the vessels grew so heavy with fish that they had to be paddled, wobbly with weight, back to shore, where the squirming masses were dumped into huge pits dug into the beach. A portion of the harvest was roasted fresh over an open fire, a delicacy to celebrate the end of winter and the beginning of another season of subsistence and renewal.[4] The rest of the fish were strung by the women to dry on long sticks[5] or dumped inside cleaned-out canoes filled with fresh water that was brought to a boil using heated stones. From these steaming converted canoes, hooligan oil was skimmed and cooled in seal bladders, where it would age. To render a single gallon of oil required upward of six hundred fish,[6] and so the harvest involved even the children, who gathered fish from the seaweed along the water's edge[7] and fetched snow from mountains to mix with the oil and berries to make Indian ice cream.[8]

By the time of the *saak* harvest in the spring of 1885, Shaaw Tláa had given birth to a daughter.[9] If she were too young to help with the fish, her little girl would have been wrapped in soft rabbit skins and carried on Shaaw Tláa's back in a moose hide pack lined with moss. That she had been born healthy and strong was no accident. While pregnant, Shaaw Tláa would have averted her eyes so she wouldn't see otter or mink, whose dangerous spirit powers could harm the unborn. One of the Tlingit women would have slid an arrow down the front of her dress to encourage a quick delivery. And when her birth pains had begun, Shaaw Tláa would have entered the canvas hut where Tlingit children were born while Kult'ús circled outside, unlacing the strings of his shirt and singing a song to hasten the labor.[10]

As a young mother working among the Chilkoot women, Shaaw Tláa understood the moral obligations to the *saak*.[11] No one was to splash or make loud noises or wear bright colors. No dishwater, pots, dogs, hands, or feet should touch the water. If you went into the river unclothed, the hooligan would sap your strength and you would drown. Menstruating women had to stay away, and because the *saak* were sensitive fish, feuds and bad feelings had to be set aside.[12] When the catch was poor, the blame fell on the *gutzkakon*, the strangers from far away.[13] Said to have angered Kanagu, the legendary stone woman whose house was along the Chilkoot Trail,[14] the anemometer belonging to Carrie Willard's husband was blamed for the poor start of one hooligan run.

During the *saak* season of 1885, there was yet another potential problem—a 311-ton gunboat, the *USS Pinta*, anchored in the green waters of Portage Cove. In addition to other duties, the crew of the iron-hulled boat had been charged with ensuring that a handful of miners who had hitched a ride with them achieved safe passage over the Chilkoot Trail, where they would fan out over the Yukon watershed, searching for gold. Though their numbers were small, these prospectors represented both potential opportunity in the form of wages for packing as well as a growing threat to the Tlingit, who were struggling to maintain control of their fiercely guarded trading routes to the Tagish and other inland groups.

Among the miners on board the *Pinta* that spring was twenty-five-year-old George Washington Carmack. By the time the *saak* ran the following year, Shaaw Tláa would become Kate Carmack, his wife.

In contrast to Kate, much about George Carmack would be entered early on into the historical record, due in no small part to the fact that, unlike his wife, he was literate, and as a man of the dominant culture, his flaws were readily overlooked by those who would choose to make a hero of him. Blue-eyed and handsome despite a prominent nose that he himself joked about, George had first come to Alaska in 1882. Conscripted into the US Marines, he'd served aboard the *USS Wachusett* under the command of Frederick Pearson. Gunboat captains came and went from Alaska almost as predictably as the *saak*, and George had

George Carmack in 1883. (Yukon Archives, James Albert Johnson fonds, 82/341 #7)

been with Pearson for the entire six months of his command, from March to October of 1882. After a summer plying Alaskan waters, the *Wachusett* docked at Mare Island near San Francisco. It was from there that George Carmack jumped ship.

Though mostly good-natured, George did not appreciate being told what to do, and he was quick to feel slighted. He also was quick to lay blame. For his military desertion, he faulted Captain Pearson, who had refused George leave to visit his sister, Rose, who had taken ill. George's mother had died when he was three years old, and following the death of his father when George was eleven, Rose, who had been married at age fourteen to a man twice her age, had raised her younger brother.

Because his parents had traveled from the Midwest to California in the mid-nineteenth century, people would later say that gold was in George's blood. But his father left Illinois in 1859, more than a decade after a nugget plucked from the waters near Sutter's Mill had triggered the California Gold Rush. What George's father had been after in California was not precious metal but dirt, as in farmland—good, black soils warmed by steady sunshine and moistened with gentle coastal rains.

After the elder Carmack's death, Rose's husband James Watson had put George to work on his small ranch in the golden hills of San Benito County, one hundred miles southeast of San Francisco. George developed a distaste for ranching, but after his abrupt and illegal exit from the *Wachusett*, he had few options. If military authorities were to catch him, as was the case with one-fifth of the Marines who went AWOL, he could face imprisonment and hard labor. To collect the $120 reward on a deserter's head, even friends, wives, and mothers had been known to surrender the wayward.[15]

A staunch Baptist, George's sister would never have given him up to the authorities, but she did chide him for his "strange notions" and rash decisions. "I wish you would hurry and sow your wild oats and settle down with me," she wrote to her brother shortly after he'd granted himself permanent leave from the Marines. "You don't know how earnestly I pray that you will not walk in forbidden paths."[16]

After deserting his post, George hid out on the far side of the Sierra Nevada range, in the high desert of Tulare, where he had cousins. Compared to what he'd seen in Alaska, he was unimpressed with the landscape. "If a country needs sinking below Hades, it is Tulare," he wrote. To get there required traveling a hundred miles over "the dustiest road you ever saw." Upon his arrival, he'd waded through dust and sand to reach what passed for a hotel—he called it a "shebang"—only to have the innkeeper turn him away.

His account of what happened next is classic Carmack—colorful, self-aggrandizing, and almost certainly untrue:

> "Have you got any blankets?" a bystander asked.
> "Why yes, sir," George replied.
> "Come with me then," the man said.

> "Shouldering my blankets, I followed him," George wrote. "After wading through dust again, we came to another shebang. And what was it? It was an undertaker's shop. There stood a great grim coffin looking at me just as much as to say I am just your fit, and so it was, for I tried it."[17]

Flat broke, George took work herding sheep. Dirty and greasy, but thankfully not lousy—the Tulare plains were crawling with lice—he emerged from his tent each cold desert morning to face another day of drudgery.[18] Eventually, he saved enough to pay for passage back to Alaska aboard the steamship *Queen*, which left San Francisco at the end of March, 1885.

George arrived ten days later in Juneau where, with the help of the local Tlingit, prospectors had located veins of gold five years earlier. He could have worked for $2.50 a day at the stamp mill, where water-powered stamps crushed ore so that the gold could be extracted from it. But the lakes were the place for him, at least for the summer, meaning the lakes where the Tagish made their home, on the inland side of the Chilkoot Pass. Equipped only with a gold pan and some luck, a fellow might find some color all on his own there, or so George had heard.

What stood between George Carmack and his chance at fortune were the Chilkoot Tlingit, led by L'unáat,[19] who "got their backs up and would not let some men go over. . .There are about 12 men up at chilcat now waiting for the Boat to cool the Indians down," George wrote to Rose in May 1885. "But they are all right now," he added, "for they [the Indians] have a Holy Horror for gunboats."[20]

If the Tlingit had a "holy horror" of gunboats, it was with good reason. To start with, the 1867 transfer of Alaska from Russia to the United States remained a sore point. At Sitka, Tlingit leaders had relinquished only a few acres to the Russians—as they saw it, the Russians had only occupied other portions of the territory by invitation of the local people, for the mutually beneficial purpose of trade. How, then, could they sell lands that didn't belong to them in the first place?[21]

That the so-called new owners were Americans was a special difficulty. Sixty years before Seward finalized the Alaska Purchase, not far from where the *Pinta* now hunkered in Chilkoot Inlet, seventy Chilkat men had been killed in a reported attempt to board and loot a "Boston" rig. "They [the Tlingit] are proud and independent in manner, and are said to cherish peculiar hatred to Americans," wrote Colonel Robert Scott in 1867. "Small parties of Americans should be very cautious in dealing with these Indians."[22]

In May 1885, it would fall to Shaaw Tláa's brother-in-law L'unáat to determine what to do about George Carmack and the other prospectors aboard the *USS Pinta*. The larger events that played into this particular crisis had begun far from the shores of Alaska, which had joined the Union at a bad time. In the aftermath of the Civil War, America was struggling to pull itself back together. The federal government was a mess. During the presidency of Ulysses S. Grant, graft, bribery, and pay-offs were common. Money changed hands not simply to gain political power but also to gain advantage in expansive and potentially lucrative ventures along the American frontier, where land speculators wiped out seemingly infinite herds of buffalo and Indian tribes were systematically cut off from the lands that had traditionally sustained them. Aside from exploiting the western frontier, the collective national attention was fixed on advances in technology, communications, and industry. Managing Seward's 586,412-square-mile icebox was the least of the nation's worries.[23]

In the absence of any other American authority, the US Navy more or less ruled Alaska on behalf of the US government; having taken great pains to orchestrate the Alaska Purchase, William Seward had advised Congress to run the region as a temporary military district until a viable economic base could be established. The military administered policies that turned as quickly as the commanders of the gunboats patrolling the waters, and the soldiers assigned to Alaska proved a rough, undisciplined sort, plagued by boredom.[24] As head of the Presbyterian missions' effort in the new Alaska district (Alaska would not become an organized territory until 1912), Sheldon Jackson complained that it would take twenty years to undo ten years of evil inflicted upon the Indians by the soldiers, with syphilis and a molasses-brewed rum known as hoochinoo being chief among these problems.[25] The Tlingit, too, declaimed the debauching effects of liquor and the white man's easy way with their women.[26]

Gloomily prophetic over what might transpire, the *New York Tribune* extrapolated from what had gone in the American West, proclaiming that to kill one of "Seward's Indians" would require an expenditure of $300,000 by the US government.[27] From a financial point of view, a more expedient solution to the so-called "Indian problem" had been to wipe Tlingit villages off the map. In the Kake War of 1869, the military demonstrated this method by sending a gunboat to destroy three Native communities. The conflict was eventually settled when a local trader took it upon himself to provide the restitution that the US military in its wisdom had failed to offer—thirteen blankets and one coat, a total outlay of about $50.[28]

In a rare show of interest by a federal official, Commissioner of Indian Affairs Vernon Coyler traveled to Alaska at his own expense to witness firsthand the tensions that had brought on the Kake War. His recommendation: the authority of the military over the Indians must be removed at once. "A greater mistake could not have been committed than stationing troops in their midst," he wrote concerning Anglo-Indian interactions. "They mutually debauch each other, and sink into that degree of degradation in which it is utterly impossible to reach."[29]

Anchored in Chilkoot Inlet, the *USS Pinta* was proof that such pleas had been ignored. Among other functions, the military had deemed itself responsible for negotiating safe passage on behalf of prospectors like George Carmack, tempted by reports such as that of Reverend Robert McDonald, missionary of the Anglican Church in the Mackenzie River Valley, who had reported finding gold so thick along one creek that he could scoop it up with a spoon.[30] Fort Selkirk trader Robert Campbell had also noted gold in the region. But the trading companies, most notably the Hudson Bay Company and the

Alaska Commercial (AC) Company, had not wanted their traders distracted by gold. The real money, they believed, was in furs. For their part, the Tagish and other inland groups had little interest in gold. Coveted for making weapons and tools, copper was the metal they valued, and for trading, you couldn't beat furs.

US Navy Captain L. A. Beardslee commanded the waters closest to the two Tlingit-controlled routes, the so-called Chilkoot and Chilkat trails. A shrewd and capable straight shooter, Beardslee blamed *hooch* for Alaska's "Indian trouble," and he blamed the federal government for allowing the hooch. He also questioned the motives of white settlers who demanded a naval presence in the region; their interests, he maintained, appeared to be have more to do with a ship's substantial monetary disbursements for various services the settlers provided than with the actual protection offered.[31]

When Beardslee's proposal that Alaska be allowed to govern itself went unheeded, he charged local Tlingit leaders with enforcing the peace, and he applied Tlingit logic to the problems he was called upon to solve. Petitioned by nineteen miners seeking passage over the Chilkoot Trail in 1880, Beardslee made them pledge to carry no hooch and to eschew direct trade with the "Stick Indians." In negotiating such passage, the Tlingit made no secret of their terms—at their discretion, you might visit, but staying required an invitation, and if anything of value was to leave the Interior for the coast, it had to pass through a Tlingit middleman.[32]

When two of the miners violated their end of the agreement by trading directly with the Sticks, Kohklux begged Beardslee to intervene before the men were killed. The captain and his lieutenant negotiated a settlement that also included a payment of two hundred Chilkat blankets to end a blood feud with the Chilkoot that had dragged on for more than a year. In no small part, this peace was aided by the notice taken of two new and powerful weapons of war mounted to the aft of the ship under Beardslee's command: howitzer and Gatling guns. It took little imagination to envision the damage that could be done to a fleet of wooden canoes by ten rotating barrels of bullets.[33]

These were among the threats bearing down upon the people of Shaaw Tláa's new home, and in particular, her brother-in-law L'unáat, during the spring of 1885. A single Gatling could wipe out a fleet of warriors. A single gunboat could take out an entire community. A single barrel of hoochinoo could incite bloody clan warfare. Diseases continued to fell the young, the old, the healthy, the weak, with the shaman helpless against them. And with each passing spring came more white men, demanding passage over the mountains so they could hunt for gold. Of the two routes inland, they preferred the Chilkoot, a route that though steep and difficult was short and direct compared to the Chilkat Trail, accessed through Kohklux from the village of Tlákw.aan.

Rising chief to his Uncle Daanawáak, called "Silver Eyes" because of the spectacles perched on his nose, L'unáat was still feeling his way with leadership of the Chilkoot Tlingit. Photographed on the occasion of the 1881 settlement of the blood feud with the Chilkat, he wore a traditional woven blanket around his shoulders—possibly one that was part of the restitution—and a tall felt hat on his head. Of the four Tlingit leaders photographed, his expression is most alert; a piercing gaze tops his frown. Articulate, kind-hearted, but also quick-tempered, Shaaw Tláa's brother-in-law had high expectations of himself and everyone else, as he once demonstrated by storming into the Presbyterian mission house, dragging his young successor outside, and throwing the boy to the ground because he had whacked a flopping fish in the head with a rock, a transgression that could have caused the whole village to suffer the effects of horrific rains.

Under the Tlingit reckoning regarding communal property and communal liability, L'unáat was responsible for the safety of every person who trekked over the Chilkoot Pass. Faced with increasing pressure from the gunboat commanders, he had been allowing prospectors to use the Chilkoot Trail as long as they paid in something other than hooch for the Indians to pack their supplies, and as long as they promised not to trade with the Sticks. But sometimes the white men couldn't be trusted.

As George Carmack wrote in the spring of 1885, L'unáat had drawn a firm line with the first twelve prospectors to arrive—no more white men were going over the pass unless they paid a guaranteed rate per hundred pounds for the services of Chilkoot packers. When the prospectors refused, L'unáat warned them to leave or they'd be killed.

When the *Pinta* arrived with even more prospectors, the second chief knew he'd need leverage to negotiate with the military officials. In a practice that typifies middle-ground interactions, Tlingit leaders were in the habit of carrying with them letters to recommend them to strangers. But the letters already in L'unáat's possession were less than impressive—one was an I.O.U. for tobacco, and the other elaborated on his weakness for falling in love with white women.[34] What L'unáat needed was a real letter, with a genuine recommendation, that would give him an edge with the captain of the gunboat.

To get it, he set out over the Chilkoot Pass to Lake Bennett, a journey of two days or more, depending on the conditions of the sloppy spring trail. At the head of the lakes where the Tagish lived, he tracked down a prospector who had reliably and fairly compensated Chilkoot packers for their services. In pencil, the prospector scribbled a note saying that as second chief, L'unáat was the "best one in the tribe." He added that in packing for him in three trips over the pass, L'unáat had "always acted on the square." His closing words: "Use him right and he will Do the same as near as an Indian can." On the back of the letter, the prospector wrote "White Men Please Read."

L'unáat hurried back over the summit to Lynn Canal, where a colorful Tlingit canoe delivered him to the *USS Pinta*. Impressed with the endorsement, the ship's lieutenant added his seal to the prospector's letter, along with a note stating that the Indians were to receive a flat rate of $15 per hundred pounds for packing over the pass. As the leader charged with overseeing the operations, L'unáat was to be paid extra.[35]

In return for this seal of approval and promise of a guaranteed wage, L'unáat was obliged to carry with him another letter, this one written and signed by the commander of the gunboat:

> This country is free to all White men to go through in the pursuit of their business; it is for your interest to have them here because they bring you wealth by your contracts to work for them. If any of the White men desire to do their own packing they must not be interfered with. The chiefs of the Tribe and the headmen of families are by me held responsible for the good conduct of their people, and the White Chief, who governs the whole country, is very angry with you for this ill treatment of peaceable people passing through your country. Should there be any disturbances or outrages that call for my interference, I shall punish the offenders to the full extent of the law.[36]

CHAPTER FIVE

Peculiar Privilege

At first, the complications that arose from the longing for gold had only a peripheral effect on Shaaw Tláa. L'unáat's negotiations with the crew of the *Pinta* offered new perspectives in interacting with outsiders who had vastly different ways of seeing, knowing, and communicating. In 1879, a Chilkoot shaman had summed up this challenge by saying, "It has always seemed to me while trying to speak to traders and those seeking gold-mines that it was like speaking to a person across a broad stream that was running fast over stones and making so loud a noise that scarce a single word could be heard."[1]

In a narrative all too familiar in Anglo-Indian relations, each time L'unáat thought he had reached an agreement with a representative of the Great Tyee, chief of the outsiders, the terms inexplicably shifted. Within a year of his negotiations with the crew of the *USS Pinta*, Chilkoot packers still weren't being paid the wages promised. Worse, L'unáat was beginning to lose control of the trail.[2] His packers simply couldn't keep up with demand, especially as coastal families were being drawn from their *k̲wáans* to work at salmon canneries across the Lynn Canal, in Pyramid Harbor.

Beginning with the 1883 Schwatka expedition, L'unáat had allowed Tagish packers related to the Chilkoot by marriage to be hired on, but they were to work only on the inland side of the mountains. By the spring of 1886, half of the two hundred packers camped on the coastal end of the trail were Tagish, and they were packing along the entire route, not just on their side. Among them were Shaaw Tláa's brother, Keish, and in all likelihood, also Shaaw Tláa herself; nearly half the packers that year were women and children.[3] Like the other women, Shaaw Tláa carried fifty to one hundred pounds on her back over *Shaa Shakée*, the Chilkoot Pass, while children hauled food and cooking utensils. Even dogs, normally used only for sledding, carried packs over the trail.[4] Among Yukon Indians, packing with sacks made of tanned skins or finely netted sinew was traditionally done by women, so Shaaw Tláa was earning wages for the same sort of work she would have done in helping her family move from camp to camp.[5]

Demand for packing services was especially high in 1885 because of a gold strike on the Stewart, a river that empties into the Yukon more than four hundred miles downriver from Shaaw Tláa's childhood home. More than half of the seventy-five men looking for gold in the Yukon that year were headed there, where from only one gravel bar the two men who'd make the initial discovery had extracted $6,000 in gold, the equivalent of a handsome year's wages; seven miles up the Stewart, four other miners had made a haul of $35,000.[6]

Even with the women and children and dogs, even with the large Tagish contingent, L'unáat was forced to also allow a few Tlingit relatives from the southern panhandle of Alaska to pack for hire over the Chilkoot Trail. By the following year, in June 1886, a record ninety-three miners had gone over the Chilkoot Trail. They broached the summit in groups up to twenty-five strong, with an average of six packs to the man. That season, certain Tlingit and Tagish packers earned up to $3,000, paid in silver, not gold, which they did not trust.[7]

Simple economics would suggest that as demand for the services of packers went up, so would their wages. In L'unáat's letter from Lieutenant Nichols, the number fifteen, as in $15 per hundred pounds, had been traced over and over in pencil. Still, with every new batch of prospectors, L'unáat found himself negotiating all over again for wages he believed only fair, given his personal liability for the outsiders and the extreme conditions over which his people were packing an average of four hundred pounds of supplies for each would-be miner.

Always a hard worker, Shaaw Tláa was pushed to a new level of physical endurance when she hired out to pack supplies for the prospectors. Each time she strapped on a pack using leather bindings that went around her forehead and waist, she face a precipitous climb—from sea level, the Chilkoot Trail rises nearly 4,000 feet in less than eighteen miles. Through the coastal rainforest of tall, ancient Sitka spruce and western hemlock, she followed a trail that was mucky and wet, climbing in many spots alongside the rushing green-gray waters of the Taiya River. Past the tree line, where the forest gives way to high alpine flowers and hardy mosses and lichens, she had nothing to walk on but large, irregular rocks, with few level places to rest.

For final half-mile to the summit, she had to scale huge boulders, a steep climb that required her to lash herself to other packers using lengths of strong, plaited rawhide. Even on the warmest summer days, she had to cut footholds in the snow near the summit.[8] Beyond falling, the dangers were legion, including avalanche, blizzards, dense fog, and bears. Even Frederick Schwatka, while inconsistent in paying his packers, admitted that they labored mightily in their duties, leveraging loads of more than a hundred pounds using nothing more than deerskin bands around their heads.[9]

With the wages she earned hauling supplies for men eager to find gold, Shaaw Tláa was able to purchase the best trading goods at the best prices—sugar, fabric, beads, pots and pans, canned goods, needles for sewing. All these items and more were available at a trading post across the Chilkoot Inlet from Lḵoot, at the mouth of the Taiya River, in a place called *Dayéi*, rendered as Dyea, the jumping-off point for the Chilkoot Trail. Newly arrived in Alaska, the owner of the store was a shrewd and sometimes combative entrepreneur named John J. Healy, whose actions would affect Shaaw Tláa's life in multiple ways, up to and beyond the Klondike discovery.

Like Alaska's district governor and his syndicate of New York and Boston investors, Healy was banking on reports of gold trickling out of the Yukon. Before coming to Alaska, he had knocked about in the West, where he and his partner made a chance discovery that led to a small rush for gold along Idaho's Salmon River. Though he failed to find enough color to inspire him to keep looking, he learned how much and how fast prices rose once a mining stampede got rolling—the price of a horse had risen within hours, from $30 to $125, while flour went from $40 to $100 a sack.

After twenty years in the West, Healy considered himself an expert in dealing with Indians, to whom he referred—rather typically, for a frontiersman—as "hostiles" and "fiends." He thought that the federal government was too sentimental when it came to Indian policy, whereas the army "understood the Indian and his social need for war."[10] Prior to setting up his post in Dyea, he traveled the western plains of Canada, where he established Fort Hamilton—not a military installation but a trading post, fortified with guns and blockades against possible attacks by the "hostiles," an installation known to locals as Fort Whoop-Up.

Situated on a river bluff with a sweeping view of the prairie, Healy's Fort Hamilton was protected by a heavily fortified gate, a mountain howitzer, and an alarm bell. From his days as an Indian agent in Montana, Healy had discovered the large profit potential in trading whisky to the Indians. Through a Fort Whoop-Up wicket, an Indian could exchange a buffalo robe for two cups of whiskey, watered down but spiked with red pepper so it still had a kick. According to his son, adopted by Healy upon the death of the boy's Indian father, the fort was a "jolly home of American desperadoes."[11]

The Dyea trading post had only been open a few months when Healy got in the middle of a fracas between the L'unáat and Charles

Seghers, a Catholic bishop on his way to reestablish a mission hundreds of miles down the Yukon River. The problem began when a prospector refused to pay the Chilkoot packers anything more than $10 per hundred pounds for carrying his supplies over the mountains.[12] L'unáat countered with $13 per hundred pound, two dollars less than the rate promised in his letter from Lieutenant Nichols. When the prospector refused to budge on the price, L'unáat ordered the Chilkoot to take their canoes and go home.

Two days later, L'unáat and his packers returned. By this time, additional white men had arrived, also in need of passage and packing services—two Catholic priests and Bishop Charles Seghers. A slender, studious Belgian immigrant, Seghers was unknowingly carrying more than the gospel into Alaska and the Yukon—his parents and four siblings had died of tuberculosis and he, too, was infected.[13] In front of John Healy's trading post, Seghers joined the prospectors in their demand that packing wages not exceed $10 per hundred pounds. L'unáat waved his letter with the seal of Lieutenant Nichols. Fifteen dollars, it said. Moreover, it declared that L'unáat was a good and reliable man, a fine chief who should be respected.

Bishop Charles Seghers begged to differ. L'unáat was not a good man; he had allowed his packers to return with full knowledge that the rate which had been offered was $10 per hundred pounds. Now he wanted $13. According to the bishop, this made L'unáat a liar.

Had he known that L'unáat's diplomacy and patience were reaching a breaking point, Seghers might have taken more care with his words. He'd spent time with the Indians of Vancouver Island and was not completely ignorant of the ways in which cultural differences might be accommodated. In state-run societies, the terms of a contract were negotiated between the two parties doing business, not dictated by the terms of some old letter. But to the Tlingit, the letters signified the terms on which significant relationships had been established, and contracts were fluid arrangements that could and should shift, not arbitrarily, but to accommodate forces beyond human reckoning: wind, rains, snows, tides, the spirit world. As more was required—by weather, by a labor shortage when the *saak* or the salmon were running—more must be paid.

In this particular contract dispute, L'unáat did not take kindly to the bishop calling him a liar. His response was to chuck the religious official lightly under the nose, a blow that some would later describe as a slap. The prospectors in Seghers' party readied their rifles. To those white men who were unarmed, Healy handed out more guns, along with advice not to let the Natives surround them. The outsiders retreated to Healy's store while approximately a hundred Tlingit and Tagish packers, some armed with knives, went off to confer.

Following a two-hour standoff, L'unáat returned to offer a packing rate of $12 per hundred pounds, which the outsiders accepted. The bishop, who had not planned on having to pay anything, had to borrow money from Healy for his share.[14]

But the matter didn't end there. Bishop Seghers reported the affront to Alaska's district governor, who traveled in person to Lk̲oot to arrest L'unáat, assisted in his mission by none other than John Healy, who would later be named US marshal in the region. To the governor, L'unáat again asserted his right to charge what he deemed reasonable for white men to use the trail that belonged to the Chilkoot. The governor in turn insisted that fees could be charged only for packing, not for use of the trail, and in any event, he was not going to tolerate an assault on a bishop. To reinforce his point, he had L'unáat jailed in Sitka, though he freely admitted to his superiors that there was no evidence on which to bring him to trial.

Not surprisingly, the editors at the *Sitka Alaskan*, a newspaper owned by the governor, lauded this maneuver. "The protection of whites from Indian aggression is far more important than any sentimental reverence of the red man's peculiar privileges," the editors wrote.[15] The editorial reaction was consistent with complaints that dated back to 1869, the year of the eclipse: "The Indians rule and their fashions are law in that land . . . at present the Indians govern to suit their own interests."[16]

The notion that a people should govern themselves with an eye to anything other than their own interests was a thin disguise for the real problem, which was that the Chilkoot, with labor supplied in part by Shaaw Tláa and others in her family, were conducting a "very large trading business" that interfered with the profit motives of the newcomers.[17] During a time when the interests of the sprawling monopolies of the American "robber barons" superseded the general good, it was still an outrage that a small band of Indians might make money from working a trail that for centuries had been under their control.

Enticed by the potential for profit, entrepreneurs in Juneau formed the Chilkoot Pass and Summit Railroad Company, a venture that would have put the Tlingit and Tagish packers out of business. But between the precipitous canyons and steep final approach to the summit, the Chilkoot Trail would prove unfit for laying tracks.[18]

Ever on the lookout for opportunity, John Healy got his hands on a double-masted schooner, the *Charlie*, to transport prospectors from Juneau to Dyea. In 1886, he hired an "old sea pirate" to captain the vessel and none other than George Carmack to serve as second mate.[19] Healy and Carmack had first met in Juneau, a haphazard town spawned by Alaska's first gold rush. "Its houses appear as if they had fallen pell-mell from the sky," wrote Bishop Seghers when he passed through Juneau. "One house is turned to the west, another seems to be looking for the rising sun, a third turns its back to the water and its front to the mountain."[20] What it lacked in street-front aesthetics, Juneau made up for in hustle and bustle, and Healy liked that. Even a knocker—Healy's term for those who downplayed opportunity—could see that the town was booming, thanks to gold.

After three months exploring the prospects in Tagish lake country during the summer of 1885, George Carmack had passed the coldest part of the winter shipwrecked west of Juneau on Admiralty Island, where he subsisted on clams and suffered a bad bout of rheumatism.[21] When he finally reached Juneau, his plan had been to save up over the winter in order to fund another prospecting expedition into the Yukon. Then a letter came from his girlfriend in California. "Darn Becky said she wished I was back there, as it seems awful lonesome," he wrote to his sister. "It appears that people don't appreciate me until I am gone."[22] With Becky's letter, George changed his mind about future prospecting. "I don't think that I will go in there [the Yukon] again if can get good wages here. I will stay here [in Juneau] until I make a grubstake for Becky and me."[23]

But Becky's interest in George Carmack soon waned. Jilted, he turned again to prospecting. Though he'd found only scant gold that would have to be worked with expensive hydraulics, he proclaimed the Tagish lake country the finest he'd ever seen, with fine water, good land, abundant wood, and—during his visit in 1885—long, sunny days. As far as prospecting, George prided himself on his pragmatic outlook, especially compared to other gold-seekers. "Some men have come up here expecting to find gold laying around on the beach, and some of them have got fooled pretty hard," he wrote. "One young man drowned himself and another shot himself because someone did not fill their pockets with nuggets the day they landed."[24]

Crewing aboard the *Charlie*, George delivered supplies to Healy's trading post in Dyea during the first part of the summer of 1886. He also helped build the trader's house, a simple log structure, nothing like the fortress at Fort Whoop-Up. No doubt George also got an education in Indian relations from Healy, who was never shy about speaking his mind. As the Hudson Bay Company's tight-fisted control of trading along Canadian waterways had irked Healy, so did L'unáat's monopoly on traffic over the Chilkoot Trail. Healy wanted to improve the trail by laying logs through the wet spots and then charge a toll for its use.

Until he accomplished this task, Healy aimed to do as he'd done in Montana and Alberta: he'd figure out who were the bad Indians and who were the good ones, and he'd ally himself with the latter. To assess complex cultural interactions through this simple dichotomy—good Indian, bad Indian—was a favorite strategy of outsiders such as Healy, whose impressions of Natives came from the American West, where some groups were indeed more hostile and warlike than others, although more often than not it was their proximity to the point of incursion, otherwise called the frontier, that forced their defensive stance.

Confronted with Healy's intentions regarding the Chilkoot Trail, L'unáat was backed into a corner. It was his duty to preserve Chilkoot dominance in the region, retaining a balance of power that had been worked out over centuries of trading and alliance-building. From Healy's perspective, that made him a bad Indian, with the slap to the bishop as evidence, should any be required. On the other hand, Healy determined that L'unáat's Tagish relatives, including Shaaw Tláa and her brother Keish, were good Indians. Held in check by their more wealthy Tlingit relations, they were also thought to hold a grudge that Healy believed he could work to his advantage—Shaaw Tláa's father, the Tagish Deisheetaan chief, had reportedly once called the Chilkoot "all the same dog," gesturing to indicate a vicious snapping.[25]

Healy also surmised that once he wrested control of the trail from L'unáat, he would still need Indian packers to generate income. Conveniently, the Tagish packers, forbidden from direct trade by the Tlingit, were used to getting paid half of what they were worth. In short, to ally himself with the Tagish clans would be a win all around for John Healy.

Close as he was with George Carmack during the summer of 1886, Healy's advice regarding Indian relations would also have included the advantages of taking an Indian wife. Given the wild goings-on at his Fort Whoop-Up, Healy had left his first wife, Mary, and their children back in Montana, which conveniently freed him to take an Indian woman into his household while in Canada. Through this Indian wife, he enjoyed the benefits of sexual attention, and he was also able to forge alliances with the locals, all while learning more about how the Indians thought and behaved—an education that proved useful for turning profits in trading. When he was done with Fort Whoop-Up, Healy would leave his Indian wife to fend for herself.

CHAPTER SIX

A Troublesome Question

Against the backdrop of George Carmack's education in Indian relations and John Healy's ambitions to undo L'unáat's hold on the Chilkoot Trail came events of even more direct and immediate consequence for Shaaw Tláa: both Kult'ús and her daughter fell sick, most likely in the late summer or early fall of 1886. As with each wave of disease that passed through coastal villages—smallpox, scarlet fever, measles, mumps, influenza—the long-haired "Indian doctors" proved mostly helpless, no matter how many blankets were offered in exchange for their assistance.

As a traditional remedy, there was Skookum Root, coming from a plant that grew high in the mountains, with a sturdy stalk and glossy, long leaves. When digging the root, Shaaw Tláa knew to speak to it with respect: "Grandmother, I want you to do your best for my husband and daughter. Do your best. I'm picking you for medicine."[1] When the Skookum Root failed to cure Kult'ús and their daughter, Shaaw Tláa likely called on the missionaries, despite conflicting ideas about whether they cured or caused such sickness.

But nothing could save her husband and daughter. Statistically, their deaths were part of a mortality rate that, according the governor of Alaska, indicated "the gradual extinction of the native people."[2] In grief, Shaaw Tláa blackened her face with charcoal and joined in singing, in slow, sad tempo, the mourning songs that made a trail for the dead to find their way to the afterworld.[3] Of the food shared by her coastal relatives, she threw some in the fire, feeding it to the spirits of her departed husband and child. Following cremation, their ashes were stored in a wooden chest inside a spirit house, surrounded by a fence to keep their restless spirits contained.[4]

Despite her loss, Shaaw Tláa bore her grief stoically, knowing that if she cried too much, the souls of her husband and child would lose their way to the other world, since they, too, longed to be reunited with her. On the fourth day after her husband's death, she hung his moose hide belt in a spruce tree to ensure that her next husband would live long. After a Crow woman combed and washed her hair, she was free from a widow's restrictions, though for a full year neither she nor anyone else was to mention the name of her husband or child.[5]

By tradition, the elders of the Wolf moiety—or Eagles, as they are called on the coast—would have decided whom Shaaw Tláa should next marry; in all likelihood, her new husband would be a relative of Kult'ús. But Shaaw Tláa's mother had already lost too many children. She sent for her daughter to come home. It was there, on the inland side of the mountains, that George Carmack would become part of Shaaw Tláa's life—but not before he first married someone else.

After helping build John Healy's cabin, George had teamed up with a cheerful prospector named Barney Hill. In July 1886, the two of them traveled from Dyea over the Chilkoot Pass to Lake Bennett, where George built a boat so they could float through the lakes and down the Yukon River (then called the Lewes River, in its upper reaches) to look for gold. The boat was sturdier than the oblong box George had cobbled together the previous summer to transport seven prospectors over the lakes and rivers. "What water it didn't push ahead, it pulled after it," George said of that first boat. "It took Lake Bennett twelve hours to fill up again after we got across."[6]

Floating down the Yukon, going north, was a lot easier than poling back up it. But the waters were rising with summer melt from the mountains.[7] Some 250 miles short of the Stewart River, where most prospectors were trying their luck that season, George and Barney Hill turned up the Big Salmon River, the boat cutting "some odd figures" as they poled upstream.[8] Finding the current strong and the gravel bars under water, George decided he'd had enough. He sold his outfit, leaving Barney Hill behind, and he turned back on foot, packing cross country toward Dyea with three other miners.

The prospecting season was short, and none of them wanted to get caught on the inland side of the mountains when winter set in, bringing temperatures that in some spots would dip to eighty degrees below zero Fahrenheit. That meant they had to get out while they could still get passage over the Chilkoot Trail. "That was some trip," George later wrote. "Our grub gave out and we had to live on grouse, rabbits, hawks, and Hoot owls. We found an Indian cache that had over a thousand dollars' worth of furs, blankets, and other goods, but all we found in it that we wanted was about a pint of red beans, which we cooked with just a little salt, but they surely tasted good to four hungry men."[9]

Finally, George and his companions reached the blue-green waters of Lake Bennett, where they had the good fortune to run into Bishop Charlie Seghers, no worse off from having been "slapped" by L'unáat. "We surely dug a post hole in his bean pot," George said. "I am sure he must have got an extra sparkle in his crown for the way he treated us boys."[10]

Also at Lake Bennett was Shaaw Tláa's family, camped along the north shore, at the place called *Todezáané*, "blowing all the time." The caribou came through at that time of year, and the crisp autumn winds were good for drying meat. It was *K̲usi.áat K'áchk'w* moon, a crucial juncture in the subsistence cycle during which large game were hunted and cached for winter. Having gone home at her mother's request, Shaaw Tláa joined the other

Tagish women in harvesting cranberries and crowberries, which both taste best after a hard frost.

Somehow, George got separated from his traveling companions. He was starving, and Shaaw Tláa's family had food. As the nights grew cold, they took him in, hungry and ragged and weak. He wanted one of them to escort him over the Chilkoot Pass, but it was too late in the year, they told him—even a "good strong Indian" wouldn't risk it.[11] Through John Healy, George already knew Shaaw Tláa's brother Keish, called Skookum Jim; among Healy's so-called "good Indians," Jim was known for his strength, courage, adventurous spirit, and keen sense of duty.[12] He was also brother-in-law to L'unáat in two ways: through Aagé's marriage and through his own marriage to L'unáat's sister, Daakuxda.eit, meaning "like a pearl."[13]

As John Healy strategically courted the Tagish, Jim also recognized the benefit in allying himself with white men—he could bypass, on the sly, transactions for which L'unáat demanded a cut. He was hardly the first to recognize such opportunities. While floating the Yukon in the summer of 1886, one prospector claimed to have encountered Indians so eager for a direct trading alliance that they grabbed the gunwale of the white man's boat and refused to let go.[14]

Though they followed seasonal subsistence rounds, the Tagish clans had begun spending the cold, subarctic winters in more permanent homes the way the Tlingit did, log structures from which the men could run trap lines and still return to their families every few weeks. East of Todezáané, where the wind blew all the time, in a quiet, sheltered place girded by low mountains, George Carmack was invited to spend the winter in *X̲aayhít*, or Warm House, one of two Tagish clan houses on the east bank of a wide, tranquil stretch of a shallow river later called the Six Mile, connecting Tagish and Marsh Lakes.[15] Above the interior door was painted a large beaver, in honor of the origin story of the Deisheetaan, the clan led by Jim and Shaaw Tláa's father.[16]

The result of what George Carmack later termed the "rude hospitality" shown to him by the Tagish people during the winter of 1886 was a marriage, arranged in the traditional way with

Shaaw Tláa's niece, whom he called Kitty.[17] Kitty would have had no more say in marrying George Carmack than had Shaaw Tláa in marrying Kult'ús, but that doesn't mean she didn't find the blue-eyed prospector attractive. The newlyweds were even able to communicate, after a fashion—from his short time in Sitka and Juneau and his friendships with John Healy and Skookum Jim, George had picked up some Chinook, the pidgin trading language used up and down the coast.

In a brief ceremony required for him to marry a Wolf, George was inducted into the Deisheetaan clan, making him of the Crow moiety. Although he lacked furs for paying the bride price, the marriage proceeded in the usual Tagish way: he and Kitty began sleeping together and appearing as a couple in public. As was expected of new husbands, George helped with hunting and other preparations for winter—and in doing so, learned Tagish ways of thinking and acting—exactly the sort of education John Healy had hinted would come from taking an Indian wife.

For the Tagish clans, the marriage also had advantages, forging an alliance that might one day allow them to bypass their Tlingit relatives and trade directly with John Healy, a maneuver that would be to their economic advantage. In the complex trading network that stretched from Alaska's Pacific Coast to the shores of the Arctic Ocean, the farther removed any group was from direct trade with the Russians, the Hudson Bay Company, or the Americans, the more likely they were to receive from their neighbors inferior goods at inflated prices.

Though Kitty's union with George appears to have been the first for a Tagish woman, among prospectors and fur traders (although official Hudson Bay Company policy discouraged it) there had been many such marriages. As with all matters of love and allegiance, the motives and circumstances were many, but there was an overarching pattern: After mucking around for a few years in the North, a man would grow attached to the place and the lifestyle and the prospect of fortune around the next bend. At the same time, he would tire of the company of the same few men, and the longing for female companionship would become too strong to ignore.

How did love factor into these matches? J. Bernard Moore, who with his father later founded the town of Skagway, near Dyea, followed the typical pattern. After three years of lonely travel up and down the Yukon River, he was invited to a potlatch by Chilkat chief George Shotridge (son of Kohklux). "I was twenty years old, with no great and serious thoughts of the future," Moore later wrote. "I felt light of heart, though lonesome at times, living in and seeing only the present."[18] Across the warm, crowded clan house, as Tlingit dancers swayed and rocked, back and forth and sideways, Moore locked eyes with a pretty girl of fourteen. She ran off, but when he visited George Shotridge after the potlatch, he met the girl whom he later called Minnie, granddaughter of Kohklux. Soon, the two were married.

George Carmack's marriage to Kitty was short-lived—within a few months, his new bride had died. Certainly her family, including Shaaw Tláa, grieved their loss; to what extent George did isn't known.

Because all of Tagish life was organized around family units, no person of marrying age stayed single for long; when a husband or wife died, a new marriage was arranged for the surviving spouse. So it was that three weeks after Kitty's death, Shaaw Tláa became George Carmack's next wife.[19] Thereafter, she was known as Kate Carmack.

As with each of their former marriages, the ceremony was brief; in the Tagish-Tlingit way, Kate and George were recognized as wife and husband as they began living together according to arrangements agreed upon by Kate's family and their new son-in-law. How Kate felt about entering this new relationship even as she was grieving the loss of Kult'ús isn't known.

Outsiders would later contend that Kate was privileged among Indian women because she married a white man, and that she had sought out George as a husband because she considered herself "too good" to marry among her people.[20] No evidence supports either notion. In one sense, Kate was only acting as any good Tagish woman would, reordering her life for the benefit of her family and clan. But in arranging her marriage to a white man, her family also demonstrated their confidence in her strength and ability to adapt. To become the wife of George Carmack—of any white man, for that matter—would require her to improvise, adapting her established ways of behaving to new situations.[21]

Although Kate may have known of George from the time he'd spent with John Healy, she wouldn't have known what to expect of him as a husband.[22] He might be like George Dickinson, the white trader who ran a store at the Haines mission with his Tlingit wife, Sarah. Then again, Kate's husband might turn out like one of the downriver fur traders, who fathered children with their Native wives and then left them.[23] Or he might turn out to be like Ben Moore, who went to great lengths to care for both Minnie, the Tlingit woman he called his "little girl wife," and also for her parents.[24] That George Carmack had stuck with the Tagish after Kitty died was perhaps a good sign, indicating some genuine feeling for the land and its people. Then again, his staying on was in keeping with his general lack of direction, not to mention the perceived financial benefits of an Indian marriage, as extolled by John Healy.

Before winter fully set in, Kate returned with George to Dyea, where her new husband helped pack for a few hardy prospectors who were returning for the winter after restocking supplies.[25] As it turned out, the winter would be especially ugly, as demonstrated by the journey of a Tutchone Indian, dubbed "Indian Bob," and a prospector, Tom Williams. In what became known as Tom Williams' Death March, the pair were delivering a message that would indirectly affect where Kate would move next.

Late that fall, there had been a big gold strike on a tributary of the Fortymile River, some six hundred miles "down north" on the Yukon River, on what might or might not be the Alaska side of the border. This strike marked the first time prospectors had consistently found good quantities of the coarse gold they'd been seeking in the North—more promising by far than the fine dust George Carmack had panned from the streams near the Tagish lakes in the summer of 1885, and more plentiful even than what had been discovered that same year along the Stewart River. Fortymile promised the sort of gold that could make a person rich.

The prospectors who found it had managed to backtrack from the Fortymile River to the Stewart River just as winter set in. When American trader Arthur Harper saw their gold, he knew he had to get word to his business partner, who had traveled to California in hopes of persuading the Alaska Commercial (A.C.) Company to front more supplies for their post. Though the A.C. Company was more interested in furs than in gold, Harper was confident they'd see the profit potential in supplying the prospectors who were sure to come in droves when word got out about the Fortymile discovery.

The problem was how to get word of the strike to California. Mail went out via the Yukon River only a few times a year, always during the summer, when paddleboats came up the river from St. Michael, on the Bering Sea coast. From Dyea, the mail went out year-round, every month or so, but the usual route to get to Dyea from the Stewart River involved a good deal of travel by water, and the rivers were already frozen, which meant a long and hazardous overland journey was required. For this, Harper recruited "Indian Bob" to guide prospector Tom Williams, who volunteered to take the mailbag to the coast.

Whatever Bob was paid for his troubles, it wasn't enough. When he and Tom set off by dog team from the mouth of the Stewart River on December 1, 1886, they made good time at first, but then a Chinook wind blew in, bringing rain that left a slippery sheen of water over the Yukon River ice.[26] Three days in a row, Bob fell through, going in over his head where the ice was weak. By Christmas, they were creeping along at the rate of only nine miles a day, dodging huge ice chucks frozen into the river, and their dogs' feet were cut and sore. Then came the bitter cold. By New Year's Day, when the pair crossed wide, ice-locked Lake LaBerge, they had resorted to feeding the dogs from their dwindling supply of flour. By mid-January, they were traveling through ice fog, dense condensate that pushes toward the ground in periods of extreme cold.[27]

Through temperatures that froze quicksilver, used by prospectors to mark forty below Fahrenheit, the pair pressed on to Tagish Lake, where Bob tried but failed to convince some of Kate's relatives to travel with them over the summit. Though this might have been the perfect excuse for Bob to give up, he pressed on—he'd promised to get Tom Williams to Dyea, and he aimed to do it. Through strong headwinds and blinding snow, he led Williams up the Chilkoot Trail. But a violent blizzard forced them to stop. Without food or shelter, they abandoned the sled and forged into the storm, packing on their backs their few remaining supplies, along with the precious mailbag containing the letter that explained the specifics of the gold strike. Making only five miles in two days, their dogs dropped off one by one.

At Stone House, a rock outcropping below the Chilkoot summit, Indian Bob and Tom Williams holed up in a snow shelter. Williams became feverish. Five days later, they ventured out again, but Williams collapsed in the swirling snow. Leaving everything behind, Bob hoisted Williams onto his back and struggled on toward Dyea. After five days of arduous trekking, he met up with some of L'unáat's clan, who delivered them to Healy's store. "Bob was about all ice," George Carmack wrote. "But we managed to save him."[28]

Tom Williams was beyond saving, but in the final hours of his life, he repeated what he'd told every miner he'd met along the way—there had been a big strike at Forty Mile, and they'd better get over there. "Gold all same like this," was how Indian Bob described it, sifting dry beans through his fingers to illustrate.[29]

After Bob was grilled for specifics on where the mail sack might be found, two search parties were sent out, but they returned empty-handed. John Healy, who had been away when Bob staggered into his store in Dyea, loaded him onto his new schooner and took him to Juneau to have his toes amputated. As Healy spread the news about Fortymile gold, a group of Juneau miners handed over $125 to Healy, reward money for whoever could find the mail sack containing the letter with details of exactly where the wealth could be found.

Upon his return to Dyea, Healy succeeded where the first two search parties had failed—he discovered the mail sack near the summit, next to one of Bob's dead, frozen dogs.[30] From Juneau, elated miners sent Bob home with some cash and a Yukon sled. Only later did questions arise over the gold Tom Williams had stashed in the mail sack. Implicated in its disappearance, a furious Healy refused to provide any explanation for what had become of the gold.[31]

The prospects along the Fortymile River and its tributaries—soon to be known as the Forty Mile district—were enough to tempt any prospector, even one as unfocused in his search as George Carmack. But for him and his new wife, it would take another death—a violent one—to spur them on.

CHAPTER SEVEN

We Claim Them All

Encouraged by the news for which Tom Williams had given his life, a small rush of miners decided they had to get over the mountains as soon as they could—and that at first meant more opportunities, in the form of packing, for Kate and George. The earliest group that headed to the Forty Mile district bucked strong northeast winds to cross over the Chilkoot Trail on April 1, 1887. In the soft snow, they sank up to their shoulders as they fought through blizzards and drifts and dodged avalanches. From a distance, their packers, who may have very well included the Carmacks, looked like tiny black spots as they heaved their packs to the summit and then slid down a two-foot trench to strap on another load. For the worst part of the climb, the last half-mile to the top, they cut stairs into the snow. When the sun finally came out, they had to fight snow blindness, a painful condition brought on by the glare of light off the stark white landscape.[1] As if in mourning, the packers rubbed on their faces a mixture of soot and grease to deflect the light.[2]

During the spring of 1887, the *USS Pinta* again anchored offshore at Dyea, her crew ready to intervene in any fracas that might arise between L'unáat and the hundreds who now clamored to cross the Chilkoot Trail.[3] Eager to get to the gold, these new prospectors had little patience with L'unáat. "The Indians compel every miner to pay toll for going through their country," complained the editors of the *Alaska Free Press*. L'unáat, they said, "makes the demand for the toll, and all the miners pay rather than having trouble with the Indians, as this tribe is the strongest one in Alaska. Over two hundred men have went in this spring, and combined they have paid one dirty, thieving, Indian about $300 for the privilege of travelling about thirty miles through the woods of Uncle Sam's domain."[4]

In a report filed that same year, Lieutenant Alexander McCrackin disputed the claim that L'unáat was charging a toll for passage over the Chilkoot Trail. "I could find no person who had paid toll or who it had been demanded," wrote McCrackin.[5] Toll or no toll, there was money enough to be made from packing—plenty to keep Kate and George in Dyea, where packers stood to earn upwards of $1,000 for the season. By virtue of his marriage to Kate, George was the only white man L'unáat allowed to pack for wages,[6] with Tlingit packers from as far away as Sitka eager for the privilege.

A portion of Kate's earnings that summer came from the Canadian government, which upon receiving news of the Fortymile strike had developed a sudden interest in the region called, rather unimaginatively, the "Unorganized Northwestern Territories." On both sides of the American-Canadian border, governance beyond the gunboat had been haphazard at best, with the exact location of the boundary that separated Alaska from Canada yet to be determined—it was thought to divide the Forty Mile district, but no one knew exactly where.

Enter George Dawson, a field scientist who suffered a spinal deformity from tuberculosis, and William Ogilvie, a seasoned, steady Scotsman who had hired on as a Dominion Land Surveyor after his emigration to Canada.[7] Upon his arrival in Dyea with his surveying crew, Ogilvie requested the services of 120 packers to carry seven tons of supplies over the Chilkoot Trail, pushing the limits of how many able-bodied men, women, and children that L'unáat could supply.[8] Among those assigned to the task were Kate, Jim, and George.[9]

It was on this expedition that Jim proved himself worthy of the name "Skookum"—he astounded Ogilvie by packing 165 pounds of bacon in a single load to the top of the mountain. At the summit, Ogilvie's Tlingit packers quit. Desperate, the surveyor asked George Carmack to send for the help of additional Tagish packers. It wasn't easy, since the Tagish knew that L'unáat was in charge of such arrangements. But George had a sense of humor, and among his Tagish relatives, ridicule was acceptable along clan lines—a Crow could make fun of a Wolf, and a Wolf could make fun of a Crow. So George teased his Wolf relatives about kowtowing to L'unáat. They had just as much right to pack on the interior side of the mountains as L'unáat had to pack on the coastal side, George told them. Finally, according to Ogilvie, "nine of them came over, and in fear and trembling began to pack down to the lake, at the bargain rate of $5 per hundred pounds."[10]

Despite the fees and the rigors of the route, the Chilkoot Trail was still the most expedient way to reach the lakes, where travelers could build boats and then float the Yukon River to their destination. Given the difficulties of passing over L'unáat's trail, Ogilvie was pleased to learn from Canadian boat captain and adventurer William Moore of an alternate route to the Interior, one Moore knew of through Kate's brother, Skookum Jim. Needled for details, Jim clammed up, saying that "a great evil would befall him if he said any more."[11]

Finally, after much prodding, Jim gave in. With the Moore family patriarch, Jim retreated from the Ogilvie expedition to a spot five miles south of Dyea, a place called *Shgagwei*, meaning "Wrinkled Up," owing to the effect of the north wind on the water. Fom there, Kate's brother led William Moore over a section of the mountains that Jim claimed was good for hunting goats and picking berries, but not much else. For seven days, the pair beat their way through the brush, barely able to make out the trail as they climbed up and over the Coastal Mountains toward Lake Bennett, where they met up with the Ogilvie expedition.

Though John Healy predicted that Jim's route, later called the White Pass Trail, would amount to nothing, Moore couldn't stop talking about the possibilities. The first five miles were level bottom land, thick with trees. In the next nine miles, through a canyonlike valley, the brush was even thicker. But though the final three miles to the summit were difficult, the ascent was not nearly as steep and rocky as the approach to the Chilkoot summit. Best of all, L'unáat appeared to have no hold over this trail.[12] Moore had such faith in its prospects that he and his son applied for homestead rights at *Shgagwei,* a place that after the Klondike discovery would become the boomtown of Skagway.

When summer ended and there was no more packing to be done, George helped Healy repair the schooner *Charlie,* which had run aground in Skagway Bay during a spring tide.[13] Then he and Kate returned to spend the winter of 1887 hunting, trapping, and fishing with Kate's family. While the trapping of furs to trade was mostly handled by men, women snared rabbits and other small game as well as stretching the hides to the traders' specification, so whole families often spent at least part of the winter on the move, holing up against the weather in brush shelters and tents. But the fish that could be speared in Tagish Lake were an important source of fresh food, so Kate and George also spent part of the winter near Tagish Lake, at X̱aayhít, her father's Deisheetaan clan house,[14] built of vertical planks of split spruce fitted into a timber foundation with a roof of split spruce and spruce bark, with the floor excavated to accommodate a cooking fire. Though the house was neither as large nor as elaborately decorated as a Chilkoot clan house, Kate and George had their own sleeping space.[15]

Kate's life might have continued in this way for some time, following seasonal rounds divided between two economies, the old and the new—the period from freeze-up to break-up devoted to trapping and other subsistence activities, and summers spent earning wages by packing for prospectors going in and out of the Yukon. But in the summer of 1888, everything changed.

In his 1887 report to the Department of the Navy, Lieutenant Commander J. S. Newell proposed an alternative solution to the problems he attributed to L'unáat's control of the Chilkoot Trail.

"There is no doubt that in course of time, with sufficient force, the Indians could be severely punished and brought into subjection," he suggested. "Dependent, as they are, for food upon tidewater, they could be driven into the interior and their supply of fish—the main article of diet—cut off entirely, or so reduced as to impose upon them great suffering."[16]

In a turn of good fortune for Kate's Tlingit relatives, the government failed to act upon the lieutenant's advice. Newspaper editors in Juneau proposed yet another solution—in lieu of a railroad, some enterprising man should blast out the toughest "little three miles" to the summit and set up a pack train on the Chilkoot Trail.[17] For this enterprising man, they had to look no further than John Healy. He had set up a toll road in Montana, and he wasn't about to let the Indians interfere with his plans to set up another along the single best route to the gold country, on a trail that happened to start more or less on his doorstep in Dyea.

In hopes that horses and mules could replace the Native packers, Healy sent men to start improving the Chilkoot Trail. L'unáat's demands that these men cease and desist from their modifications to the trail went unanswered. In response to reports that Indians on the trail were again discouraging miners from proceeding to the summit, the *USS Pinta*'s commander sent Lieutenant Alexander McCrackin to get a firsthand look at the Chilkoot situation, while another lieutenant, George Emmons, was dispatched to Tlákw.aan to meet with the Chilkat chief, Kohklux, and assess relations between the Chilkat and the Chilkoot.

Following the McCrackin expedition, L'unáat made a formal appeal to federal authorities, requesting a legal opinion regarding the rights of the Chilkoot in relation to the trail. While there were larger issues at stake, L'unáat's chief complaint was personal, against John Healy, as he recounts a dramatic incident that Kate likely witnessed:

> Mr. Healy wishes to take away our road or trail to the Yukon, which my tribe does not like, as we made it long ago, and it has always been in my tribe. We fixed the road good, so

that the miners would not get hurt, and Mr. Healy is putting sticks or logs on it, so he can get pay for people going in over our trail, and we do not want to see that.

When the miners come here, I talk kindly to them, but some of them begin to swear, and then they say I began the quarrel. I always treat the miners kindly, and when they do their own packing I tell them that they had better let the Indians do their packing, so the miners will not hurt themselves on the trail, and some of the miners tell me that it is not my business, which hurts my feelings.

When the miners treat me right I will and do treat them as my children. I am glad Mr. McCrackin went over the trail with me to see our work on the trail and what we did and how we treated the miners. Not long ago I was nearly killed by a white man John (Wilson) who has since gone to Juneau. John made Healy's house and then did packing over the trail. My tribe had borrowed lots of money from Healy and were going to make money by packing to repay Mr. Healy. We had arranged to pack for some miners when John rushed in and took one of the packs and said he was going to do the packing. John had been doing lots of packing and I asked him kindly, saluting him at the same time, to please not to pack this time, but to let my men do so, so that they could get some money to repay Mr. Healy.

John replied by calling me a _________ and I then called John the same name. John then rushed and took one of the miner's guns and wished to shoot me, when the miners took their gun from John. These miners were very good friends of mine and they said they were going to tell Captain Newell the real facts of the affair. George Carmack and a lot of my tribe saw the whole affair.

When the miners go in I would like them to arrange with me instead of the other men of my tribe, so as to save time and misunderstanding, as the Indians come to me anyhow as chief. My tribe claims the winter trail over the river Schkat-Quay [Skagway]. We have three trails to the Yukon, and we claim them all.

> I do not object to miners doing their own packing, but I hate to see them doing work they are not used to. I like to see white men, such as George, pack for miners, and have no objection to their packing. I have no objections to Stick, Chilcat, or any other Indian or white persons packing over our trails, but I and my tribe do object to Healy, or any other person, claiming our trails and monopolizing the packing.
>
> We used to get all the furs from the Stick Indians, but they now trade with Mr. Healy, which ought to satisfy him without taking our trail. I ask $10 for a half pack to me for my general supervision and responsibility of the packing, as I feel myself bound to see every man and pack through safe. I have never asked or demanded toll from any person and do not do so.[18]

With no definitive lines marking precisely which areas were overseen by which Tlingit group, L'unáat in this letter made a bold, preemptive claim to all three viable trails in the region—the Chilkoot Trail, the White Pass (revealed by Jim to William Moore, this winter route that began in Skagway was within the general area used by the Chilkoot), and the Chilkat Trail (a claim Kohklux would surely have contested).

Where other outsiders remarked on L'unáat's bad temper and overbearing manner, Lieutenant McCrackin reported that Kate's brother-in-law showed great kindness, shouldering a pack at no cost for a miner who was struggling to reach the summit. He proposed to his superiors that L'unáat's claim to the Chilkoot Trail had more merit than Healy's. If the Tagish (or Sticks, as he called them) were to stay on their own side of the mountains—they were technically British subjects, after all—and if the US gunboats remained at the ready, the lieutenant believe a reasonable peace could be achieved.

This would prove to be wishful thinking. In March 1888, the district attorney issued a murky opinion in response to L'unáat's letter. To the question of whether the Chilkoot might enjoy exclusive use of the trail, he cited the 1867 treaty with Russia in which Alaska lands were transferred free of reservations or privileges that might favor certain parties, such as the Natives who were there first. As to whether the Chilkoot had earned exclusive packing rights by having made and maintained the trail, he acknowledged the inherent unfairness of Healy stepping in to make money from their efforts, but he proposed no way to settle the matter. The easement rights L'unáat claimed for the Chilkoot were surely protected under the 1884 Organic Act, the district attorney noted, but how to enforce them was another issue altogether.[19]

Absent a definitive ruling, Healy encroached even further on what L'unáat considered his own right and duty as second chief. Complaining that Aagé's husband liked to spend his money in Sitka instead of at the Healy & Wilson Trading Post in Dyea,[20] John Healy recruited Tlingit packers from Sitka to break L'unáat's hold on the Chilkoot Trail. When the Sitka recruits arrived, a hundred Tlingit men squared off in Dyea, where around Healy's post there was a ragtag collection of some one hundred tents, brush huts, and log homes, one of which belonged to Kate and George Carmack.

Kohklux's son George Shotridge joined L'unáat in confronting the packers from Sitka. L'unáat offered two options—the Sitka Tlingit could either go home or they could pack and pay a 30 percent royalty to the Chilkoot. Chief Jack, leader of the Sitka contingent, refused both alternatives. He told his men to strap on their packs. When they did, L'unáat slapped Sitka Jack's son in the face. Knife drawn, Jack rushed L'unáat. In the tussle that followed, both were wounded, Jack more severely than L'unáat.

Both sides retreated, but through the night, skirmishes between the two camps broke out. In the morning, it was decided the opposing groups would line up, each with their leader at the head, and fight until the matter was settled. Painted for war, the chiefs met in front of Healy's two-story log trading post. As John Healy, his wife, Healy's partner Edgar Wilson, a sailor, and a young couple watched from inside the store, Sitka Jack and L'unáat advanced with drawn knives, followed by men armed with rifles and knifes.

In fierce fighting, several men on both sides were wounded. As blood from their initial skirmish seeped from their bandaged wounds, Chief Jack and L'unáat slashed at one another. At one point, L'unáat staggered and rushed for the trading post door, but Healy refused him entry. Sitka Jack struck L'unáat with the butt end of a rifle, and Kate's brother-in-law collapsed to the ground. L'unáat's teenaged son exacted revenge by slipping a knife to its hilt into Sitka Jack.

Men from each tribe transported their chiefs to shelter. Sitka Jack died, and so did L'unáat, leaving three widows—his two Sitka wives plus Aagé. The Chilkoot clans blamed L'unáat's death on John Healy. Not only had he created the problem by bringing the Sitka Tlingit to Dyea, but he had also refused the wounded chief entrance to his trading post. In response to demands for retribution in the form of blankets and other goods, Healy barricaded the doors and windows of his post. From inside, he and one of his companions transformed the structure into a stockade, cutting small holes through which they could keep watch and shoot as needed. The Chilkoot threatened to set the building on fire.

It was a long night. The next day, twenty-two sworn and armed deputies were hastily dispatched from Juneau to Dyea to calm the situation. They arrived to a flurry of small white flags stuck on poles. Among themselves, the Tlingit had reached an uneasy truce: the Sitka Tlingit could haul supplies for the miners, but they would pay the commission L'unáat had demanded.[21]

After L'unáat's death in what became known as the Packer War, John Healy wisely left his partner in charge of their store and departed Dyea to set up a new trading post across Lynn Canal, near the Pyramid Harbor cannery. With her daughter widowed, Kate's mother brokered an agreement with L'unáat's family: Aagé would be allowed to return home, but she would leave Susie, one of her two daughters, on the coast.

Following the Packer War, neither Kate nor George would ever again hire out to pack supplies over the Chilkoot Trail. They spent the rest of the summer of 1888 traveling with Jim and their nephew Charlie, trading for furs down the Yukon River. They also did a little rocking for gold here and there along the Hootalinqua (Teslin) River, where they found only skim diggings, fine gold washed onto the sand by high spring waters.[22]

When summer drew to a close, they returned with Kate's family to Todezáané, on the shores of Lake Bennett, to hunt caribou and dry the meat for the winter. Once the snows fell, Jim and George trapped marten and other fur-bearing mammals. They lived on cached caribou, sheep, and moose meat, building open fires to warm themselves and bolting a piece of canvas to trees for shelter when it snowed. After a winter of living mostly out in the open, Kate's husband found himself "tough as a piece of shoe leather."[23]

Spring brought another surge of prospectors, all headed for Forty Mile, not a stampede exactly, but a steady stream that would amount to another three hundred outsiders in the Yukon by year's end. Had Kate's husband been more strongly motivated by gold, he would have hastened to Forty Mile too. Perhaps he had been persuaded by John Healy that there was a surer livelihood to be had by "mining the miners." Perhaps he was deserving of his reputation for laziness.[24] Perhaps he wanted to find his own way.

It may have been Sed Wilson,[25] the prospector who married L'unáat's widow, Aagé, who eventually convinced George to take up a more earnest search for gold. Like Kate's husband, Wilson had gotten himself into a predicament that required rescue. While attempting a winter crossing over the Chilkoot Pass, he and a fellow miner had become trapped in a blizzard. With nothing to eat but raw corn meal and dried dog salmon, they turned their dogs loose and never saw them again.[26] After that, Wilson cast his lot with the Tagish people, entering into a marriage alliance with Kate's widowed sister, Aagé. But unlike Carmack, Wilson did not linger with his wife's family. After the ice went out in 1889, he and Aagé floated the Yukon River toward the Forty Mile district[27] to prospect for gold.

That same summer, George and Kate headed for the Big Salmon River, where six years earlier Frederick Schwatka had reported that gold might be found in placer deposits along any bar or bank,[28] though whether in sufficient quantities to justify the staking of claims remained to be seen. With them went Jim, Charlie, and in all likelihood Jim's wife, now called Mary, sister to L'unáat.[29] Jim's motivation for joining George's expedition was his duty to look after his brother-in-law, who knew little of the ways one should act in the wilderness; as a favored nephew, Charlie went almost everywhere with Jim. As they had the previous summer, they would also do some fur trading with groups more removed from the coast, with plans to return home well before freeze-up.

Although a person could predict with some certainty where and when muskrats and marten and salmon and caribou could be found, one never knew about gold. In contrast to the Tagish seasonal rounds, George's prospecting venture was a different sort of wandering, the destination undetermined, the goal intangible. Worked out of granite or quartz by repeated cycles of freezing and thawing, gold sinks into some streams but not others—miners might pan good pay out of one section of a creek but not the next. Moving waters carry it along until dense clay, heavy gravel, or solid rock stops it. As new forces shape the earth and creeks go dry, the precious metal is worked back into bedrock and embedded in veins along hillsides—though again, precisely where, no one knows.

That summer, George and his Tagish relatives were placer mining, a method aimed at finding gold in the most obvious places, the beds of creeks and rivers into which it had tumbled. "You can't imagine a person's feelings when at this kind of work," wrote one prospector. "Take a pan of dirt, wash it down to about a handful of dirt, then it gets exciting and you are afraid to make a miss dip of water and lose part. Then as colors begin to show up your heart commences to go quicker and quicker until it is finished. Then a big sigh, dry the pan and weigh it out."[30]

With Jim, Mary, and Charlie, the Carmacks floated the Hootalinqua River to the Thirtymile River and then started up the Big Salmon River. For gold, George had his eye on the headwaters, located in the Big Salmon Mountains. In general, Kate and her family were wary of unfamiliar mountains, where a powerful Mountain Man with a distinct dislike of ordinary humans ruled over the weather and wildlife.[31]

At the junction of the Big Salmon and Yukon Rivers, they came upon a fish camp belonging to a group who spoke Tutchone, an Athabaskan language that Kate mostly understood. They warned of a specific danger in the mountains George wanted to explore: a Kushtaka, a land otter man. Lustrous and rare in the upper Yukon, land otters were feared for their malevolent, supernatural powers. If you had the bad luck to trap one, you had to make sure you apologized to it immediately. If you got lost, a Kushtaka would appear in human form, urging you to return with him to their village. If you succumbed, you risked turning into a Kushtaka yourself, which also could happen if you drowned. The land otter man was especially dangerous to women—if Kate touched one, she risked becoming possessed by its spirit.[32]

George believed the Tutchone warnings were a hoax, a ruse to scare him away in the same way that, primarily to protect trading advantages, Yukon Indians had sometimes exaggerated dangers to warn away explorers and traders.[33] For George's Tagish relatives, the situation was different. Territorial boundaries between the Tagish and the Tutchone and the Inland Tlingit—between all Yukon Indian groups, for the most part—were porous. As the Chilkoot had claimed the passes through the Coast Mountains, the Tutchone claimed the Big Salmon Range, in that they considered themselves stewards of the land. The Tagish would have been welcome to hunt and fish there as long as they showed due caution and respect.[34]

Undeterred by the warnings, George packed a light blanket, a gun, and some dried meat and tromped into the mountains alone, not bothering to bring the tools necessary to prospect for gold. Sent to follow him, one of the local Tutchone "wore out his moccasins," George later wrote, trying to keep up.[35] From the Tutchone perspective, to track a prospector as he trekked alone into the mountains would have been entirely reasonable. Once he broke away from the rest of his group, George's intentions, his trustworthiness, even his mental stability would have been suspect. Odds were that at some point he would need to be rescued—the Indians had helped more than one foolhardy miner out of a bad spot.

With her relatives, Kate waited at the mouth of the Big Salmon River for her husband to return. Five days passed, then six, seven, and eight. Perhaps George had passed out upon hearing the land otter's whistle; if that happened, he wouldn't wake for a long time. Perhaps upon meeting the Kushtaka, he had forgotten that only tobacco juice or metal could turn it away. Or perhaps the Kushtaka had lured George into becoming one of its own, in which case he would be lost forever.

After ten worry-filled days—for Kate, if not for her husband—George finally returned, having traveled only fifty miles before he'd run out of food. Though he'd found no gold in the Big Salmon Mountains, he was convinced he would, and he wanted Kate, Jim, Charlie, and Mary to return to the mountains with him.

Jim and Charlie flat-out refused. With derision, George told them to go home, where there were no bad spirits.[36] That left Kate in a bad place, caught between her brother, who understood the right ways of acting, and her husband, whose inexperience led to foolish choices. Though Jim had a duty to protect her, they were prohibited by brother–sister avoidance patterns from frankly discussing the situation.[37]

It was up to Kate to decide for herself which was the better course: to let George go off on his own or stay with him.[38] A loyal Tagish wife remained with her husband. But George was prone to foolish decisions, being little more than a child in terms of how he understood the natural world. And though it was summer, winter was right around the corner, as it always is in the North, and Kate and George had done nothing to prepare.

CHAPTER EIGHT

SOMETIMES WE HAD PLENTY

FOLLOWING THE DISCORD OVER THE KUSHTAKA, Kate watched as Jim, Charlie, and Mary prepared to turn back, most likely on foot, toward Marsh Lake. If she went along, she would spend the remainder of the long summer days with her mother, sisters, aunts, and nieces at fish camp, cutting and putting up salmon for winter. But she knew better than to leave anyone alone in the wilderness. Her people traveled together—beyond tradition and duty, this was simple good sense.

Even so, to stay with her husband under these circumstances would be in many ways an exceptional choice. In an ordinary marriage made to strengthen alliances, a Tagish woman might never leave her immediate family. And in an ordinary marriage, if a wife did go off with her husband, as Kate had with Kult'ús, she could rely on relationships with her in-laws to sustain her. In remaining with George, she would have no one to rely on except herself.

As a Tagish woman, Kate was hardly subservient; though women were not formal leaders, their views were respected within their households and clans.[1] She and George reached a compromise: instead of returning home with her family, she would stay with him, but she was not going to venture into the mountains where the Kushtaka roamed. Instead, the Carmacks pointed their boat downriver, toward the Forty Mile district, where Aagé had gone with her new husband.

At a rate of three to five miles per hour, the Yukon River carried Kate farther and farther from her home. As the river widened, the current grew swift, the boat dodging hazards that included sandbars, mud bars, and gravel bars, which are tough to avoid and even tougher to get off of. Kate remained vigilant, for wherever the river undercut its banks, sweepers—trees shorn from the land—had the potential to knock the unwary from a boat. Aside from the sweepers, the banks were so thick with poplar and willow and alder and spruce that finding a spot to raise even a basic camp for the night—a piece of canvas slung over a pole—could prove tricky.

The days on the river were long, the sun barely dipping under the horizon for a few hours in the dead of night. The mosquitoes were ferocious; Kate blackened her face with soot and grease to stave them off. Only on the warmest days would the ever-present hordes of buzzing insects retreat, returning with a vengeance at dusk. When rain chilled the air, the mosquitoes might also subside, but only if the rain was substantial and hard. Some days, the pests darted from thick banks of fog that rolled over the river.

At Five Finger Rapids, the Carmacks steered their boat between a stunning but treacherous formation of towering rocks where screeching gulls nested. Past these rapids, the river braids, flowing past ribbons of white ash that stripe the steep cliffs along both sides of the river, evidence of a large volcanic eruption hundreds of years earlier. In a picturesque valley, they passed a log home surrounded by several brush dwellings that belonged to families who spoke Tutchone.[2]

A mile past where the Pelly River meets the Yukon, the Carmacks passed three brick chimneys—all that remained of Fort Selkirk, the Hudson Bay post raided by Kohklux and other coastal Tlingit. In the vicinity, Indians still gathered occasionally for seasonal trade fairs, where they traded as they always had. At a summer village downriver from Fort Selkirk, local speakers of

Tutchone cut and dried salmon in the company of a large number of dogs. Still farther downriver, past where the White River dumps its pale, silty waters into the Yukon, they passed the mouth of the Stewart River. With the discovery of gold at Forty Mile, the trading post once run by Arthur Harper and his partners was now deserted, the vacant cabins windowless, the doorways gaping.[3]

As the Carmacks continued downriver, thick thunderheads would pile up in the afternoon sky. When these broke loose in a storm, the fresh scent of rain mixed in the aftermath with the stench of charred wood from forest fires started by lightning; often, these huge fires would burn until the first snow fell, filling the summer air with smoke and sometimes reigniting in the spring.

Two days' journey from the Stewart River, the river the local Hän called the Tr'ondëk,[4]—later renamed the Klondike—empties into the Yukon. At the mouth of the Tr'ondëk, Kate and George passed a summer fish camp of moose hide tents, smokehouses, fish wheels, and drying racks, a place called Tr'ochëk by the Hän, who were river people (the word *Hän* means *river* in their language). By virtue of the way the trading was set up—the Tlingit trading with the Tagish, the Tagish trading with the Tutchone, and the Tutchone trading with the Hän—gestures and the Chinook pidgin language introduced by the Hudson Bay traders were the easiest way for Kate to communicate with the Hän.[5] She asked in the Chinook trading jargon whether they had seen her sister Aagé, wife to a *Boston*, an American, who was looking for *chickamen*, gold.

Beyond the bare-sided bluff downriver from Tr'ochëk, they passed the remains of Fort Reliance, another short-lived trading post established by Arthur Harper, who, with his Native wife, would soon befriend George and Kate. At Fort Reliance, there had been a deadly misunderstanding between the traders and the local people. Before leaving the area for the winter, one of Harper's partners had mixed arsenic with grease and set it out to kill mice. While he was away, some of the local Hän broke into the store. When three women ate the grease and died, the Hän blamed the traders for their deaths. Another of Harper's partners settled the matter by allowing the family of one of the victims to keep one of his dogs.[6] After that, Fort Reliance was boarded up and never reopened. When Kate first saw it, there was nothing left but a dilapidated house and collapsed roofs from three or four small cabins.[7]

Fort Reliance was the point from which prospectors still measured distances along the Yukon, so upon reaching what remained of the post, Kate was within forty miles, more or less, of the Forty Mile district, where she hoped to meet up with her sister Aagé. Across the river from the abandoned Fort Reliance, in the semi-permanent village of Nuklako, the Hän welcomed visitors who floated past by firing from muskets, an old Russian custom that had migrated inland from the distant western coast of Alaska.[8]

From Nuklako, the Yukon River swings tightly to the west, its wide waters brown and rippling. Past the prominent "old wife" rock that sticks up from the river bottom, past the "old man" bluff on the opposite shore, the river carried Kate between high limestone cliffs and then past another Hän settlement near the present-day town of Eagle.

Finally, after more than six hundred miles on the river, the Carmacks reached the community of Forty Mile, on the flat, treed delta where the Fortymile River empties into the Yukon. Alongside the most recent trading post set up by Arthur Harper and his partners stood a hodgepodge of mud-chinked, sod-roofed cabins and Hän summer tents made chiefly of moose hide. As had the Tlingit when the Willards established the mission at Haines, some of these local Hän had moved to Forty Mile to help build the mission and school.[9] For fresh meat, the miners at Forty Mile depended mainly on caribou harvested by the Hän and sold at ten cents per pound.[10]

While the Hän stayed mostly near the new town, the prospectors, including Aagé and Sed Wilson, were spread out over a vast network of creeks that crisscrossed the region. Because prospecting in the fast-moving waters was a hit-and-miss venture, miners would chase up and down these creeks, searching for sweet spots. Some got lucky—from one claim purchased for $300, the new owner took twenty-seven ounces of gold in a mere two hours—but overall, the big payloads in the Forty Mile district were proving elusive.

Kate's new brother-in-law was trying his luck near the south fork of the Fortymile River, at Franklin Gulch. In the late summer of 1888, farther from home than either of them had ever traveled before, Kate and her sister were happily reunited. But their joy was short-lived. As autumn came, turning the aspen leaves golden and the arctic willow red, the entire Forty Mile district faced a crisis. The *Arctic*, the riverboat that was to have brought the last of the season's supplies from St. Michael, had wrecked on its way up the river.

Panic spread—with winter fast approaching, the miners had been counting on dry goods to carry them through. From their elders, Kate and Aagé knew the dangers of famine. During the especially bad winter of 1841, Yukon Indians had been forced to eat moose skins, pack cords, bear skins, and leather sled trappings in order to survive.[11] Even in normal years, late winter and early spring could be lean times, especially in places like Forty Mile, where the moose and caribou had been over-hunted both by outsiders and the Indians who sold meat to them.

To get through the winter, the Yukon Indians worked together, year round, to harvest and preserve food. But at Forty Mile, the miners were obsessed with gold. Even with the help of Indian wives like Kate, who snared rabbits and gathered greens and berries, the miners were depending on the supplies that should have come on the *Arctic*. In anticipation of what would later be dubbed Starvation Winter, Arthur Harper's partner called a miners' meeting. He presented two options—some could wait out the winter at Forty Mile, subsisting on a bag or two of moldy flour per household and whatever game they could kill, and the rest could board the last steamer headed downriver in search of an outpost that had received supplies, riding all the way to St. Michael if they chose.

Proper Tagish brothers-in-law would have stayed together under these circumstances;[12] it was certainly what Kate and Aagé would have preferred. But for whatever reasons—personalities, or perhaps a particular falling out—George and Sed weren't close;

they prospected independently, each with his own partners.[13] So when pressed to decide how to spend Starvation Winter, each husband chose a different course. Sed opted to winter at Franklin Gulch, while Kate and George, in the company of some fifty to eighty miners, boarded the aptly-named *New Racket,* a steam-powered paddle wheeler bound for St. Michael.

Short on provisions, the *New Racket* steamed out of Forty Mile on October 10, 1889, in a race against the coming freeze-up, which would bring a halt to all river travel. It was a dicey journey. The boat was too small to sleep on, so after appointing a few men to cook, the miners agreed they'd camp each night at a well-timbered spot where they could cut cordwood for the steamer, though on their very first night ashore one crazed miner wandered off and had to be rescued. A few days later, as the river pilots, local Hän, debated over which channel to take, the boat and the barge it was towing were pulled in separate directions, requiring some of the men to wade into the (literally) freezing water and use poles to pry their vessel off a sandbar.[14]

Near the confluence of the Tanana River and the Yukon, a measure of relief appeared for the passengers in the form of prospector and trader Gordon C. Bettles, whose future wife, a Koyukon Indian, would one day count herself among Kate's friends. Bettles was the one who had warned the Forty Mile miners of the crisis, dispatching an Indian who had paddled four hundred miles upriver to announce that they would not be getting their winter supplies. Bettles's own small trading post, called Showman's House,[15] was well stocked.[16] Kate and George were among the sixteen refugees who opted to spend the winter there instead of riding all the way to St. Michael.[17]

At Showman's House, George partnered with fellow prospector Howard Hamilton (H. H.) Hart to build a rough cabin in which they would spend the winter. Small but sturdy, the long-bearded Hart had gone West from Indiana, then ventured north seeking fortune. That winter, he and Kate and George heated their little cabin with a mud stove, also called a Russian furnace, cobbled together with rocks and clay. A sod roof helped keep in the heat.

In January, the quicksilver froze for a week, meaning the temperature had plunged past forty below zero. Close as they were to the Arctic Circle, the winter sun rose and set within a three-hour window.[18] On those dark winter days, the only light inside the cabin came from a Yukon lamp, a twisted strip of cotton stuck in a bottle with oil rendered from wild game. On warmer days, Kate added to their limited supply of food with rabbits, ptarmigan, and grouse, cutting down young jack pines to lure the animals and then setting snares to catch them.[19]

When the snow finally melted in the spring of 1890, H. H. Hart parted ways with the Carmacks. But as often happened among the few people spread across the vast territories of Alaska and the Yukon, their lives would intertwine again, several times. Along the way, they would all find wealth—Hart, in fact, would amass two separate fortunes. But as Starvation Winter gave way to spring, Kate, George, and Howard Hamilton Hart were equally poor and not eager to spend another cold, dark winter in such close quarters.

At Franklin Gulch, where Aagé had wintered, the men had managed to kill forty caribou on a hill that they named Bloody Mountain. With Labrador tea and berries, Aagé and the other Native wives helped stave off scurvy. They also made bone butter by boiling down the caribou antlers and bones—with added salt, the mixture turned smooth and buttery as it cooled.[20] Thick, warm blood soup was another hearty favorite. After the river ice broke in the spring of 1890, Aagé's husband began extracting an average of six to seventeen dollars in gold each day from the paystreak at Franklin Gulch—enough to get by on, but no fortune by any stretch.[21]

Meanwhile, George Carmack teamed up with yet another prospector, George Mock of Davenport, Iowa, a man ten years his senior. Son of Prussian immigrants, Mock cited ill health as his reason for striking out for Wyoming in his early twenties. There and in Montana, he rivaled the exploits of John Healy, working stints as a stage driver, a cowboy, a ranchman, a miner, and an Indian fighter before heading north in 1887.[22] Kate followed as her husband and Mock worked Nugget Gulch, a tributary of the Fortymile River that turned out to be on the US side of the border, a location that put her two days' journey from her sister. Eventually, Nugget Gulch would prove a rich creek for its length, with most of its gold concentrated near the steep-terraced gravel along the hillsides near the Fortymile River.[23] But for George Carmack, the prospecting was hit and miss. "Sometimes we had plenty," he wrote, "and sometimes we didn't have anything."[24]

More reliable was Kate's income from sewing moccasins and mittens for the miners. At home, she would have prepared the skins of caribou and moose using a flesher, made of either a large animal's leg bone or an old metal gun barrel, to scrape off any fat, blood, or meat. Then she would have used a sharp blade to cut off the hair and even out the thickness of the skin. Once these steps were completed, the hide had to be thoroughly washed in a stream or lake and then draped to dry. When winter arrived, she would have hung the hide out in the cold to soften and bleach it, then soaked it in a solution of water and rotted caribou or moose brains. After repeated wringings, the skin was stretched over a frame and scraped smooth until it was fully softened and sometimes smoked to a golden color.

Tanning was a laborious process, one best accomplished with the help of other women, and so at Forty Mile, Kate likely purchased tanned hides from the local Hän. After marking her pattern for mittens or moccasins in red ochre on the inner side of the skin, she cut it out with a knife. The traditional way of sewing was to use your fingernails to split into fine strands the dried leg sinew of a caribou, which you would then wet and roll against the side of your leg until it was thin and pliable. You would then punch holes with an awl in a tanned hide and wet the sinew so it would slide through.[25] But at the Forty Mile trading post, Kate had access to steel needles and cobbler's thread, which made her work easier.

The mittens and moccasins Kate sewed were in high demand among prospectors, who recognized the superior warmth these items provided. Other women sewed also: At Forty Mile, several miners had taken Indian wives, who on the average were less than twenty years of age—sixteen years younger than the average age of the husbands.[26] Several of these wives were Koyukon women from hundreds of miles down the Yukon River. Because of early contact with the Russians who made their way around the coast of Alaska to exploit fur trading opportunities, these women were familiar with the ways of outsiders. One of them, a trader's wife, even organized social events like the so-called "squaw dances" at Forty Mile, where Native women, married or not, were expected to dance with the miners to the music of a lone fiddler.[27]

So-called "squaw men" such as George Carmack were often viewed with disdain, as exemplified by one prospector who wrote, upon learning his friend had married a Native woman, "What a pity that a fine specimen of a man should have fallen so low as to marry a squaw."[28] But on a broader scale, long-term relationships between Native women and their white husbands were fertile ground for the sorts of exchanges that facilitated cooperation and new sets of cultural practices, a process of accommodation that would be cut short when the rush to the Klondike began.

Like early fur traders, Kate's husband and others who married local women enjoyed the benefits of wives who in addition to cooking and sewing and warming their beds could snare rabbits, sew skins, and harvest edible and medicinal plants. From the families they had married into, these men also learned skills that enabled them to survive in the wilderness. And regardless of how they began, many of these relationships grew to include genuine affection, as illustrated by the case of one British miner at Forty Mile who turned down an inheritance from his older brother because he feared his Indian wife would be unhappy in England.[29]

For Kate, following George from creek to creek in the Forty Mile district meant a disruption in the seasonal rounds she'd grown up with—winter camp to spring camp to fish camp to hunting camp in the fall. As best she could, she continued the work required in each season, sewing and snaring small game in the winter, gathering fresh greens as the snow melted, putting up fish where she could, gathering berries in the late summer and fall. At Nugget Gulch, she endured two winters of bitter cold, with temperatures that often hovered near forty below zero (Fahrenheit), while she and George tried to stay warm in temporary shelters with sod roofs.[30]

Even in these conditions, Kate had cause to celebrate on December 21, 1891—the shortest day of the year, in terms of sunlight—and more significantly, the day Aagé's third daughter Mary Wilson (also called Minnie) was born.[31] Assisting with the birth, Kate would have cleaned her niece's mouth with her finger, then pulled lightly on her nose and flattened her ears to make sure she grew up to be beautiful. She would have sponged off her niece and wrapped her in soft rabbit skins. Because babies were sometimes tempted to go back where they came from, she would have sprinkled Mary with ashes from the household fire, a reminder to stay on earth with her parents.[32]

But following the great happiness of Mary's birth came great sorrow. Aagé died. No one knows for certain when or how it happened, except that it was within nine months of Mary's birth. For the first time, Kate grieved with no one but herself to wash Aagé's body and dress her in funeral clothes, no one but herself to sing the mourning songs, no one but herself to sit watch for the ghosts that might come to claim her sister's spirit.[33] Of her family, she alone was there to help care for the baby, a responsibility that must have brought her some solace.

But even that small comfort would be taken from Kate. In September, 1892, Sed Wilson decided to leave Forty Mile. In the company of several miners, he planned to pole up the Yukon River toward Carcross, where he would follow the Chilkoot Trail to Dyea and from there hire passage on a steamship.[34] Not for a moment would he have considered taking little Mary with him on a wilderness journey along the icy waters of the Yukon just before freeze-up. Naturally, Kate assumed he would leave little Mary in her care—Tagish daughters belonged with their mothers, after all, and with the families of their mothers.

Widowed miners had another option, however—to leave their children at the local mission.[35] For their part, missionaries had a special fondness for these "half-breed" children, believing them to have more "potential for refinement" than full-blooded Native children. In September 1892, a new missionary couple, William and Selina Bompas, had recently arrived at Forty Mile, and they were happy to take Aagé's daughter from Sed Wilson.

So it was that Kate was separated from her niece, her only connection to the sister she had lost in this faraway place. And whatever dreams Aagé may have had for her daughter, Mary's life would unfold in ways she could have never imagined.

CHAPTER NINE

SHOVE IT OUT NOW

KATE'S NIECE, MARY WILSON, also called Minnie, was Wolf, of the Dakl'aweidí, the Killer Whale nation. Her mother was Aagé, daughter of Gus'dutéen, daughter of Húnx̲u.aat, whose people came from Tahltan, the flat place. Led by two old men, they had gone under a glacier to the mouth of the Shtax'héen River, to a place now called Wrangell, and camped on a pebbly beach, where the clan got its name, Dakl'aweidí. From there some went up the coast to the Chilkat River and over the Bear Creek pass to where they made the village of Tagish. Their song is "Shove It out Now," sung in remembrance of when their people went under the glacier.

Had Kate raised her, Mary would have learned that this was her *shagóon*. But in the household of Anglican missionary Charlotte Selina Bompas, she would have had no way of knowing that every story began with acknowledging the people you came from. For years, in fact, she would be cut off completely from her Tagish relatives. She would never be known by her own Tagish name. Like her cousin, the daughter who would soon be born to Kate and George Carmack, she would be among a generation of children from mixed marriages who eventually lost touch with the clans of their mothers.

Mary's adoptive mother, Charlotte Bompas, who went by Selina, would be the first white woman of lasting influence in Kate's life; over and over, their paths would cross. Like Kate's, Selina's marriage had been arranged for a purpose—but in Selina's case, it was an alliance forged to advance not the exchange of furs but the procurement of souls for the kingdom of God. Alarmed by the activity of Catholic missionaries in the northern reaches of the continent, the Anglicans had decided they'd best form a new diocese, which they called Athabasca, in northwestern Canada. To the dismay of missionary William Bompas, who hated administration and other worldly pursuits, the Anglicans declared him bishop of this new diocese, the only sticking point being that as bishop, he was expected to have a wife.

With characteristic expedience, Bompas proceeded directly to England, where he proposed to his cousin, Selina. Twenty years earlier, he'd made a similar offer of marriage and Selina had turned him down. But at age forty-four, her prospects were few. Faced with a choice between spinsterhood or marriage to a man who made up in zeal for what he lacked in charm, she opted to wed the imposing, bull-headed Anglican missionary who had more or less exiled himself doing God's work among the indigenous people of western Canada.

Impulsive, self-willed, but also kind-hearted, the woman who would raise Aagé's daughter had at a young age shown little interest in the work of the church, describing missionary meetings as "the dullest affairs" led by "dismal old slow coaches."[1] A murder changed her mind. In 1871, Anglican bishop John Coleridge Patteson was killed on a South Pacific island. Set afloat in a canoe, Patteson's naked body had been hacked with a hatchet and adorned with a palm branch that was knotted five times, once for each island Native killed in a raid by slave traders. His martyrdom sparked outrage in England, where citizens demanded their government act once and for all to abolish the slave trade in its Pacific territories.[2] It also inspired individuals like Selina to honor the martyr by focusing their attentions on converting indigenous

Missionary Charlotte Selina Bompas, who raised Kate's niece Mary Wilson from 1892 to 1899. (The General Synod Archives, Anglican Church of Canada, Stringer P7517-198)

people throughout the world, with what they hoped would be more genial results.

A small, sharp-nosed woman, Selina Bompas had spent much of her childhood in Italy and was reported to carry a copy of Dante's writing wherever she traveled. Five days after her hasty marriage to the bishop, the newlyweds set off for Fort Simpson, a Hudson Bay Post at the confluence of the Mackenzie and Liard rivers in northwestern Canada. Though the setting struck her as lonely and desolate, Selina learned the local dialect, and as her husband made his itinerant rounds in the wilderness, she performed her own set of missionary duties. Taking a particular interest in Native children, she chose two girls to raise as her own. The first died while still an infant; the second, Owindia (also called Lucy), died as a toddler when Selina brought her to visit England.[3]

On August 4, 1892—a month before Mary's father, Sed Wilson, would depart the Yukon—Selina and William Bompas relocated to the Forty Mile mission, from which the bishop was to administer yet another new diocese, called Selkirk, covering an area of 200,000 square miles from the Arctic Ocean to the edge of British Columbia.[4] To Selina, one measure of the remoteness of their new location was that steamers carried their mail only twice a year, once right after break-up and once again before freeze-up. The mission house at Forty Mile sat high on a bank of the Yukon River, surrounded on all sides by mountains. Its construction had been overseen by the predecessor of William Bompas[5] and then by Native catechists who, according to Selina, had "allowed a number of Indians to have free run of the house . . . the state of filth and disorder when we took possession was really terrible."[6]

After a thorough scrubbing of her new home, Selina took up quarters in the loft, where she set up the chairs, tables, and carpets she had brought from England, along with her books and her pictures. "I sit at my window," she wrote, "and look at the beautiful Yukon flowing by so stately and yet swiftly, and at the Eastern mountains which I tell myself lie towards Salisbury! The quiet life and mountain air suit my health. There is no bustle or excitement here, but yet I have so much to do that I never feel dull."[7]

Among the projects that busied Selina Bompas soon after her arrival was Kate's niece. "It is very merciful of God to let me have charge of another little Indian child," Selina wrote. "It was very painful at first, as she is just the age of my dear little Lucy the year we went to Fort Norman, and one seemed living over the past again, and at times almost forgot the interval of deep sorrow. But she is quite unlike my little 'Owindia,' except in some of her quaint Indian ways. She is really a lovely child with passionate black eyes. Her mother was a Chilcat Indian—a tribe which has always been very warlike, and given at times a great deal of trouble." Selina was wrong, of course, about Mary Wilson's Chilkat heritage, but this sort of confusion among outsiders concerning Native groups was common.

Though compliant enough as she grew older—a development Selina would no doubt attribute to the tempering effect of her household—Kate's niece was a spirited toddler who inadvertently played into the Janus-faced thinking about Native Americans in the late eighteenth century, that somehow indigenous people more than any others embodied both the best and worst of human nature.[8] "Minnie's fits of passion are fearful," Selina Bompas wrote. "I was quite frightened the first time I saw her in one of them, when the small creature threw herself on the floor and rolled backwards and forwards across the room, roaring as loudly as she could. She clings to me with great affection, and if she wants anything coaxes very prettily by putting up her mouth to 'kuss.' One day last autumn she was thirsty, so with the pluck and independence of her nation and tribe, she toddled alone down the bank to the river's brim and there lay down and drank, sucking up the water with avidity. It was such a pretty picture! The great Yukon River rolling on its turbulent course of more than 2,000 miles, and the tiny child quenching her thirst out of it as if it had been only a saucer."[9]

Kate would have been less than amused by her niece lapping water straight from the river. Unless your clan had a special relationship with a particular body of water, you were to approach it with caution—if while anywhere near a waterway you made loud noises or were disrespectful, you risked drowning.[10] But Kate had no opportunity to teach this to Mary. With little gold to show for his three years of prospecting, George wanted to return to the Big Salmon River and try his luck. So only days after Sed Wilson gave Mary to Selina Bompas, George and Kate also left Forty Mile, boarding the *New Racket* on September 2, 1892, for the final leg of its voyage upriver before freeze-up.[11]

The month was *Kaxwéix Dísi*, the Highbush Cranberry Moon, a busy and important time of drying salmon, picking berries, and gathering plants in preparation for winter.[12] In the Yukon, autumn comes and goes in a matter of weeks; you wake to a chill, one that sometimes brings frost, the nights fully dark, the skies filled with stars that are washed out in the twilit nights of summer. The golden blaze of birch along the river fades as autumn winds blow the leaves from their branches. Rosehips swell and ripen, filling the woods with a tangy, pungent odor, and cottony seeds cover red fireweed stalks that only weeks before bobbed with purple flowers.

Despite her sorrow at leaving her niece, Kate also had cause for joy. Each mile they traveled up the silty river was another mile closer to home. The sternwheeler wouldn't take them all the way there—it would dock downriver, and from there they'd have to travel either on foot or in a small boat, but with any luck she and George would arrive at her father's clan house in plenty of time for Kate to be with her family when she gave birth to her own child, due in January.

Aboard the *New Racket* with the Carmacks was Bishop Bompas, bound for Fort Selkirk, where he had recently dispatched Reverend Thomas Canham and his wife, Charlotte Sarah Canham, to establish a new mission. One might assume that embarking on a 225-mile river journey in the company of the tall, stern bishop whose wife had just taken her niece would be impossibly difficult for Kate. But the situation was more complex than that. While Kate was sorry to be leaving Mary behind, Selina Bompas had no children of her own, and the giving over of a child to the childless was common among indigenous people of Alaska and the Yukon.[13] It was also too soon to realize the long-term cultural loss that would result from the well-meaning efforts of church officials like Bompas to "re-educate" Native children.[14] And though blunt and gruff and ever-paternal, Mary's adoptive father in particular would prove a fierce advocate for the Natives he perceived as being under his care.

As the sternwheeler chugged upriver, the bishop revealed to Kate and her husband that the Canhams were "in a mess" about their house at Fort Selkirk.[15] Eager for someone to saw lumber and get out logs to help speed the construction, Bompas hired George Carmack on the spot. Once again, Kate would have to adapt, giving birth without Tagish women to assist. Fort Selkirk was a good ways downriver from her family, near the confluence of the Pelly and the Lewes, as that portion of the Yukon River was first called by outsiders. Ten thousand years earlier, this region had been the eastern edge of Beringia, the land bridge that opened between Asia and North America during the final big Ice Age.[16]

Well before trader Robert Campbell established his ill-fated trading post at Fort Selkirk, Indians from all over had gathered there to trade: obsidian from the St. Elias Mountains, copper from headwaters of the White River, chert from the Tagish lakes region.[17] The Tlingit came, too, bringing dried clams, hooligan oil, and seaweed to exchange for caribou hides and the pelts of marten and other fur-bearing mammals; beginning in the 1790s, they also brought blankets, tea, tobacco, and guns obtained from trade with the Russians. After the 1852 raid on Fort Selkirk, the Hudson Bay Company ignored Campbell's pleas to rebuild the post. But American trader Arthur Harper had been in the country long enough to recognize the potential in setting up a store where so many groups traditionally came to trade. Thanks in no small part to his Koyukon wife, Seentahna, also called Jennie, Harper had a rapport with the Indians that Robert Campbell had never enjoyed.

When Kate arrived at Fort Selkirk in September of 1892, Harper's post on the south bank of the Yukon River consisted of the log store, where he and Jennie lived with their family, surrounded by a few small cabins for use by those who traveled to Fort Selkirk to trade. In one of these cabins, Kate set up housekeeping. Until freeze-up, George ran logs from Joe LaDue's sawmill downriver, logs with which he and Henry Davis—a prospector who with his Native wife was friend to the missionaries—raised the walls of the Anglican rectory.

While George worked on the rectory, Kate renewed her acquaintance with Jennie Harper, whom she'd first met in 1889, during Starvation Winter.[18] Married to white men, their circumstances were similar, though Kate was childless at the time while Jennie was busy with five small boys. Like Kate, Jennie Harper had followed her white husband far beyond the region in which she'd grown up. Daughter of a Koyukon leader known as Chief Larion, one of the men responsible for the Nulato Massacre,[19] Seentahna had met and married thirty-nine-year-old Arthur Harper when she was only fourteen years old. With high cheekbones and long, dark hair, she was tall for a Koyukon woman, making her a bit of an oddity, which may have been one reason she was given to a white man in marriage. Another reason may have been famine—by marrying off young women to traders, the band would have fewer to feed.[20] Her wedding, like Kate's, was accomplished the traditional way: with little ceremony and no papers, she and Arthur Harper began living together and raising a family.

An Irish immigrant and staunch Catholic with large hands, a rectangular face, and deep-set eyes, Jennie Harper's husband appeared older than his years. Along with Jack McQuesten and Al Mayo, he had been among the first to prospect for gold along the tributaries of the Yukon. Traveling in separate groups, each had come overland in the 1870s through Canada, following the Yukon all the way to its mouth while avoiding Robert Campbell's mistake of venturing too far into Tlingit trading territory. When the rigors of the North proved too much for their initial companions, McQuesten, Mayo, and Harper joined together to represent the interests of the Alaska Commercial (A.C.) Company, trading furs for manufactured goods—beads, guns, teakettles, blankets, fabric, tobacco, and ammunition—[21] as they ventured into places the Russians and the Hudson Bay Company either had either abandoned or failed to go in the first place.[22]

Unlike Healy's, Harper's Indian marriage had not been a strategy lightly taken up only to be abandoned.[23] He raised a large family with Jennie, and following what appears to have been a friendly parting of ways with McQuesten and Mayo, he formed a new partnership with prospector Joe LaDue, which led him to Fort Selkirk in the fall of 1890.[24] Described by a passing geologist as one of the best informed and most genial men he'd met in the country,[25] Harper was something of a loner, even by Yukon standards, and so the remote outpost of Fort Selkirk, at the junction of the Pelly and Yukon rivers, suited him well. Unlike Healy's Fort Whoop-Up, there was no whiskey traded at Harper's post, which was a fort in name only. Relations with the locals were genial, due in no small part to the presence of Harper's Koyukon wife.

Besides their husbands, Yukon Indian women usually had one special friend or partner with whom they were very close.[26] During her years of wandering with George in the Forty Mile district, Kate had little opportunity to develop one of these friendships, so the presence of Jennie Harper was welcome.[27]

Jennie's labor came first, nearly one year to the day after Aagé's. Ideally, a woman from her husband's side of the family would have helped with the birth, but at Fort Selkirk, Jennie had made do without this assistance; if anyone joined her in the birth hut, it would have been Kate Carmack and Helen Davis, the Koyukon wife of the man who was helping George build the rectory. On December 22, 1892, Jennie Harper gave birth to her eighth child, Walter,[28] a boy who would make history when at age twenty, he became the first man in recorded history to summit Mount McKinley, the tallest mountain in North America.[29]

Three weeks after Walter's birth, on January 11, 1893—a quiet day in the Goose Moon *T'aawák Dísi*, one day among many devoted to sewing skins and repairing the gear that would be needed when the ice broke in the spring, a day when the feeble light of the winter sun barely breached the horizon before conceding to the deep cold of night—Kate retreated to the birth hut. To comfort her during her labor, she had Helen and Jennie, who caught the baby and cleaned it and straightened its limbs.[30]

The child—Kate's second, George's first—was a girl. Kate called her Aagé, "daughter of the lake," after her sister. For the child's English name, George drew from a character in a book that belonged to missionary Thomas Canham, a man of letters. So it was that the daughter of Shaaw Tláa, daughter of Gus'dutéen, daughter of Húnx̱u.aat, whose people came from Tahltan, the flat place, and whose song is "Shove It out Now," became known as Graphie Grace Carmack.

Once a Tagish woman had a child, it was time for her to quit traveling around with her husband.[31] At Fort Selkirk, Kate was still hundreds of miles from her father's clan house, but she was much closer than she'd been at Forty Mile. Even better, her relatives came to the Pelly River each winter to trade, and the little cabin where she took care of Graphie Grace was located near the junction of the Pelly and Yukon rivers.[32]

During the winter of 1893, the worldwide financial outlook was grim, the only bright spots being the impressive discoveries of gold in South Africa and Australia. Squeezed out of employment, let alone wealth, by the ever-widening gap between rich and poor and the overall vile state of the economy in the US mainland and beyond, more and more would-be miners were taking their chances in the North. Most were cut from the same cloth as George Carmack—independent, directionless, with little to hold them back home. A good number found the country hard and the prospects slim, especially since those who were in the right place at the right time had already snatched up the best claims before newcomers arrived. Still, a person could hope to get lucky, on some other creek, with some other gold.

At Fort Selkirk, 1893 proved a profitable year for Jennie Harper's husband: that winter, he purchased over 9,000 marten, plus ten bales of lynx and fox skins. "They got their furs cheap," wrote Helen's husband, Henry David, referring to Harper and his business associates, "for if an Indian wanted a rifle, they stood it on the floor and [stacked] their skin[s] to the top of the rifle. Sack flour came the same way, flat ways on top of each other. Robbers, I say they were."[33,34]

When the ice went out that spring, George Carmack moved his young family from Fort Selkirk to a spot twenty miles from Five Finger Rapids, just above where the Big Salmon River empties into the Yukon, a part of the river that's thick with sandbars and islands. There, Arthur Harper had staked Kate's husband for a half-interest in a trading venture, a franchise of sorts on the Fort Selkirk store. On a large, flat patch of riverbank,[35] near a vein of coal noted by geologist George Dawson during his 1887 expedition, George built a small log cabin, a post people called McCormick's Post or Stick George's.[36]

Among the calico, rifles, beads, and canned goods supplied by Harper, Kate made yet another home. Like Jennie Harper, she became a storekeeper's wife. While tending Graphie, she kept sewing—prospectors on their way to Forty Mile were always in the market for well-made mittens and moccasins, and the Selkirk people got lots of moose and caribou upriver every fall, so she had plenty of access to skins.[37] Though away from her family, she at least enjoyed some of the material goods her wealthier Tlingit relatives took for granted—though at inflated prices, since she and George were so far from the coast.

Owing to a combination of bad luck and failed navigation, George's trading post venture was short-lived. After posting a sign on the door that said *Gone to Fortymile for grub*, George "lost his boat and everything" on the river.[38] Bishop Bompas hired him again, this time to help build the schoolhouse at Fort Selkirk, a small log building that would also serve as the church.[39] For the next two years, the Carmacks stayed in the general area of Fort Selkirk; since her marriage to Kult'ús, it was the longest Kate had lived in any one place. George still did a little prospecting, but only in passing, on trips downriver to Joe LaDue's sawmill. Nothing came of his efforts.

By this time, most of the serious prospectors in the North had moved down the Yukon River, from Forty Mile to Circle City, a new boomtown in Alaska. The Circle City rush had been set off by two Koyukon men who discovered gold in 1892 at Birch Creek, where Carmack has prospected only a few months earlier. The discoverers initially tried but failed to keep their find a secret;[40] by 1894, hordes of prospectors had extracted over $400,000 in gold.[41] Very little of the riches went to the Koyukon men, however, since they'd failed to properly file their claims.

In lieu of serious prospecting, Kate's husband tended the Fort Selkirk store when Arthur Harper and his family went downriver during the summers of 1894 and 1895 to deliver furs and restock on trading goods at St. Michael. Again Kate assumed the role that Jennie Harper had taken for two decades, that of a shopkeeper's

Native wife, whose presence encouraged a deeper level of trust among the Indians who came to trade. But she rarely enjoyed visits from her family, who had mostly relocated to Dyea, where the packing opportunities were too lucrative to pass up.[42]

In the fall of 1895, Arthur Harper returned from his summertime travels without Jennie or his children. He had sent the children to school in California, following the example of his former trading partner, Jack McQuesten. It was a decision that had sat well enough with McQuesten's Koyukon wife, who had attended a Russian-run mission school. But Jennie Harper was outraged. She left Arthur and with her youngest child, Walter, she returned to the village of Tanana, where she told friends and family that at least Arthur Harper would not get his hands on her youngest child.[43]

Whether Jennie had acted rightly was difficult to judge. The elders said you were supposed to stay with your husband, and yet who could fault her anger, when her children had been sent thousands of miles away to be educated by someone else? One thing was certain—without Jennie, the winter would be especially lonely for Kate. But before the snows fell again, she would have more company than she knew what to do with, with her life transformed by gold.

CHAPTER TEN

Good Gold, Lotsa Gold

In addition to wealth, one of the key outcomes of what became known as "Discovery Day" in the Klondike—August 17, 1896—was a mosaic of stories that frame the event, dramas in which Kate plays various roles from supporting actress to chief protagonist, depending on the cultural context.

In the prevailing versions of the rush to gold in the Klondike, the heroes are rugged, independent, and irascible frontiersmen; women, if mentioned at all, serve to underscore the tension between adventure and domesticity as men explored and asserted themselves in the Frozen North. Where they could, the prospectors acquired and profited, the ultimate goal being to retreat from the wilderness to a comfortable existence improved by wealth.

Outside the Native community, most tales of the Klondike discovery feature George Carmack as the central figure, though in some, he is aided by Kate in the role of "Indian princess." In one classically Victorian rendering, Kate keeps the gold a tantalizing secret before eventually revealing it out of fear of losing her husband:

> Still always uppermost in his [George's] mind was the quest for the gold that he felt sure was not far away. Kate saw that

> this would sooner or later take her loved one from her, for with her young child she could not follow on all of the hard trips in search for the bits of metal that were her only rival in her husband's thoughts. Why should she not tell him where the creeks were that ran for miles over golden pebbles? That would make him happy and then, [once] he had all of it that he desired, he would stay contented at home with her and cease those tiresome wanderings for the metal whose lack made him so unhappy . . . She could not see him unhappy, and one day an excursion was planned that would lead them to the place where the mosses trailed over golden sands and the waters of the rippling creek looked like Chablis as they took alternately the color of the moss and gold on which they ran.[1]

In yet another version, the innocent play of Indian children becomes the providential clue that leads Kate's husband to the gold. As the story goes, George Carmack, weakened and sickly, is rescued by "Skookum Charley." While the "Eskimo" women tend to him in their "igloo," their children play a game with rocks taken from a nearby stream. From the metallic ring of one of these rocks striking a steel pick, George recognizes that the quartz must contain gold. He traces the rocks back to their source, and the rush to the Klondike is on.[2]

Spread by newswire to papers throughout North America, the most outlandish of these discovery stories reads like a classic fairy tale. In it, Kate promises to show George where he can find gold on the condition that he pledge his love for her. Ostensibly told in Kate's own words—a curious mix of fake Indian-speak, romantic cliché, and terms Kate could not have known—the narrative reveals much about nineteenth-century American attitudes toward Natives, women, and wealth:

> One night at dance in frozen country I first see white George. He talk to me and press my hand. He tell me how he walk about all over big, frozen country many, many months, and

he tell me how he never find so much as one little piece of great gold which make white man's heart glad.

Then he press my hand some more and love came into my heart and I remember some things I hear my brother Skookum Jim and my brother Tagish Charlie say. I think of what they tell me of a place where gold is as thick as the sand when one digs on the shore of the Meiozikaka, and I say: 'Whiteman, meet me by the river at midnight and I tell you something to make your heart glad and love will come to you for Tagish Kate.'

White George he shake his head to show me he no believe Tagish Kate, but all same he came to river at midnight. I took him out in my canoe, away out in middle of river where no red man can hear and I whisper in white George's ear: "I know spot where gold is thick like sand."

I tell paleface George he love me, me show him gold. He shake his head and say he no believe Tagish Kate.

Then I tell him how my brothers, Skookum Jim and Tagish Charley, have found place where they get heap much gold, and I tell him how they go and bring me back necklace all made out of little gold stones. When I see paleface George's eye grow bright by light of moon and when he press my hand with his big strong hands I take one, two, three gold stones from under my dress and show them to him. George look at them and his eyes grow big. He swear he love Tagish Kate. I ask him if he make Tagish Kate his squaw. He says yes, yes, many, many times. He take me in his arms; he kiss me and say he love me. Tagish Kate believes and is happy, very, very happy. Then comes wedding and plenty much to eat.

Now is September and in frozen country we must wait, wait for summer before we can go and find gold. Then me tell my brothers, Skookum Jim and Tagish Charlie, that my white chief George know where gold is. They very mad, but me, no care. Me love paleface George, my chief.

Then when summer came we make peace with Skookum Jim and Tagish Charlie, and one day all start together to place

> where gold is. Long, long time to get there. One day we came to Rabbit creek and George he lay down and sleep. While he sleep I fill pan with sand and put it beside him. He wake up and see pan and wash out dirt and in it is gold all same like three dollars. George glad. He find heap much gold and love Tagish Kate and buy me heap nice clothes.[3]

In the age of yellow journalism, this was hardly the first fabricated story to make news, but it does complicate the matter of determining what part Kate actually played in the discovery that set off the rush to the Klondike. To add to the difficulty, there is no single clear and consistent explanation of the events from George Carmack himself that led up to his scratching a Discovery claim into the trunk of a birch tree near what became known as Bonanza Creek.[4]

Instead, what passes for George's own account of the Klondike discovery is a heavily embellished tale that reveals more about the American sense of destiny, achievement, fortune, and individualism than anything else. The author of this oft-quoted publication was not George Carmack but George T. Snow, a first-rate theatrical man who took on the project of gathering the accounts of early prospectors on behalf of the Yukon Order of Pioneers, a group that he himself had founded. Born in Boston in 1847, he took the stage name of George Snow after he ran away from home. Following two solo prospecting trips into the Yukon in 1888 and 1892, Snow returned with his wife and two children, who had the distinction of being the first white family to cross over the Chilkoot Pass. At Forty Mile, he opened a theater, complete with San Francisco "music-hall girls" and a stage set with Chippendale chairs, plush curtains, and pier glass.[5]

In order to fashion what eventually came to stand as George Carmack's version of how gold was found in the Klondike, Snow worked from George's handwritten notes, which end with an account of the winter of 1895–1896, short of the actual discovery event in August 1896. From there, Snow made good use of his theatrical inclinations to complete the story. Nowhere is Kate mentioned—not in George's handwritten account nor in Snow's colorful rendition—though a great number of firsthand sources place Kate at the Klondike River during the summer of 1896 alongside her husband, as she had been for the previous decade.[6]

As a preface to the discovery, Snow positions George Carmack on the banks of the Yukon River at Fort Selkirk in May 1896. "The sky above the eastern rim of the Palisades was glowing with a soft light, presaging the birth of a new day," Snow writes in a style Carmack himself never used. "Over the Palisades the morning star was drowsily blinking and falling to sleep, as I gazed with wonder and awe on God's miracle of dissolving night into day . . . As I watched the flaming banners thrust farther their streamers of scintillating fire above the mountains, I felt my blood begin to tingle with new life and strength. I had a premonition that something unusual was going to take place in my life."[7]

Right then and there, Snow writes, George flips a coin, a silver dollar, the only "cheechaco" money he has. Heads, and he'll venture upriver; tails, he'll go down. Through the coin toss, Lady Luck directs him downriver, past the Klondike to Forty Mile. On the night of his arrival, he dreams that he's watching grayling shoot the rapids. All at once, the small fish scatter, and two huge king salmon stop directly in front of where George is sitting. Instead of scales, the salmon are covered in gold nuggets, and for eyes they have $20 gold pieces.

This means he'll make money catching fish to sell to the miners, George decides, and so he heads back up the mighty Yukon to the Klondike River, where the Tr'ondëk Hwëch'in keep their fish camp. As he poles his boat close to shore, a yellow-breasted bird lands at his feet. Lifting the tiny creature in his hands—the bird shows no fear—George determines it's yet another sign of luck.

In Snow's account, Jim and Charlie then happen upon George and his fish traps at the mouth of the Klondike. Seven years have passed since they've seen one another, Snow writes—seven years of bad luck for Jim, foretold by George when Jim's wife dropped a mirror on a rock and broke it.[8] For the benefit of readers, Snow recounts a new version of how George and Jim first met, a rendition that characterizes Jim as the stereotypical "mighty Indian":

> It was a very warm day and the Sun was blazing; a light North-West wind began to filter across the [Chilkoot] summit, cooling the heat waves in its course; the scintillations of the ice crystals on the surrounding glaciers, the towering giants of embattled rocks, thrusting up their hoary heads toward the dome of Heaven, gave one a feeling of intense awe . . . Suddenly Skookum Jim rose and stood looking toward the hills, with steady eyes. His head was bare and his shirt was unbuttoned at the throat, exposing his great chest and neck of bronze. There was something in his attitude which suggested the silent strength of the North.[9]

Reunited at the Klondike River, Snow writes, Jim, George, and Charlie are soon greeted by Bob Henderson, who tells them about the color he's found at nearby Gold Bottom Creek. "I don't want any Damn Siwashes staking on that creek," Henderson says, according to Snow. This, of course, doesn't sit well with Jim and Charlie.[10]

Never mind, George tells them, we'll find our own creek. And so they set off. Though the terrain is unfamiliar, George takes the lead. As he pans for gold in a stream, he quotes from Shakespeare, "To be or not to be, that is the question." Explaining to his companions that he's making "Boston man's medicine," he directs them to spit in his gold pan for luck. As he swishes the waters, a streak of bright yellow gold appears.[11]

But true hero that he is, George has high standards—he won't settle for any old gold. He insists they keep looking, but the going is tough. "Climbing up the steep side of a mountain without a trail and with a pack on your back, struggling over fallen trees, floundering thru Devil Clubs and interlaced underbrush, is heart breaking work and exacts the uttermost toil of your body," writes Snow on Carmack's behalf. "Well: a weakling has no business to play in that kind of game."[12]

At last, George's strength, fortitude, skill, and endurance converge in the discovery foretold by the aggregated good-luck omens. From a high bank, he recognizes the promise of gold in the creek below:

> Throwing off my pack, I walked down to the rim, as soon as I reached it, I stopped and looked down, my heart skipped a beat. I rubbed my eyes with the back of my hand to wipe away a misty film that enveloped the pupils, then I reached down and picked up a nugget about the size of a dime, then I put it between my teeth and bit at it like a schoolboy who had found a quarter in the garbage can.[13]

A first-class theatrical spectacle follows as George celebrates with Jim and Charlie. "We did a war dance around that gold-pan, it was a combination war dance; composed of the Scotch hornpipe, Indian fox trot, syncopated Irish jig, and a sort of a Siwash Hula-Hula."[14] The reveries then fade to a reflective interlude around the campfire, where " . . . the two Indians sitting with their blankets over their shoulders, their lean, bronze features lit up by the gleaming camp fire, began to chant a wild weird song of praise to the Great Spirit."[15] After Jim and Charlie fall asleep, Snow depicts Carmack recapping the American vision of wealth and happiness, his musings punctuated for effect by celestial wonders:

> In all that eleven years of strenuous, unceasing battle with the un-subdued North-land, I had imbibed a grim optimism, which found expression in undertaking to accomplish things which seemed at the time almost impossible of achievement. At last my hopes were about to be realized. A grim determination entered my soul to hold on in spite of every obstacle, until the treasure chest I had un-earthed lay unlocked before me. Already my brain was occupied with half-formed projects for the future. A trip around the world with a congenial companion. A beautiful home with kept lawns, shrubbery and flowers. A sum invested in government bonds, the income of which would be sufficient to enable me to enjoy the good things of life in a decent way and keep me comfortable for the balance of my life.
>
> I was getting sleepy, so I rolled in-to my blankets and lay looking up at the scintillating stars, gleaming in the great arching dome of the un-clouded Yukon sky: The Great

> Dipper, nearly over-head, circling thru the vast expanse; a falling meteor flashed for an instant across the heavens and disappeared; then I fell into a dreamless sleep.[16]

For Kate and the indigenous people of the North, the discovery that would threaten their way of life was, quite literally, an altogether different story, one that was grounded in the same actions that defined their everyday existence. As those who knew Kate would tell it, gold was found in the Klondike that day because her brother Keish, known as Jim, acted on his family obligations and went looking for his sister, whom he hadn't seen in two years. The extent to which fortune was found—and lost—by Jim and his family, including Kate, was determined by a series of encounters between Jim and his spirit helper, a frog, that was connected to an elusive figure called Wealth Woman, who pointed the way for Jim—not George Carmack—to discover gold in the rust-colored waters of what was then called Rabbit Creek.

Post-discovery, outsiders would portray Kate's brother much as Snow had, as a stereotypical Indian who wanted nothing more than to be white. It's true that in nearly every photo that survives him, whether the backdrop is a rustic cabin or a pile of dirty tailings from a mine or a San Francisco photo studio, Jim appears dapper in his three-piece suit, with a gold watch chain dangling from his vest pocket. But fashion aside, Jim's heart was in the Yukon, with his people. Those who knew him recall a man who was dutiful, reliable, truthful, and capable.[17] Though admired, he was humble,[18] and he enjoyed a good joke, even if it was on himself.[19]

With his Tlingit wife, L'unáat's sister Daak̲ux̲da.éit', Jim had a son, Kal.ens', and a daughter, Saayna.aat, also called Daisy. By 1894, he was living much of the time with his family at Dyea, where his reputation as an iconic outdoorsman was offset by stories of his laughable blunders, like the time he boiled beans all day long, hoping for a nice meal, only to find that all he'd cooked was a mighty strong pot of coffee.[20] Another time, it was said, Jim had some laundry to do, so he set a big pot of water to boil on his Yukon stove and then went to the trading post for some soap, which in those days was carved off of big fifty-pound blocks. Not sure of the right word for soap, Jim pointed to a big slab and gestured with his hands to show the storekeeper how much he wanted. Back at his tent, he shaved slivers into the water and stirred in his clothes. After they'd boiled a good while, he scrubbed them on a washboard he'd made out of poplar. But instead of getting clean, his clothes got greasier and greasier. When he prevailed on his neighbor for help, she informed him that he hadn't bought soap—he'd bought cheese.[21]

More significant to Kate's story was a series of events that correlate directly with the discovery of gold in the Klondike: Jim's encounters with Wealth Woman, who at times took the form of a frog helper. The first of these appears to have occurred around 1891, the year Aagé's daughter Mary was born in the Forty Mile district. It was in the fall, the season of *Kaxwéix Dísi*, the Groundhog Mother Moon, when the lengthening darkness brings frost and the crisp air precipitates a flurry of activity in preparation for winter—putting up late-run fish for the dogs and hunting mountain sheep, with the meat to be dried and cached before the snows come.

That fall, Jim was hunting for sheep with his nephews Káa Goox̱, later called Dawson Charlie, and Kootseen, later called Patsy Henderson, or Paddy; both were sons of Kooyáy, one of Kate and Jim's sisters. Cold and wet from fighting wind and waves as they paddled the expansive waters of Lake Bennett, Jim, Charlie, and Patsy built a large fire on the shores of a smaller lake where they always camped before going over the Chilkoot Pass. Over the crackle of burning driftwood, they heard an unusual sound, the cry of a baby: *Waa A*, and then again, *Waa A*. Judging the cries to be coming from about halfway up the lakeshore, they set out to investigate. As Jim led the way through the darkness, the crying grew more distinct. Patsy, only twelve at the time, became frightened and began to cry himself.

At that point, the baby's wailing ceased. Hearing only silence, the three of them returned to their camp, but they were too distressed to sleep.[22] Back at their village, the old people told them they'd come close to meeting Tl'anaxéedakw, or Wealth Woman, an iconic figure known to the Tagish and Tlingit as well as to the Haida and Tsimshian, Native groups that lived along the southern coasts of Alaska and British Columbia.[23]

Although there are many versions of the Wealth Woman legend, the one that would have been most familiar to Kate begins with a child born to a young man and a lake woman. After the child is stolen, it begins to terrorize whole villages, gouging out eyes, where according to the Tagish way of thinking, the soul resides. In one community, a new mother emerges from her birth hut to discover that only she and her baby have survived an attack by the lake woman's child. Before departing the gory scene, she clads herself in copper jewelry, dentalia, and a marten skin robe taken from her uncle's treasure box. In this way, she becomes Wealth Woman, a mystical figure who perpetually wanders the forests, clutching her baby as she floats a few feet from the ground.

On each person who meets her and precisely performs a complicated set of actions, Wealth Woman bestows riches. When Jim heard the baby's cry, he should have followed the sound until he found the mother and child, then stripped naked, tossed urine at Wealth Woman, grabbed her baby, and held it while allowing its mother to scratch his skin four times with her golden fingernails. After Wealth Woman defecated four gold-colored balls,[24] Jim should have returned the baby and then fasted and bathed for four days, telling no one what happened while at the same time making wishes for wealth. With all that accomplished, he would have achieved lasting fortune.[25]

The impossibility of getting all of this right gets Jim—and anyone else who meets Wealth Woman—off the hook when it comes to finding and keeping wealth. Alluring though riches might be, the legend proves that they're impossible to attain and hold on to, even for a man like Jim who has gone hand-to-hand with a bear. And this is just as well, since wealth for the Tagish meant literal burdens that tied you to one place, when the real actions that sustained you required that you kept moving with the salmon, the caribou, and the mountain sheep.

But even close encounters with Wealth Woman could result in good luck. In Jim's case, leading the expedition toward the cries in the night proved that, beyond his physical prowess, he had spiritual strength, and a man with such strength was well positioned for contact with one of the more powerful and dangerous animals in Tagish reckoning—the frog, shaman of the animal kingdom, which was to be treated with the same deference you would show to a human shaman.[26]

Three years after his first Wealth Woman experience, it's said that Jim went out from his small log home in Dyea to relieve himself in the night. He heard a noise, *whoo, whoo,* like the sound of sand being poured. He tracked the noise to a ditch where sand had been dug up for spreading on top of the moss roofs of cabins. Far from the water, a big frog was jumping against the sides of the ditch, trying to get out. Jim found a board and propped it inside. When the frog leapt onto it, Jim carried the board to a creek, where he set the frog free.[27]

The following year, a drunken man kicked Jim in the stomach. The wound festered, and Jim became bedridden. Burning with fever, he pulled off his bandages to air the wound. It was early summer, and Jim's wife was packing for prospectors over the trail, so Jim called for the help of his neighbor, La.oos Tláa, also called Maria Johns, a relative of both Jim and Kate. When she arrived, there was a frog on Jim's stomach, licking the sore place. Though frogs were especially dangerous to women, Maria was young and strong, and she knew the proper way to respond. To thank the frog, she gifted it with silk thread, beads, and down feathers, and she found a board for it to hop onto. Within a few days, Jim was completely healed.[28]

From a subsequent incident, Jim discovered that his frog helper may have actually been Wealth Woman, in the form of an animal spirit. In the fall, when the ground had frozen but snow had yet to fall, Jim traveled through *Shásh Zéitítí* ("grizzly bear throat"), the pass between the hunting camp at Todezáané and Tagish Lake, to visit his mother.[29] As he camped at Crag Lake,[30] halfway to his destination, a shining, translucent woman appeared to him in a dream. She wanted Jim to marry her, but he told her he already had a wife. The woman then stretched her gold walking stick toward him, explaining that he had saved her when, in the form of a frog, she was starving and near death, and that she, as a frog, had in turn saved Jim when he was sick. When she pointed her walking stick in the direction of what would become known as the Klondike, everything within sight turned golden. Jim would find luck there, she promised.

When Jim woke the next morning, he was covered in a foot of snow. He continued on to where his mother was staying, and after determining that she had plenty of wood and food and grandchildren to keep her company, he went home. There he was told he'd been gone for eleven days, though by his reckoning, it had only been four.[31]

A salmon with gold coins for eyes; a broken mirror that brings seven years of bad luck; a little bird that lights unafraid in George Carmack's hand; a meteor that streaks across the heavens as he reflects on his fortune; a crying child, Jim's frog helper, and a golden woman who points the way to riches—in both cultures, George's and Kate's, the discovery event is presaged with signs and wonders.

What actually happened at the moment of discovery? Who plucked the first nugget from Bonanza Creek? From a Western perspective, the act of discovery matters quite a lot—there develops an obsession over narrowing the event to the actions of a single individual. Within the Tagish culture, right ways of behaving within the known world matter most, and these favor humility over the glorification of individual achievements.

George Carmack's version of the Klondike discovery changed often, especially as George Snow shaped it into what some would eventually accept as the definitive version of the history-making event. From those who knew Kate best, her Tagish relatives, the story remained relatively consistent with the versions that Jim and Charlie shared with William Ogilvie, the surveyor who had hired George, Jim, and Kate to pack for him back in 1887.[32]

Here's what seems to have happened:[33] After the river ice went out in the spring of 1896, Jim set out in the direction the golden woman had shown him in his dream. But he was not after gold. Two years had passed since he'd last seen the Carmacks—Jim had been at Dyea while they'd been at Selkirk. When George and Kate failed to appear as planned at Dyea, Kate's family became concerned. As her oldest surviving brother, Jim was responsible for looking after his sister.[34] He assembled a search party consisting of his wife, Mary; his daughter, Daisy; his nephews Charlie and Patsy; Charlie's wife, Annie, and their children; his cousin Tagish John; and his cousin's wife, Maria Johns, who had made the gift of beads and feathers for Jim's frog helper at Dyea.[35]

Together the families rowed and poled their boats across Marsh Lake and down the Lewes River, past hills wooded with spruce, pine, and poplar to the roaring rapids of Miles Canyon, where they portaged over a high ridge to the valley below. With the faces of the women and children blackened to fend off mosquitoes, they rowed the thirty-five-mile length of Lake LaBerge, flanked to the west by formations of red rock.[36] Tagish John told his wife to look back at *Chílíh Dzéłe* (Carcross Mountain) because it would be a long time before she saw it again. Maria began to cry. What about your poor crippled mother, she asked, and my mother, and your sister? There's no one to chop wood and get water for them, and they might not live long.[37] Her distress was so great that John turned their boat back toward Tagish Lake.

The rest continued downriver. Twenty miles before Five Finger Rapids, they passed George's boarded-up trading post. At Fort Selkirk, Joe LaDue told them that the Carmacks had wintered there but had left after break-up for Forty Mile. So Jim and his companions continued on, drifting and rowing and poling. Five hundred miles from where they'd begun, they stopped at Tr'ochëk, the busy and productive Hän fish camp at the mouth of the Tr'ondëk (Klondike) River, which was staked nearly all the way across with salmon weirs.[38] The Hän, with whom the Tagish traded,[39] directed them to the far bank of the Tr'ondëk, where Kate and George had set up their own fish camp, a smattering of tents and birch-covered sheds for drying fish.[40]

Kate was elated to see her family.[41] They were still planning to return to Tagish, she told them—she and George and Graphie—as soon they were done putting up fish.[42] It was early July, and the king salmon run was just getting started. Together, they all set about working the weirs and cutting the fish and hanging the fillets to dry on racks that protected the fish from flies and rain while still admitting the proper amount of sunlight. A skilled woman like Kate could clean and cut up to fifty fish an hour, but it might take a week or more to dry a batch of filets, which had to be turned every day. Once ready, the fish were baled by the men to be either sold or cached for the winter.[43] As George told a newspaper correspondent who stopped to visit with him at the fish camp, his plan was to sell the dried fish for dog food at fifteen cents a pound. The correspondent wrote:

> The squaw man was interesting to us because he was one of a class that in the aggregate are rather numerous. The two little half-breeds were bright children, who could speak only a few words of English, as the family language was evidently of the native tongue. Their faces were painted black, as a protection against the mosquitoes, but their father seemed to have genuine affection for them, and instead of being ashamed of the connection, as might happen, he evidently took pride in them. Whatever had been his intentions when he first cast his lot with the Indian woman it was evident that he would not now abandon his family.[44]

One of the "little half-breeds" at the Carmack fish camp that summer was of course Graphie Grace, but who was the other child? Perhaps a playmate from across the river or, if Jim had reached the fish camp before the newspaperman did—the two had met while crossing Lake LaBerge—the child may have been Jim's daughter, Daisy, left in Kate's care for a day or two following their reunion while her parents continued to Forty Mile for supplies.

The busy hum on the river that summer involved more than fish—there was also talk of gold in the creeks that fed into the Klondike River. From his post and sawmill at Ogilvie,[45] between Fort Selkirk and the Klondike River, Arthur Harper's trading partner Joe LaDue encouraged such talk. To anyone who would listen, he spoke of how Canadian prospector Bob Henderson was getting two cents a pan from a tributary of the Klondike he called Gold Bottom. Two cents a pan was nothing, but where there was a little gold, there might be a lot—you only had to keep looking.[46] By one estimate, up to fifty miners were roaming the Klondike valley that summer, sniffing for the mother lode.[47]

Kate herself may even have found a little gold in one of the creeks that summer; later, George would laugh with friends about his wife finding color while she gathered firewood.[48] Such a discovery would not have been unusual. Natives had long told Hudson Bay traders of gold in the sands and gravels of creeks in this part of the Yukon.[49] In 1886, Joe LaDue and his partners had confirmed these reports, swishing twenty-five to thirty cents to the pan from the Klondike River. But at the time, the Stewart River prospects were yielding $50 to $100 a day, so few paid much attention.[50]

Upon his return from a supply trip in late July, prospector Bob Henderson found high water at the Indian River, the waterway he normally followed to reach his claims at Gold Bottom. So he turned back upriver to access an alternate route.[51] At the mouth of the Klondike, he met up with George Carmack, who was processing salmon. He told George of his discovery at Gold Bottom and invited him to stake there. Such an invitation was part of the miner's code—after staking a discovery claim on what you hoped was the best spot, you spread the word of your find so others could come in and try their luck. But Henderson also informed George that he did not want "his" creek to be staked by Indians, especially those from upriver.[52]

Their provisions having dwindled to mostly fish, it was decided that Jim, Charlie, and George would cut logs to sell at

Joe LaDue's sawmill, where they could get $25 per thousand feet; with these funds, they would purchase supplies for winter. Jim went scouting for timber that was large and easy to drag to the water. Less than a mile up the Klondike, along Rabbit Creek (soon to be renamed Bonanza), he found the sort of logs he was seeking. As he studied the creek bed to determine whether the logs could be readily transported, he found gold in the gravel. But when he relayed this news back at the fish camp, George appeared unimpressed.[53]

Jim, Charlie, and George started back up Rabbit Creek, while seventeen-year-old Patsy, who'd had a brush with death when the gun he was cleaning went off accidently,[54] stayed behind with the women and children. The intent of the older men was to check out Henderson's claim at Gold Bottom and then, on their way back to the fish camp, to gather the logs Jim had found. Partway up the river, they stashed their boat and tromped through thick underbrush in the general direction of Henderson's camp. The going was difficult, and they had to rest often. This part of the country is a maze of creeks, and during one of their rest stops, Jim and Charlie decided that for fun they'd pan one of them. In gravel dug up by Charlie and panned by Jim, they found a ten-cent gold nugget. In this, George showed some interest. If they found little of substance at Gold Bottom, they'd investigate the creek's prospects.[55]

Between there and the next creek, later named Eldorado, the three men climbed a divide. Following marks made by Henderson, they descended to where he'd set up camp. Nothing they found there impressed them, including Henderson's refusal to share any of his tobacco, for which Jim and Charlie were desperate and willing to pay. Together, they headed back toward the creek where they had found the ten-cent nugget. Hungry and tired, they made slow progress. As they drew close to the creek, Jim stalked a moose—some say it was the golden woman who led him to it—and though he missed with his first shot, he killed it with the next.[56]

As Kate's niece explains, recalling the story as Kate used to tell it, here's what happened next:

> They cook meat—big eat! They fall asleep—they eat too much!
>
> Skookum Jim wakes up: Carmack is sleeping, Dawson Charlie too, Patsy too. He wants a drink of water . . . He tells me this, you know . . . He's got hat; he wants to drink with that one. The teapot is full of tea. That's why he goes down, puts his hat in the river that way. He see something up there . . . Is that copper? He drinks water, looks again. Same big as beans you know—bigger than . . . heavy.
>
> He takes off. He doesn't know gold much, Skookum Jim. Nobody knows much gold. But George, he knows! He goes back. Dawson Charlie wakes up. 'I found something,' Jim tells him, Indian way. 'Don't know what is that. What does it look like?'
>
> 'Copper,' he [Charlie] says.
>
> 'Make George wake up now—it doesn't look like copper. Heavy, too.' George wakes up.
>
> 'You wake up good?'
>
> 'Yeah.'
>
> 'What is that, this one? That creek I found it.'
>
> 'That's gold!' Where's their sleep now! That tea is still there. They don't drink much, though. 'You see now gold!' George tells them—runs down to creek.'[57]

In the gravels of the rippling brown water, the three of them spotted more gold than they'd ever seen in one place—[58] "Good gold, lotsa gold," as Kate's nephew Patsy Henderson later put it.[59]

The rest, as they say, is history.

CHAPTER ELEVEN

A Lot of Thanks I Get

After having nearly lost a raft-load of horses and stovepipe due to the sandbars and sweepers along the Yukon River, prospector William Douglas Johns tied up one August evening next to the Carmack fish camp at the mouth of the Klondike. While the men were away, Kate and the other women were preparing for winter—cutting and drying fish, picking berries, snaring rabbits. She told Johns that George, Jim, and Charlie had gone prospecting, and he asked if she would sew him a pair of moose hide mittens.[1] She stayed up all night cutting and stitching the mittens, for which her visitor paid with a large black silk handkerchief, a bargain that, according to him, pleased Kate greatly.[2]

As for the Tagish men and George Carmack, they had gold, but they also had a moose to cut up, and they had to stake their claims along the newly named Bonanza Creek, a process that required panning the gravels at various points to determine which spots were richest. An argument followed about who would get to stake the discovery claim, which in addition to bragging rights rewarded its owner with twice as much land as an ordinary claim. While Jim claimed right of discovery, which allowed the discoverer to stake two claims instead of one, George insisted that Indians were only allowed to file ordinary claims, an assertion that proved to be one of his "stretchers." So on August 17, 1896, George staked Discovery and No. 1 below Discovery, telling Jim he'd assign him a half-interest in the double claim, though no paperwork was ever filed to that effect. They staked No. 1 above Discovery for Jim and No. 2 below Discovery for Charlie.[3]

After a five-hour tromp through the woods, George, Jim, and Charlie retrieved the boat they had stashed on the riverbank. As they floated down the Klondike River, they came upon four men towing their loaded boat through the shallows, "all fine, big, husky looking fellows; a healthy pink color glowed through the skin of their tanned and bearded faces," as Snow tells it.[4] George toyed with these men, telling them he had checked out the prospects they were after, on Henderson's Gold Bottom Creek, and found them lacking. At this, Snow writes, the men's faces turned "baby blue" with disappointment.

But when George gave up the ruse and produced a Winchester shell packed with gold, "Their eyes lit up and the whole expression of their faces changed. It was like the bright sunshine burst out from behind a black cloud."[5] In Snow's version, George also shared his news with two French Canadians, hailed to shore as they traveled down the Yukon River. In recording their response to his news, the theater man makes grand use of dialect: "I tink hees was beeg bluff," says one of these prospectors.[6] Another miner told his partner, "Why I wouldn't go across the river on that old Siwash's word." Yet another reported seeing a sign along the stream that would become known as Eldorado. "The creek is reserved for Swedes and Moose," it read. Since he was neither, he moved on.[7]

The gold George brought back to show Kate, that cartridge shell full, likely didn't impress her as much as Jim's moose, which would go a long ways toward feeding the family through the winter.[8] As for her young nephew Patsy, he said, "Why I see the gold first just like I don't care because I no savvy; I never see gold before."[9]

Straightaway, George, Charlie, and Patsy left the fish camp for Forty Mile, where they intended to record their find. Meanwhile, Jim returned to Rabbit Creek to work the gravels while also making sure no one tried to jump their claims. Within days, twenty-five miners gathered on the hillside across from No. 17 below Discovery. At their meeting, they renamed the creek Bonanza, appointed a mining recorder, and procured a length of rope with which to measure their claims—incorrectly, as it would turn out.[10]

It seemed the only person in the valley who had yet to hear about the big strike was Bob Henderson, the Canadian whose reports of modest finds at Gold Bottom accounted for most, if not all, of the men who were in the vicinity when the news of the strike at Bonanza began to circulate. By the time Henderson finally learned of the discovery from eight men packing over the hills near his camp, Bonanza Creek had already been staked "from one end to the other."[11]

"Henderson has always bitterly resented Carmac's neglect to send him word of the new discovery," William Ogilvie later wrote, "as he—Henderson—says Carmac promised he would do, if he found anything better than where they were working on Gold Bottom."[12] In what became accepted as George Carmack's version of the events, Snow lays the blame for this squarely on Henderson. "As far as I ever heard, Henderson's claim never did show up over two or three cents to the pan. His childish, unreasoning pregidice would not even allow him to stake on the same creek with the despised 'Siwashes' so his obstinacy lost him a fortune."[13]

In what must have been an embarrassing moment, Kate's husband discovered upon his arrival at Forty Mile that the gold he'd so proudly displayed in the rifle cartridge was worth only $12, while the fee for filing the claims was $15.[14] Still, the gold was enough to show off at the local saloon. Snow makes good use of this culminating scene of the discovery narrative to reiterate the qualities of the American frontier hero:

> . . . some one shouted 'Have a drink, George,' and "Pass out the hootch, Bill,' and other similar greetings, some of

which would not look good in print. They were a rough bunch, rough in dress, rough in speech, and rough handed, but just as great hearted and manly as they were rough. Real men, every one of them, with muscles and sinews like iron bands, developed by continuous and arduous exercise. There was no adventure too strenuous or dangerous for them to undertake. They possessed the kind of power and strength that made men invincible, with characters broadened and strengthened by the hardships and privations they had been forced to endure, in their unequal struggle with the mighty forces of Nature in the unknown and desolate wilds.[15]

The story continues with George fortifying himself with a few drinks, then producing his cartridge shell and announcing his strike. One "big, husky miner" immediately discounts it as a scheme of Harper and LaDue to start a stampede up the river. After assuring the "big rabbit-eating malemute" that Harper and LaDue know nothing about the discovery, George dumps out his gold. Upon examining it closely, the naysayer makes a speech that, in the spirit of the man who confesses too much, attempts to dispel George's long-standing reputation for playing loose with the truth:

"Is that some of [the] Miller Creek gold that Ladue gave you?" asked my big friend, getting up and striding to the bar . . . then his mouth dropped open as though his lower jaw had been unjointed, and his voice sounded like a Stick Medicine Man with congested lungs, delivering an incantation.

"Holy Makuluk boys, this ain't no Miller Creek dust. I know the gold from every creek in this country and this ain't like none of them," and putting out his ham-like hand, he said: "Put 'er there, George, I've known you since '88, and I've never known you to lie to a whiteman or a Siwash, and I can lick any hootch-guzzling, salmon-eating son-of-a-gun that says you lie now."[16]

Soon, the town of Forty Mile began to empty; even those too drunk to set out on their own were reportedly shoved into boats and turned loose on the river. When George, Patsy, and Charlie returned to the Klondike, Kate and the rest of the family abandoned the fish camp and relocated with them to the claims along Bonanza Creek. There, the men built a ten-foot sluice box with pole riffles in the bottom and constructed a low dam to divert water through it. On their backs, Jim and Charlie hauled gravel from a bank fifty feet away, while George tended the sluice box, glowering, it was said, at passersby who, in keeping with another miners' tradition, stopped to work a pan of his pay dirt. Though their methods were crude, it wasn't long before family had more than enough to pay the filing fees for their claims; within three weeks, they'd netted some $1,400 in gold.[17]

The shores of the once-quiet stream were soon overrun. By the first week in September, nearly every miner in the vicinity had found his way to Bonanza Creek, where encouraging finds were occurring in rapid succession. On the last day of August, five men decided they'd try their luck at the "Swedes and Moose" creek that emptied into Bonanza south of Discovery. There they found gold in abundance; before they were through, each of their claims would produce over a million dollars. From the supposedly worthless five-mile creek they named El Dorado, a total of $30 million in gold would be taken, worth more than half a billion in today's dollars.[18]

It was reported that the claims of George Carmack, the man who started it all, were the richest of all, although serious prospectors suspected that, owing to Carmack's crude sluicing techniques, a good portion of the gold from his diggings was being washed downstream. And there was a larger, more ubiquitous problem—no one really knew where the best gold was. In the unglaciated Klondike valley, the actual mother lode had eroded out of hills that had once been mountains. Dispersed into creeks, the gold sank into sand, and as the creeks shifted and layers of sediment built up, most of the precious metal ended up well below the surface, near bedrock. How much one claim paid when compared to another was a matter of chance—until you worked the gravels, you could never know for sure how much your claim would be worth.

By September 24, 1896, the day the discovery party returned to Forty Mile to file their claims, the river was close to freezing. If Kate traveled with them, she would have seen the twelve-by-fourteen-foot log cabin that had gone up where she and George had kept their fish camp, a structure hastily erected by Joe LaDue and three of his associates. Around the bend, the whine of a saw and the pounding of hammers sounded over the quiet sloshing of the river as LaDue's sawmill churned out lumber for the first cabins being raised in Dawson City, the town site LaDue had staked out of the wilderness.

As had been the case with every new settlement in Alaska and the Yukon, whether established by the Russians, the Hudson Bay Company, the Alaska Commercial Company, or by individual traders like Harper and Healy, the question of Native rights to the land was never addressed. LaDue had only to pay a $50 survey fee plus $10 per acre to secure title to the lands traditionally occupied by the Tr'ondëk Hwëch'in. On these, he platted the town named after hunchbacked Canadian geologist George Dawson, who first traveled through the region in 1887.

The claims filed by George Carmack and his Tagish relatives at Forty Mile that September were twice the size of what was allowed by law for a discovery party of only three men: Discovery parties of four or fewer could file no more than 1,000 feet total. But George filed a 1,000-foot claim, and Jim and Charlie each filed five hundred-foot claims, for a total of 2,000 feet, a size allowed when six or more people were present at the time of discovery. Apparently, Kate, Patsy, and one of the other wives (Mary or Annie) were counted by George as having been on scene when the gold was first discovered, though from all other evidence the women and Patsy had been at the fish camp on the day the initial claims were staked.[19] Another of George's "stretchers," this accounting would encourage those who later claimed that Kate herself had discovered the first nugget at Bonanza Creek.

Having barely accomplished the filing of their claims within the sixty-day deadline, the Carmacks and their Tagish relatives would spend the winter assessing the extent of their fortune.[20] Following a big September snowstorm, October was unusually mild. As the winter snows began to fall, some three hundred men were shuttling up and down the Klondike Valley, staking and filing claims, setting up canvas tents, and stripping the landscape of spruce and cottonwood used to build and heat cabins and to fire the digging that would proceed once the ground froze solid. Nothing she'd experienced in the Forty Mile district prepared Kate for such a wholesale denuding of the earth.[21]

The amount of gold pulled from the Klondike in those first few months suggested that Kate's wanderings with her husband were over, at least for a while. In the men occupying the tents and shacks that sprang up along the creeks, she found a burgeoning market for hand-sewn mittens and hats to satisfy the miners who continued to pour in as word spread of the wealth hidden in the gravels of the Klondike watershed. She and George had

Kate Carmack, Graphie Carmack, and George Carmack in front of their log cabin on Bonanza Creek, 1897. (Yukon Archives, James Albert Johnson fonds, 82/341, #15)

sometimes wintered in tents, but she now did her sewing in the warmth of a hastily built cabin.

Cabins like the one occupied by the Carmacks were simple dwellings, rarely larger than fourteen by eighteen feet, built of spruce logs that, owing to frozen soils, were no more than nine inches in diameter. Chinked with moss, the walls were covered by low-pitched sod roofs. Windows, if any, were fashioned out of flour sacks or clear ginger ale bottles. Unless by chance the cabin's owner had come by a real Yukon stove made by a tinsmith, heating and cooking were done on the same sort of baked-clay Russian furnace Kate had used while waiting out Starvation Winter at Showman's House, though because so many now needed fuel, the wood they burned in the Klondike was mostly green. Water was melted from ice chipped from the river. Blankets and furs served as bedding on bunks, and light during the long winter nights—in this part of the Yukon, winter daylight lasts only a few hours—was by candle; when the candles ran out, a wick was stuck in a can of bacon grease and burned.[22]

After freeze-up, the miners used a winter mining method pioneered nine years earlier at Franklin Gulch by prospector Fred Hutchison, one of the discoverers of Forty Mile gold, who had been following a pay streak under the creek when winter forced him to abandon his pursuit. Figuring he'd get a head start on spring, he chopped a hole in the ice. As he worked, the ice froze deeper and deeper until he'd unwittingly fashioned an ice-lined dam that extended all the way to the creek's bottom. There he built a fire and dug out gravel that he piled up to work in the spring, when there would be plenty of water for sifting out the gold.

With this innovation, the lazy winters once passed by miners became the stuff of nostalgia. The smell of wood smoke filled the valley. All around Kate's new home, fires thawed the frozen ground, which was worked laterally to access "winter diggings," the ones too deep to be reached in the short summer season.[23] Excavating these gravels, her husband and brother and nephews shoveled their way through layers of long-ago history: sand, black sand, and gravel washed from the hills by centuries of run-off and rain; white ash, blown from a tremendous volcanic eruption 1,200 years earlier, an explosion of such wide and frightening impact that it prompted some of Kate's ancestors to migrate toward what would become the American Southwest;[24] fine rock, coarse rock, coarse gravel, gravel laden with quartz; muck—and finally, to bedrock, where the gold lay.[25]

By December, the cold leveled off into what passes for a mild winter in the North, with plenty of days at twenty and thirty below zero (Fahrenheit), but only a few that were colder.[26] Outside, fires burned through the night, thawing ground to be shoveled the next day. When the temperatures hit thirty below, these emissions formed a thick, eerie fog that settled over the valley. Though different from what Kate had been raised with, she had experienced similar cold during her years at Forty Mile, cold that checked her breath and turned her skin dry, cold that sucked moisture from snow that rustled with every step she took in her skin boots, which were made warm with fur and dry grass stuffed inside.

Following Bonanza Creek, Eldorado was fully staked, and then the smaller creeks—Adams, Skookum, Little Skookum, Irish, French, Nugget. Once the creek claims were taken, prospectors began working bench claims in the adjacent hills, where they hoped to find lode-bearing quartz. By January, Alaska's Circle City District, where $900,000 in gold had been taken the previous season, began to empty.[27] Cabin prices dropped to $500, and sled dogs could hardly be bought at any price. Those who couldn't get dogs pulled their own sleds across frozen rivers and through icy valleys to the Klondike.[28]

Food was a problem all over the valley that first winter. In their rush to stake, many miners had failed to stock up on provisions, and the steamers had long since been pulled ashore for the winter. Flour freighted from Forty Mile sold for $40 to $60 per fifty-pound sack. Beef was $1 to $2 per pound, a small fortune in those days—and it might have been higher if not for a butcher who had driven cattle over the grease trail north of the Chilkoot with the idea of selling the beef at Forty Mile. Owing to a number of catastrophes, he fell short of his destination, stopped by freeze-up right in front of the brand-new town of Dawson City, where he happily made a small fortune selling fresh meat.[29] One neighbor of the Carmacks had only a seven-pound pack of oats to get him through the winter; Skookum Jim kept him alive by sharing dried salmon, moose meat, and fresh fish.[30]

Kate and her sisters-in-law were among six women along the creeks that winter.[33] One other was forty-six-year-old Hattie Wills, a white woman who had come north alone in 1895 with the idea of finding her own gold. Upon news of the fortunes being extracted from the Klondike creeks, she was one of the first to set out from Circle City for Dawson, where she acquired a claim that yielded a quarter million dollars in gold. The others were Mrs. Ethel Berry, the wife of the man who'd been tending bar at McPhee's saloon in Forty Mile when George Carmack swaggered in to announce the Klondike discovery, and Mrs. Salome Lippy, who with her husband had the good fortune to arrive in the Yukon as word of the discovery was beginning to spread.[32] But even in the remote gold camps of the North, white women rarely socialized with Native women in the same ways they socialized with each other. After Jim and Charlie's wives went home, Kate's closest friends would be the Native wife of prospector Joe Powers, neighbors to the Carmacks, and Jennie Cook, a Tagish-Tlingit relative (likely a sister or niece of Jim's wife), who was married to prospector Henry T. Cook.[33]

In February, the Carmacks again met up with William Ogilvie, the Canadian surveyor who had employed Kate, George, and Jim to pack for his crew over the Chilkoot Pass back in 1887. Hired to re-survey the hastily staked claims along Bonanza Creek, Ogilvie found that George had shortchanged himself: the maximum length allowed for a discovery claim was five hundred feet, but owing to the meandering of the creek, George had mistakenly acquired only 462 feet. Jim's claim, No. 1 above, was found to be too long, so a fractional claim was surveyed out of the upstream end and assigned to his nephew, Patsy.[34]

Though small, a fractional claim could yield great wealth. As Ogilvie made his adjustments, one in particular ignited plenty of talk along the creeks. It was taken out of No. 2 above Bonanza, the claim adjacent to Jim's. Finding it wider than the law allowed, Ogilvie surveyed off a pie-shaped fraction. As a civil servant, he did not feel entitled to register this slice of land for himself, so it was awarded to one of the chainmen on his crew. The chainman tried to turn it for a quick $900 but got no takers, since the parcel was only eighty-six feet wide at the base. Forced to work it himself, he sank a shaft and pulled up no gold—it appeared the claim was a blank, as the miners called it. Then he sank another shaft. Within eight hours, within easy view of the Carmacks, the owner of the fractional claim extracted $46,000 in gold. Eventually, he would pull a whopping half million dollars' worth of precious metal from this tiny parcel of land, making it the richest per square foot in the Yukon.[35]

The gleanings from this little claim affirm a basic principle of mining: gold tumbles downstream, so the mother lode is more likely above Discovery than below. Why, then, had George Carmack taken No. 1 below Discovery for himself instead of No. 1 above, which was assigned to Jim? Perhaps it was because he and his Tagish relatives worked their claims as a collective, aggregating their proceeds, so the matter of individual ownership didn't matter all that much—as long as they stayed together.[36]

While Ogilvie was surveying the claims along the creeks, the Carmack collective hit pay—their fires finally reached gravels that yielded $5 of gold to the pan. For a day's work, they were getting $50, and that didn't count whatever gold was in gravels too frozen to work; these were left on the "dumps" for spring cleanup. "Every body here are millionaires," George wrote to his sister, Rose. "It is something wonderfull the pay has been located for four miles now and some of the claims they think will pay half a million and not one of them are blanks." With the four of them working—George, Jim, Charlie, and Patsy (to his sister, George does not mention that his companions are Indians)—he predicted they would take out $16,000 to $20,000 that winter; within a year, he hoped to have opened up enough that he could let someone else work his claims through a lay—a lease agreement.

There would be a big rush come spring, George wrote to Rose. Anyone could see it—anyone, that is, for whom the actions of exploring, acquiring, and profiting could be summed up in a single word: stampede. From the Tagish perspective, a stampede meant the thundering of caribou, spooked by some alarming change in their surroundings. That so many people would rush blindly into territory that they were ill-prepared to work and inhabit would be summed up with a different word: foolishness.

Changes loomed, greater than any Kate could imagine. Outside the Yukon, news of the Klondike spread via letters from family and friends. At first, it was slow to take hold, even when miners wrote as Fred Brewster Fay had: "The stories told are not exaggerated. One hundred dollars to the pan is very common." Still, by spring 1,500 miners were waiting in Seattle for boats to carry them north to Juneau and then on to Dyea, where they would travel through the Chilkoot Pass and float downriver to the Klondike.[37] To be sure, this was more than had ever before been lured North in a single season, but it was a drop in the proverbial bucket compared to what would follow.

One boat loaded with six hundred stampeders departed Seattle on March 12, 1897; several others followed in its wake. A correspondent for the *Alaska Miner* wrote from Seattle that excitement over the Klondike was at a "fever heat."[38] As the rush hit Dyea, Native packers struggled to keep up with demand; an inspector with the Northwest Mounted Police reported it took him several days to secure packing services to get over the mountains.[39]

In June 1897, George wrote again to his sister, urging her to travel to the Klondike with her husband and to come as quickly as they could. The spring clean-up was turning out better every day, he said. Though the creek was low, they had put in a big lift wheel to raise the water in order to sluice the gravel dumped over the winter. A single drift, one and a half times longer than their sluice box, had yielded $3,000 in gold.

"We sold one of our claims," George wrote. "We got $13,750, and we still have a claim a piece." It was Charlie's claim, No. 2 Below, that had been sold, but the language George used in his letter to Rose—"we sold," "we got," "we still have"—affirms that the claims were indeed managed collectively, an arrangement that would have suited Kate and her family, with the Tagish economy grounded in sharing. While Jim and Charlie did at times carry large amounts of gold on their persons, Kate's husband appears to have been the self-appointed guardian of their cumulative windfall.

In the letter to his sister, George said that while he could sell out his own interest for $25,000, he figured he could make twice that by working it himself or by having someone work it for him.[40] If Rose and her husband would rent out their small California ranch and come north with $400 or $500 (in silver, to pay the Native packers), George offered to save a patch of ground for them to work. The following year, they would leave $4,000 to $5,000 richer for their troubles, he promised. Bring your sewing machine, he advised his sister, along with plenty of thread and needles, including the razor-edged kind for sewing buckskin; she would be able to make at least $1,000 sewing and washing for the miners.

It was within the context of these instructions that George first made mention to Rose of his ten-year marriage to Kate: "My wife had (now don't faint) my wife had more work than she could do all last winter but she is getting to high toned to work now."

For Rose and her husband, George laid out additional details for the expedition that tens of thousands of would-be prospectors would mount through the lands occupied by the Tagish and other indigenous groups of the North. Bring good warm underwear, George advised, and good woolen mitts and socks, along with gumboots (no. 10, Goodyear, no leather soles) and overshoes. They could buy Canadian moccasins in Juneau, but George warned they must be purchased three sizes too big, to accommodate three pairs of socks. At Fort Selkirk, they could buy moose skin for making mittens. Bring plenty of good "mosquito bar," and "good solid clothes," he advised, as "every body with starched shirts and stove pipe hats are ducked in the river."[41]

Bring a couple of cans of good dried potatoes, he suggested, along with honey sealed up in two coal oil cans and at least a hundred pounds of bacon. If they had room, they should bring some dried fruit and sugar, and Rose's husband, James, should bring tobacco. "You can't bring too much of such stuff," George wrote, "as it is cheaper to have such things packed over the summit than they are in here."[42] Honey, for instance, was selling in Dawson for $3 a gallon, while the going rate for tobacco was $150 per pound.

Graniteware dishes were best, as they wouldn't break. With the rain on the coast, they'd need gumcoats and a rubber blanket to wrap their bedding in, as well as blankets and a good warm quilt. "Bring a little medicine," George advised, "and start with a couple of bottles of good brandy so you can take a nip when you get in to camp wet then you wont take cold but dont let the Indians see it for they love fire water do not be afraid they are harmless tell them you are my sister and you are all right but dont be to familiar with them."[43]

In Juneau, they should purchase an eight-by-ten-foot tent and a sheet steel stove and enough boat lumber, nails, and pitch, along with a saw, so they could build a square-ended scow once they got themselves over the mountains; a boat twenty feet long and four feet wide and eighteen- to twenty-four inches deep would carry a ton of supplies. Bring a rifle, George advised, in case they had a chance to shoot a moose or bear while floating the river.

After hiring Indians to pack over the Chilkoot summit—the going rate was now $15 per hundred pounds—they should "paddle their own canoe and go gallagher," except when they reached the canyon at Whitehorse, thirty miles below Marsh Lake. There they should take no chances. At the big eddy at the head of the canyon, they should land on the right bank and portage their supplies to the far side of the rapids, then run the boat through. After loading up on the other side, they should cross back to the left and portage again around the next set of rapids, where they would have to drop the boat along the bluff using a 150-foot length of rope. After that, the difficult stretches would be behind them, except for the Five Finger Rapids, which weren't all that treacherous by comparison.[44]

Whatever it took, George warned, they must reach Chilkoot summit by September 1; otherwise, they'd never make the creeks before freeze-up. Next spring would be too late; he himself planned to sell out and get out of the North the following summer. "If you should get here dead broke, I can stand it," he wrote. "I have lived of from you a good many years, so I guess I can support you for *one* winter, there are lots of men going out this summer with from ten to twenty thousand and some with fifty thousand that did not have a dollar a year ago but little thanks I get for finding it for them."[45]

In closing, Kate's husband wrote, "I want you here to cook a good Christmas dinner." And as an afterthought, he scribbled a note in the margin and circled it—"My wife is irish and talks very Broad pigin English, but I have the prettiest little daughter you ever saw."

CHAPTER TWELVE

TREACHEROUS INSTINCTS

To post the letter mentioning his "Irish" wife, George Carmack traveled to Dawson City, a town that had grown up from the marshy moose pasture he and Kate had occupied only ten months earlier, now a mucky mess with a "villainous odor" caused in part by the dumping of human waste into the river.[1] In July 1897, John Healy, who'd followed the gold to Forty Mile and now to Dawson, would set up a sawmill to compete with LaDue's; between the two, the whine of saws would reverberate day and night. While some prospectors still lived in canvas tents, several hundred buildings had gone up along the streets of the new town: supply stations, restaurants, hotels, stores, and, of course, saloons. As Dawson's population swelled to 6,000 that year, there would be dance halls, more saloons (and for balance, five churches), plus a detachment of the Northwest Mounted Police.[2]

The Carmacks' friend Arthur Harper had moved to Dawson; one of his sons, in fact, had been among a group of men who paddled out into the Yukon right after break-up to retrieve the body of a prospector who had drowned.[3] But Kate would never again see Jennie Harper. Within a year of their separation, Arthur had remarried, this time to an Alaska Native woman from

St. Michaels, where he conducted his annual exchanges of furs for trading goods.

In the summer of 1897, the Klondike River was clogged with hastily constructed boats of the type George had described in his letter. On the upriver bank, the Hän seasonal camp had been replaced by the tents and cabins of miners in what became known as Klondike City; later, it would be called Lousetown or, more nicely, South Dawson. Having witnessed the lesser stampede at Forty Mile, Chief Isaac foresaw sudden and drastic changes for his people, so he transferred the songs and dances of the Tr'ondëk Hwëch'in to Tanacross, hundreds of miles downriver, for safekeeping.[4]

Bishop Bompas, who oversaw a small church and school established in Dawson by one of his missionaries, noted that what passed for progress in the region could hardly be considered such for the Indians. Petitioning for the displaced Hän to be granted an official and permanent reserve, he wrote, "The whites occupy most of the ground and rob it of its treasures. They hunt and chase off the wild animals and so deprive the Indian of his means of subsistence. It has been argued that the Indians are no losers by the arrival of the whites, because they can make money by working for them. This is to persuade one who has been robbed of his property that he is no worse off because he can still make a living by hard labour."[5]

Starting with his arrival at Forty Mile, the bishop had long advocated for segregating the Indians from the miners through the establishment of "Indian villages," a policy of separation that was a longstanding practice of the British.[6] The problem, as Bompas saw it, was the bad influence of the miners on the Hän in the form of alcohol and the debauching of their women. Native wives like Kate were obviously exempt from the segregation proposed by the bishop, but its effect would be to make her something of an oddity in a place she had occupied before virtually all others except the Hän.

As he appealed for a separate Indian reserve, Bompas clashed with an outsider whose view toward all Indians was resoundingly negative: Commanding Officer Charles Constantine of the Northwest Mounted Police, sent north to secure order in Canada's far-flung Unorganized Northwest Territories. From the start, Constantine was unimpressed with Bompas and his flock. Of the Hän at Forty Mile, his first post, Constantine wrote, "A lazy, shiftless lot [who] are content to hang around the mining camps. They suffer much from chest trouble and die young." He imposed a ban on Native drinking, then did his best to ignore the Indians entirely, writing that he was only following orders "that the Indians were not to be recognized in any way which would lead them to believe that the Government would do anything for them as Indians."[7]

Despite the ban on Native drinking and the sale of alcohol to Natives at Forty Mile, problems had continued, owing in large part to the old devil hoochinoo, a fermented concoction of molasses, sugar, and dried fruit. Citing "much drunkenness of whites and Indians together with much danger of the use of fire arms," Bompas had initiated a meeting between the Forty Mile Hän and Commander Constantine back in 1895, but little was accomplished. When the Hän complained of the miners selling whiskey to their people and shooting their dogs, Constantine suggested they avoid whiskey and tie up their dogs.[8]

In 1897, Constantine represented the rule of law over Kate and everyone else in the Klondike. When Bishop Bompas proposed that local Indians be compensated $2,000 for the land that was now Klondike City, Constantine fired back with his assessment of how the Indians were benefitting from the stampede.[9] "The idea that the Indians would be driven from the neighbourhood by the encroachment of the Whites is absurd," he wrote. "The Indians have expressed themselves as greatly pleased at the arrival of the miners as it means plenty of food, plenty of money and better times generally for them. They will always have a ready market for their game and in summer can make good money as boatmen and packers. The lowest wage at which these Indians will work is $4.00 per day."[10]

As for the complaint that the Hän fisheries were being ruined by the alarming number of newcomers setting nets in the river, Constantine wrote, "It certainly would be a gross injustice to debar the whites from fishing and make them extremely dependent upon a band of Indians who will neither fish nor hunt so long as they can buy food. The Whites are the providers and workers in this country and should enjoy all privileges."[11]

There was plenty of room for the Indians, the Commander proposed, on one of the small islands in the middle of the Yukon River. As for the forty acres to which the village of Tr'ondëk had been temporarily relocated, Constantine wanted that land to be set aside for the Northwest Mounted Police, whose ranks swelled as news of Klondike gold spread.[12] "I don't propose to be bluffed," he wrote, ". . . by an arrogant Bishop who thinks the only people worth considering are a few dirty Indians too lazy to work, and who prefer starvation."[13]

Constantine was hardly the first "Indian hater" Kate had encountered, but he was the first in a position of real authority over her. The facts of her life counter each of his prejudices—she worked hard, sewing for the miners even when the family no longer needed the income; she had helped save George from starvation; and if she had a weakness for hoochinoo, it went unrecorded during her years in the Klondike. For that matter, the behavior of the vast majority of the Hän likewise disproved Constantine's assessment. Nevertheless, the commander got his way with the forty-acre reserve in town—it was given to the Northwest Mounted Police. When the thirty families of Chief Isaac's band were relocated to a separate reserve at Moosehide, three miles downriver from Dawson, they continued their seasonal rounds of hunting and fishing while also selling meat and tending sled dogs for the miners and doing occasional contract work in town.[14]

Kate and other Indians were hardly the problem in Dawson; the boomtown suffered from a huge (and growing) influx of prospectors who made their own trouble. Visiting the town in the fall of 1897, Selina Bompas remarked on "crowds of people passing all day long, all busy and intent on making money . . . The labour involved in working the 'claims' is not to be told, and many lives are lost and many strong men broken down. Oh! the pitiful stories one hears of treachery and dishonesty. And so many come in quite unprepared for the rigorous climate, and go through so much misery and privation. One poor man here had both hands and feet amputated from frostbite, and another has lost his right hand and left foot . . . The shady characters are numerous, and keep the police pretty busy. Last time we heard there were sixty prisoners in gaol."[15]

By the time George's sister received his letter with instructions for coming north, people the world over were hastily assembling grubstakes in hopes that they, too, would get rich in Klondike. "THE STEAMER PORTLAND HERE! BROUGHT DOWN HALF A TON OF GOLD!" screamed the headlines of the July 18, 1897 special edition of the *Seattle Times*. Lugging satchels bulging with gold, miners disembarked from the steamer; one lucky fellow was rumored to have come out with a quarter of a million dollars in gold dust. In San Francisco, a second vessel, the *Excelsior*, attracted similar attention as Klondike miners hauled their riches to shore.[16]

The news couldn't have come at a better time. While the United States led the world in manufacturing, industrialization had come at a price. Ordinary workers had virtually no hope of achieving economic independence; their labors generated nothing that even remotely resembled wealth. The economic depression that began in 1893 had only worsened. Farm prices had bottomed out, and unemployment was 14.5 percent in some parts of the United States.

Before the Klondike discovery, the prospectors who'd been lured north by rumors of gold were much like George Carmack: lower class drifters with little to tie them to home. The Klondike would attract thousands more like them, but the electrifying news of gold would also draw a fair number of middle-class professionals discontented with the small financial return for their labors.[17]

With only a modest income from a small ranch that was little more than a hobby farm, George's sister might well have been tempted to join the stampede. But her husband, well into his sixties, was not well, so Rose slipped George's letter into her Bible and prayed for his safe return to California, when she would finally meet his "Irish wife."

During the winter of 1897–1998, Kate and everyone else in the Klondike faced another shortage of food, the population in Dawson and along the creeks having increased more than tenfold over the previous year. Even as the prices of ordinary commodities dropped, fancier goods became more expensive—by March 1898, the price of flour had fallen from $75 per sack to $10, while the price of butter had risen from $1.25 to $8 per stick.

For their tidy cabin, Kate and George acquired amenities they'd never before owned. Though neither of them could likely play it, they had a "handsome organ," along with a well-stocked library of reading material, including magazines such as *Scientific American, The North American Review* and *The Review of Reviews*—though miners in general weren't a highly educated bunch, they coveted reading material. But despite these small nods to life Outside (the proper noun became used early on to describe anywhere beyond the North), Kate had yet to see an electric light or a telephone.[18] And unlike wealthy women elsewhere, she had no hired help for household chores. Once, a neighbor reported hearing her yell at George that he'd better bring in some firewood, or there'd be no dinner.[19]

As with nearly everyone associated with the early days of the Klondike, George Carmack was fast becoming a figure of legend. As reported in the inaugural edition of Dawson's *Klondike News,* which like many papers of the day was known to have on occasion played loose with the facts, George took credit for having "stuck the first shovel in the ground beside a big birch tree" to bring up a pan of coarse color:

> Carmack is a handsome specimen of the typical frontiersman, over six feet tall, with broad shoulders and a handsome face. He has a deep, serious look and is not given to talking much . . . During all the excitement and squabble for grounds, Carmack has protected his Indian partners against the speculative and wily white man. The fifteen hundred feet of ground owned by himself and the two red men of the forest is the richest spot in all the Klondike.[20]

Nowhere is there mention of how before gold entered the picture, George's Tagish relatives had seen to his survival: Jim by teaching him to hunt and trap and find his way in the wilderness and Kate by snaring rabbits and lynx, gathering berries and wild plants, sewing clothing of hides and furs, and contributing to their cash income by sewing for others.

Newfound wealth upended these relationships. Unable to read and write, Kate and her relatives now relied on George to help them navigate an unfamiliar set of tasks that included claim-filing, lease-making, and banking. They entrusted their riches to the collective he managed for the family, all of them working the claims together, their profits pooled.

For Kate's family, and for all Yukon Indians, the Klondike discovery brought change on a scope and scale beyond their imagining. With early prospectors, there had been a rough balance of power and mutual need. Now, seemingly overnight, they found themselves occupying a different sort of frontier, one in which "the *historical* reality of traditional societies is locked together for the rest of time with the historical reality of the intruders who saw them, changed them, destroyed them."[21]

Among the stampeders were some who feared the Tagish clans, having heard rumors that they practiced cannibalism and had buried slaves alive beneath the corners of their clan houses. While crossing Marsh Lake, one man reported the trepidation he experienced as several Tagish men paddled toward him in their boats, only to discover, to his great relief, that they only wanted to trade dried fish for tobacco.[22]

As a matter of course, the miners brought disease. During the summer of 1897, six of Kate's Tagish relatives died, probably of flu. After cremation, grave houses were built around the Hudson Bay Company trunks into which their bones were cached, yet another example of the cultural accommodations that were being made.[23]

The tiny seasonal settlement of Native packers camped near Healy's store at Dyea became overrun with would-be prospectors electrified by reports of Klondike gold. Many of these new fortune-seekers were a rough bunch, described by the Catholic bishop in Dawson as "men who have been running away from civilizations as it advanced westward in the States, until now they have no farther to go, and so have to stop here."[24] Relying on sketchy and sometimes blatantly false information, these stampeders would have benefited greatly from the sorts of details George had provided in his letter to Rose.

There were multiple routes to the Klondike, the most pleasant being to travel as Mary Hitchcock would, by steamer to St. Michael and then by riverboat up the Yukon to Dawson. But such a journey was expensive, and the season was short—four, maybe five months, between break-up and freeze-up. Traversing overland through Canada as Arthur Harper had done some twenty years earlier took even more time, and the hazards were many. Most prospectors chose the easier, cheaper alternative: to follow the Chilkoot Trail over the mountain pass once overseen by L'unáat and then float in hastily built boats through Tagish lake country to the Yukon River and on to Dawson.

Following L'unáat's death in the 1888 Packer War, the new L'ukaax̱.ádi second chief was unable to maintain Chilkoot control of the trail; with the advent of mining in the Forty Mile and Circle City districts, the demand was simply too great. As the stampede to the Klondike began, Native packers from towns and villages up and down the coast—Juneau, Sitka, Hoonah, Angoon, Wrangell, Kake, Yakutat—converged on Dyea to pack supplies over the mountains. Of the packing bosses who set up for business, Chief Isaac (a different Chief Isaac from the one in Dawson) had the fanciest storefront, a wooden, two-story building with windows.

For the most part, the other chiefs followed Isaac's lead regarding what prices would be charged for packing, with the fees to be paid in silver or gold coins rather than bills, which the packers still mistrusted, due to an earlier bilking that involved payment in worthless Confederate currency. As in the early days of intervention by military officers, conflicting cultural perspectives on what constituted an agreement on wages continued to plague the packing industry. In the height of the rush to the Klondike, it was not uncommon for Native packers to renegotiate prices in the middle of a journey or to abandon their initial contracts in favor of better wages being paid by someone else.[25]

In a race against freeze-up, stampeders got over the mountains as quickly as they could. But the boats from Seattle and San Francisco kept coming, off-loading prospectors who would remain landlocked until the rivers went out in the spring. Around the brush huts and cabins of the Native packers, hundreds of these newcomers rushed to stake lots in Dyea, throwing down their coats and pitching their tents on fifty-by-one hundred-foot parcels of land traditionally used by the Chilkoot. By winter, the streets of Dyea rang night and day with cursing, barking, and the neighing of horses. Where a few dozen Tlingit and Tagish packers had kept their seasonal homes, there were now bordellos, concert halls, theaters, hotels, restaurants, law offices, seamstress shops, meat markets, two newspapers, a bathhouse, a reading room, a dentist's office, an eye doctor's office, a fire department, a candy factory, and forty saloons.[26]

Kate's relatives who continued to pack from Dyea witnessed a curious scene that replayed again and again—faced with twenty-foot tides and no wharf, the crews of the ocean steamers dropped anchor three miles offshore and then dumped their cargo and passengers onto barges. When these barges got hung up in the shallows, horses trotted into the water, pulling wagons that would haul everything to dry ground. Chaotic attempts to reunite passengers with their precious supplies followed.

Given the poor setup at Dyea, William and Bernard Moore were able to cash in on the town site they had platted around the family homestead at Skagway, where deep waters facilitated the more efficient docking and unloading of ships. Windy, rocky, and with no substantial fish or large game, Skagway was a place that had been of little use to Kate's Tlingit relatives, but during the winter of 1897–1898, the population there soared to 10,000.[27]

By the time the river ice broke in the spring of 1898, the population of Dyea had swelled to 5,000, and that was only a fraction of those who would make their way toward the Klondike. Determined to be among the first to reach Dawson once the ice broke, another 30,000 to 40,000 had bypassed Dyea to spend the winter along the Chilkoot Trail.[28] On the once-quiet forest path over which Kate had trudged with her pack, there were now horses and sledges (on the lower portions of the trail) and thousands upon thousands of white canvas tents.

To accommodate the Argonauts who forged relentlessly through snow, slush, and the occasional rainstorm, an entrepreneurial father-son team treaded parts of the lower trail with logs and charged a dollar per person for those who wanted to cross their hastily built bridge over the Taiya River. A steep climb, a series of switchbacks, a narrow passage alongside a steep cliff, a descent to the river, a hike through a valley, and another river crossing brought miners to Sheep Camp, one-third of the way up the mountain. Sixty businesses sprang up at Sheep Camp during the winter of 1898, some started by prospectors and their wives who simply opened up their packs of provisions and began serving meals. If you didn't mind spreading your bedroll on the floor in a bunkroom of snoring miners, you could even stay overnight in a hotel.[29]

Where the steepest part of the trail began just beyond Sheep Camp, those who could afford it transferred their cargo to packers, many of them white men who'd gotten sidetracked in their quest for gold. Competition for the packing dollar reached levels L'unáat could never have foreseen. Forget the $15 per hundred pounds George Carmack had warned his sister she'd have to pay Indian packers. White packers were charging $30 per hundred pounds—and that was only from Sheep Camp to the trail's end.[30]

Disregarding the snow, the winds, and the unpredictable weather, a ceaseless stream of human traffic trudged up the Golden Stairs, steps that were cut into the snow along the final approach to the summit. For the lucky ones who had cash, scales were set up at the foot of the stairs to weigh the supplies to be packed or be carried by tram to the top. Those who couldn't afford to hire out the transportation of their supplies made ten, twenty, or thirty trips to the summit, ferrying what they could on their own backs, dumping their loads at the top, and then sliding down the slope to retrieve the next load. Because of food shortages in Dawson, authorities required stampeders to bring a thousand pounds of supplies into Canada. What some thought essential exceeded by far what George Carmack had suggested his sister bring: barrels of whiskey, canoes, and even French stoves weighing three hundred pounds each.[31]

On the Tagish side of the pass, additional cities of white canvas tents sprang up where intrepid adventurers were waylaid until the river ice broke. Boatbuilding was the chief activity in these makeshift communities. Winter's hush was broken by the sawing, hammering, and cursing of men who labored to cobble together their scows. Forests of balsam and spruce were razed for lumber. At Lindeman, the once peaceful lake where the Chilkoot launched their boats to float the Tagish lakes to the Yukon River on their annual trading expeditions, the tent settlement grew so large that a mayor and justice of the peace were elected.[32] Between Lindeman and Lake Bennett, where Jim, Charlie, and Patsy had followed the cries of Wealth Woman's child, tents stretched a mile deep.

The greenhorns—*Cheechakos,* in the Chinook trading jargon—were a different breed than the early prospectors, in a big hurry and disinclined to tarry with the Indians as George Carmack had done, let alone take an Indian wife. A few brought their own wives. Still fewer women came on their own or in the company of other women, traveling as the dance hall girls sometimes did. One prospector postulated that the women who went north were inspired as much by freedom as money: "She steps out of her dress into trousers in a region where nobody cares. Her nature suddenly becomes aware of a freedom which is in a way exhilarating. She has, as it were, thrown off the fetters which civilized society imposes."[33]

While George Carmack benefited from the nurturing and coaching of his Tagish wife and her family, the new breed of prospectors for the most part ignored the indigenous people, at times to their detriment, as was the case in early April 1898 when Chinook winds began to blow from the south, warming the deep, heavy snowpack in the mountains. Wary of snow slides, Tagish and Tlingit packers refused to go beyond Sheep Camp. Undaunted, the prospectors kept climbing.

On the eve of Palm Sunday, 1898, the avalanches began. The first one buried the Scales. A second slide overcame twenty stampeders. A third the next morning killed three more men. As heavy snows fell, avalanches continued to roar down the mountains, leveling three separate groups of travelers. For four days, miners dug through the snow, retrieving bodies and uncovering the lucky few who had somehow managed to survive. From the makeshift morgue set up in a tent at Sheep Camp, fifty-one bodies were shuttled to what became known as Slide Cemetery, on the outskirts of Dyea.[34] One of the victims was Anna Blystone Maxon, a cousin of George Carmack.[35]

Before the stampede, Kate's Tagish relatives had mostly stayed off the mountain during the winter. But with the trail so heavily trafficked, some now let down their guard. During the winter of 1898, Kate's sister Nadagáat Tláa and her daughters were part a Tagish group that was crossing the mountains on their way to the coast, possibly to attend a potlatch. From Bennett, the new tent town on the shores of the lake, they proceeded to the timberline, where they camped overnight. Upon setting out the next morning, Nadagáat Tláa decided not to wear her skin pants because they were making her sweat. As the group climbed above the tree line, the north wind began to howl. Blowing snow drifted over the trail. With her daughter and her baby, Kate's sister, who was pregnant, fell behind the rest of the group. Her daughter was cold, so Nadagáat Tláa settled behind a big rock to wait out the storm, wrapping blankets around herself and her children.

When they arrived at Sheep Camp, the rest of the group realized she was missing. By the time they returned with three white men and some buffalo robes, Nadagáat Tláa and her oldest child were nearly frozen. The men hauled them by toboggan to Sheep Camp and gave them hot tea, although the Tagish way was to give cold liquids to those who were cold. The baby carried in her mother's pack survived, but Nadagáat Tláa, her oldest daughter, and her unborn child all perished.[36] Several weeks would pass before word of the tragedy reached Kate and Jim.[37]

By spring, a thousand tents and forty hastily constructed buildings crowded the shores of the south end of Lake Bennett, housing a population of 2,500 stampeders. With the long-awaited spring thaw, the ground beneath the makeshift town became a foul-smelling miasma of sand, manure, and waste; in short order, the community was plagued with dysentery and typhoid fever.[38] Once the ice melted, thousands of boats passed by the Dakl'aweidí clan house on Six Mile River. Nearby, the Northwest Mounted Police (NWMP) set up a customs post. Working out of four small log buildings and several tents that sheltered policemen, horses, prisoners, and supplies, the Mounties collected the duty on American goods brought onto Canadian soil and took down the names of some 28,000 persons who came through on their way to the Klondike.[39] That Kate's brother and husband and nephew had found the gold that started such a stampede was almost too much to fathom.

In May 1898, the NWMP faced their first big criminal case in the Yukon: four Tagish men, later called the Nantuck Boys (their ages ranged from fifteen to twenty), were apprehended on charges of murder. Because they were Tagish, the young men were all related to Kate in one way or another, and while their eventual transport to Dawson would be big news in the Yukon, their arrival for Kate would portend personal grief and, on a broader scale, foretell the damage destined to rise out of the deep divide between Tagish and Western ways of knowing and doing.[40]

While traveling down the McClintock River, the four Tagish men had stopped to rest at Tl'andaake Tene, "on top of the hill road," when they spotted two stampeders. Sometime earlier, the brother and grandfather of one of the Tagish men had died, poisoned by bread baked with a white powder they had found in a can left by white men—arsenic, which they mistook for baking powder.[41] The Crow woman who had baked the bread at the request of her maternal nephew was Kate's aunt.[42] Retribution, the prevailing principle of Tagish justice, required that the clan of those responsible for the death—the white men—make some sort of restitution to the Crow clan—they could either give over items of value, such as blankets, or they could pay with the equivalent in human lives.

With this principle in mind, two of the Tagish men, called Frank and Joe, approached the prospectors, Billy Meehan and Christian Fox, who were in the process of building a boat. They all camped together that night, and the next day Frank and Joe returned with a man called Dawson. A week later, a fourth Tagish man, Jim, joined them, along with three women and two children.

To the Tagish men, this period of friendly contact was required to allow the opposing clan—in this case, the whites—to offer valuable goods in order to remedy the wrong they had caused with the arsenic. But Meehan and Fox made no such offer, so when they finished building their boat and began to float down the McClintock River, Joe and Dawson aimed their guns at the stern while Frank and Jim aimed theirs at the bow. Hit by three bullets, Meehan was killed. Wounded in the shoulder, Fox paddled with one arm to the opposite shore and followed the crest of a nearby hill to Marsh Lake, where another prospector summoned the Mounties from the Tagish Post, thirty miles away.

When the Tagish men revealed to their family and friends how they had settled this score with the white clan, one uncle urged them to go into hiding. They then traveled forty miles to Lake LaBerge, where an elder advised them to go home and not worry about what they had done—it was justice, after all. Ten days after the shootings, the Mounties arrested the first of the men, who had in his possession some of the supplies abandoned by Fox at his camp. After another ten days of surveillance at Tagish camps along Marsh Lake and Lake LaBerge, the Mounties confronted the other three men, all of whom surrendered.

Held at the Tagish Post for a month, the Nantuck Boys were the subject of much speculation and many photographs by passing prospectors; Maria Johns, wife of Kate's cousin Tagish John, wept when she saw the young men all chained together. In June, they were transferred to Dawson in order to stand trial. "Deliberately Tried to Kill Their Benefactors for Their Outfits," read the headline of one paper. "The Treacherous Instincts of the Aborigines Will Get Their Necks Stretched with Hemp" read another.[43]

CHAPTER THIRTEEN

THE MERRY JINGLE OF COINS

THE TRIAL OF THE NANTUCK BOYS COINCIDED with the arrival in Dawson of Mary Hitchcock and Edith Van Buren during the final days of Kate's preparation for her first trip outside the Far North. On July 27, 1898, the eve of the trial, Hitchcock and Van Buren caught their first glimpse of the new frontier town as their steamer approached Dawson: three long wharves crowded with people, framed warehouses going up along the riverfront, ten-foot-wide storefronts on land leased for $10 a month, and mile after mile of canvas tents.[1]

As the Tagish men bedded down that night in one of the twenty-four cells of the Dawson jail—one of nine three-sided NWMP log buildings that had gone up on the disputed government reserve— the wealthy socialites "did the town," going places where Kate, as an Indian, was not especially welcome.[2] On Front Street, they toured Belinda Mulrooney's Fairview Hotel, its grand opening set for that very evening, entering the hotel through a barroom from which Mulrooney expected revenues of up to a thousand dollars a night. Their hostess was especially proud of the damask table coverings in the dining room and the Brussels carpets and lace curtains in the guest rooms. The rooms were tiny, to be sure, with beds the only furnishings, and the lace curtains covered windows that were made of nothing more than stretched cheesecloth, but for Dawson, the accommodations were considered first class.

In a Dawson City dance hall, Hitchcock and Van Buren were afforded private entrance to a curtained box from which they could watch miners waltz and polka with girls who earned a dollar a dance if their pay was taken in alcohol or a quarter a dance if their pay was taken in cash. At the Monte Carlo Theater, the newly arrived women took in a variety show that, like the dancing, Hitchcock pronounced "thoroughly respectable."[3] Near midnight, as the summer sunlight began to fade, escorts accompanied them through the crowded streets to the steamer, where the Alaska Commercial Company graciously allowed them to sleep until their big tent was set up.

The following day, as Mary Hitchcock was affronted by the charge levied at the local bank to cash two $50 certificates she'd purchased in California, and as Edith Van Buren enjoyed a chance reunion with a man she had met on her travels in Egypt, Jim, the first of the Nantuck Boys to be apprehended, went on trial.[4] Only six weeks earlier, the Yukon Territory had officially come into being, carved out of the larger Unorganized Northwest Territories of Canada, and this trial would be the first opportunity for the legal system of the British Empire to prove its effectiveness over the miners' meetings that had previously meted out justice without state interference.

Whether Kate was in the courtroom during this trial is difficult to know; undoubtedly, she was concerned with the fate of these men she had known from birth, and she was undoubtedly aware of at least some of the cultural differences that would affect the outcome of the trial. As Frank, the youngest of the men, was called as a witness against Jim, there was some consternation in the courtroom over how he could swear on a Bible if in fact he had no concept of what the Bible represented. Through interpreters who translated into Tlingit, the second language of the Tagish men, Frank was unable to say whether he had any religion at all as the judge defined it. Further prodded, he asserted that his own death would be no different than the death of a moose, an admission that seemed to the court to prove his inability to understand the required oath. Finally, he was asked straight out whether he knew what it meant to speak the truth, to which he replied that of course he did, and so the trial proceeded.[5]

Urged to tell his version of the facts, Frank stated that all of one mind, the four Tagish men had determined that Fox and Meehan were responsible for planting the arsenic that had killed the boy and his grandfather. When pressed for details on the situation, he responded with silence, taken by observers as indifference. The defendant's version of the events, readily given at the time of his arrest, was read to him by a translator from statements transcribed by a court reporter using the testimony of an NWMP officer whose information came from another interpreter. No witnesses were called on his behalf; in fact, the murder trial lasted only one day.

In his instructions to the jury, the judge noted that no justifiable grounds for killing, such as self-defense or protection of property, had been offered by the defense. The statutes made no exceptions for what he termed the "lower orders of humanity," the judge pointed out, adding that "we have a great many Indians here and it is important that you should not lightly or carelessly consign one of them to the gallows, but it is just as important that you should not, through any mistaken idea of tenderheartedness or sympathy, omit to do that which is a very unpleasant duty."[6]

Jim was quickly found guilty. Frank's trial began and ended the following day, with a similar verdict. Having been sentenced to death, he and Jim bedded down at the jail, while Mary Hitchcock and Edith Van Buren settled in for a night of nineteenth-century glamour camping in their newly erected twenty-by-forty-foot white canvas tent. From the high ground of West Dawson, sparing them the muck and sewage of the town proper, they could look out across the Yukon at the NWMP jail where the Nantuck Boys were confined.

Enamored of the two-foot-high wildflowers and grasses, the women opted not to put down floorboards inside the tent, relishing the illusion of a conservatory as their pigeons flew about under the canvas. To the delight of their neighbors, they cranked up their gramophone, an invention most had never seen. Though Mary had armed herself with a revolver for their wilderness journey, she and Edith slept free from fear on their hammocks; owing to the failure of a clerk in San Francisco to pack air pumps, they discovered that their mattresses could not be inflated. Sheltered only by canvas, they knew that if anyone attempted to harm them, "one call from us would bring the man to justice so quickly that he would scarce have time to say a prayer."[7]

Swift justice, as the new prevailing culture defined it, was soon rendered to Dawson and Joe, the remaining two Nantuck Boys. All four Tagish men were sentenced to hang on November 1, 1898. "Not one in the courtroom but was sympathetically affected by the venerable judge's suppressed emotion at sentencing those intellectual children to death," reported the *Klondike Nugget*. The article laid out the reasons the young men deserved to hang:

> The questions put to the murderers by the judge through the interpreters showed them to be wholly deficient in the most ordinary morals. Their cunning, also, was of a low order. They could plot to destroy the two men in the boat and steal their goods but appeared to be stolidly indifferent to the results of the admissions they were making, though it was repeatedly impressed on them. Questioned about their knowledge of God or a future state, everyone was surprised to find that they knew nothing about either one. Even the "Great Spirit" and the "Happy Hunting Grounds" of the North American Indians were unknown to them.[8]

Neither did notions like the "Happy Hunting Grounds" mean anything to Kate, but it was such comparisons with "North American Indians" that would plague her as she traveled away from the North, bound for Seattle and then California where she, the "Irish" wife, with her "pretty daughter" would meet George's sister. Measured against well-worn stereotypes, the behaviors of an Indian woman of curious wealth would to some seem peculiar or even, as with the Nantuck Boys, reprehensible. Despite years of adapting to life among the miners, Kate would be hard-pressed to develop the sort of wiliness needed to find her way.

Shortly before Kate's departure from the Yukon, Mary Hitchcock and Edith Van Buren hosted their first Dawson dinner party, a seven-course affair featuring anchovy on soda biscuit, mock turtle soup, roast moose, escalloped tomatoes, asparagus salad, peach ice cream, and cake. The next day they set out on a two-day trek over a muddy, buggy trail to the creeks.[9]

At the same time, Kate, Graphie, George, Jim, Charlie, and Patsy set out from Dawson aboard a sternwheeler operated by John J. Healy's North American Transportation Company, taking with them an estimated $45,000 to $250,000 in gold.[10] Having made record time coming up the Yukon—twelve and a half days—the steamer captain wasted no time once they departed, stopping only for wood that was cut and stacked by Indians along the river, to feed the boat's hungry boiler.

For much of Kate's riverboat journey, the weather was cloudy and cool with occasional drizzle. Guided by Native river pilots earning $10 a day plus board for themselves and their families, the boat followed the Yukon River past the new village of Eagle and then through the Forty Mile district to where the waterway broadens to three-quarters of a mile, its green banks rising to heights of six hundred feet. From there, Kate traveled past the village of Tanana, where her friend Jennie Harper had relocated with her son, Walter, and Showman's House, where Kate and George had spent Starvation Winter with Howard Hamilton Hart.

Beyond that point, the boat transported Kate through country she had never seen, the landscape flattening to treeless tundra as the river widens. At St. Michael, a rocky beachfront community dominated by the warehouses belonging to competing suppliers of goods bound for the Klondike, the oceanfront could not have been more different from the coast where she'd lived with Kult'ús, hemmed in by sheer rocky mountainsides and narrow fjords and towering firs; at St. Michael, the sea opened wide to the sky, the horizon boundless.[11] An old Russian port, the village was as close as ocean-going steamers could get to the mouth of the Yukon. Though called Indians by most Cheechakos, most of its Native residents were Yup'ik Eskimo.

At the Healy Hotel, which like the riverboat was owned and operated by John Healy's North American Transportation Company, the Carmacks stashed the family's gold in the hotel safe and awaited the departure of the *Roanoke*, bound for Seattle. Two days later, a dinghy shuttled them to the steamer, anchored three miles out from the shallows. With passengers who had been aboard for up to two weeks, they waited for the arrival of another riverboat from Dawson, the *Portus B. Weare*. Joining them for the ocean voyage would be Mr. Portus B. Weare himself, one of Healy's investors, and Dr. Sheldon Jackson, a Presbyterian missionary recently returned from Siberia. He had been purchasing reindeer there as part of a project to introduce herding as a new livelihood for Natives in Western Alaska, who because of the exploits of whalers were already suffering from the over-harvesting of their traditional resources in tandem with an increased reliance on non-subsistence foods. With the advent of the gold rush, Kate's Tagish relatives were beginning to experience similar changes to their way of life.[12]

On the morning of August 21, 1898, the last of the passengers bound for Seattle boarded the *Roanoke*. As the ocean-bound part of Kate's journey was about to begin, excitement rippled from one end of the boat to the other: a valise containing over $24,000 in gold had been stolen. The missing gold belonged to four men, one of whom had leased a fifty-foot section of No. 1 above Discovery from George Carmack (although that claim in fact belonged to Jim).

Like George—and all Klondikers—the victims of the theft preferred not to hand over 10 percent of their wealth to the Canadian government in the form of a royalty tax, which was why they'd stashed the gold in their stateroom instead of entrusting it to the purser for safekeeping. Kate waited with the other passengers while the *Roanoke* was searched, but to no avail—whoever made off with the loot had done a good job of it. And when at last they set sail, Jim discovered that he, too, had been robbed—$4,000 of his gold dust replaced with buck shot.[13] Given the other excitement, and perhaps also the fact that he was an Indian, not much fuss was made over his loss.

After nine days on the ocean, The *Roanoke* tied up at the Seattle docks at 8:30 am on August 30, 1898, but no one was allowed to disembark until the police conducted a thorough search for the prospectors' missing valise. Already, some were accusing the four miners of having staged the theft, though it was unclear what advantage they would have gained in doing so. One of the victims offered as proof the testimony of George Carmack, who had been shown the valise, brimming with gold, before it was stolen. In the end, the search turned up nothing more than headlines for Seattle's competing newspapers.

When at last she was permitted to leave the steamship, Kate stepped into a scene for which not even Dawson with its crowded streets and bawdy saloons and thousands of outsiders had prepared her—soaring buildings of brick and stone, plate glass windows, smokestacks, telephone lines, railroad tracks, streetcars, electric lights. Horses clomped over streets paved with bricks. Sidewalks were jammed with people. There were bicycles, telephone wires, street lamps. Who knew how to behave in such a place?

Even George must have been amazed at the transformation worked upon the city by Erastus Brainerd, former editor of the *Seattle Press* and executive officer of the Chamber of Commerce. Early on, Brainerd had assumed the role of Seattle's chief publicist, determined to ensure that his city beat out San Francisco, Portland, and Tacoma as the chief jumping-off point for the Klondike. Within six months of an elaborate advertising campaign, Seattle had churned out five times more promotional material aimed at "mining the miners" than had any other city.[14]

With their Tagish relatives, George and Kate checked into the Seattle Hotel, a triangular building that filled a corner lot bounded by James, Yesler, and 2nd Avenues. Though the hotel was respectable enough, one had only to stroll a block or two in the wrong direction before coming upon the infamous Mug Saloon and the fancy brick building that housed an upscale brothel operated by Lou Graham, who upon her arrival in Seattle shortly before the big fire had convinced the city fathers that, done right, prostitution was good for the financial health of the town. Indeed, with the hordes of men headed to the Klondike, business was booming along what was known as "The Line," a part of the city in which, as one prospector wrote, "the Devil reined supreme."[15]

"From Klondike to Paris," read the headline for the first interview following the Carmacks' arrival in Seattle. Accompanied by his Indian wife, child (the newspaper sketch depicts five-year-old Graphie Grace as a round-faced infant), and Native brothers-in-law, George did not look the part of a millionaire, the reporter noted. George made a point of saying that he would never have dreamed of leaving Kate behind in the Yukon. "When you go off on a little journey, take your wife with you," he proclaimed. "The change will do her good, and civilization will not harm the children so long as they don't get too much of it."[16]

If the Canadian government would decrease the 10 percent royalty, George bragged that in two years he would take Kate and Graphie by private yacht across the Atlantic to the 1900 World Exposition in Paris. If the royalty remained at its current levels, however, he threatened to winter in Alaska instead of the Yukon. In the meantime, he was keeping a close eye on his Tagish relatives to ensure they did not part with any of their earnings. "He proposes to keep the wealth of the family together," the article concluded.[17]

All sorts of stories would circulate about Kate's first days in Seattle. George Carmack's family would tell of how she used a hatchet to notch the woodwork so she could find her way around the fancy hotel.[18] Another story, passed down by her Tagish relatives, told of how she got tired of restaurant food and bought a whole side of beef ribs that she saw hanging in a butcher shop in Seattle. When the packaged ribs were delivered to the hotel, she hauled them out to the alley, where she started a fire with pieces of wooden boxes and began roasting the meat. "My golly, somebody saw the fire and called the fire department," Kate's cousin Johnny Johns said. "But when they arrived and saw her sitting there just as peaceful as could be, roasting her ribs, they didn't have the heart to put her fire out, so they stood by until her ribs were all cooked, and she walked back with them into the hotel."[19]

Her Tagish relatives would also tell of how Jim attended a variety show in Seattle, where a massive woman was performing onstage—six hundred pounds, they said. Part of her act was to wander the crowd, bestowing hugs and kisses on unsuspecting men. When she approached Jim, he protested. "Oh, no-no-no, don't touch me! Please, please don't touch me. I got a wife at home. I got a wife who'll tell. No, no, I don't want a kiss! I don't want a kiss."[20]

None of these incidents made the papers, but another one did. The day after their arrival, Kate joined George, Jim, Charlie, and Patsy in tossing money from their apartment on the fifth floor of the Seattle Hotel to the street below:

> As the merry jingle of coins resounded and the pieces bounded from the pavements into the streets, men dived from the sidewalks and off passing street cars, butcher boys and teamsters hurled themselves into the air from their seats, conductors and gripmen forgot all about their charges, policemen forgot to say 'move on.' The street became a seething mass of struggling humanity. Hats were broken and lost, faces were bruised and bleeding, coats were torn and linen soiled . . . all this time Carmack and his native Alaskan relatives were splitting themselves with laughter in their apartments at the top of the hotel. Having nothing but money, they knew of no better way of becoming popular and having amusement than by distributing it in the street.[21]

Even after their coin-flinging spree, Kate and George had plenty of money. A week after their arrival, George deposited $10,000 of the family's funds with Seattle Bank. Three days later, he paid $2,500 to purchase the Togo Hotel on Maynard Street, several blocks north of the more upscale hotel where they were staying. Then he, Kate, and Graphie set out for San Francisco, where he deposited $22,000 in the Bank of California.

Though substantial, George's various bank deposits were a proverbial drop in the bucket when compared to the total amount of gold the family had extracted—and would continue to extract—from the gravels of Bonanza Creek. As for the rest of the Klondike: between June and November that year (1898), the total in gold as recorded by the US Mints in Seattle and San Francisco topped $10 million.[22]

"Mr. Carmack is quiet and unostentatious, and one seeing him on the street would not take him for the Croesus that he is," noted a reporter for the *San Francisco Call*. "He is devoted to his Indian wife and child, and has bestowed on the former nuggets in quantity, which she wears suspended around her neck or in the form of stick-pins";[23] for Graphie Grace, George bought a "handsome and expensive doll."[24] From San Francisco, the Carmacks traveled to San Luis Obispo, where George had grown up, and then to the hot springs at Gilroy, where he hoped to ease his rheumatism. From there, they would travel to Tres Pinos, where Kate would at last meet her sister-in-law, Rose Carmack Watson.

CHAPTER FOURTEEN

SIMPLY TOO GOOD

ON THEIR MODEST RANCH ALONG COTTONWOOD ROAD, between the tiny towns of Tres Pinos and Paicines in San Benito County, California, Rose and James Watson may never have known of George's plan to hire a private yacht to take his family to the 1900 Paris Expedition or of the amusement he and his wife gained by tossing coins from the top floor of the Seattle Hotel. Reunited in September of 1898 with the brother she had not seen for thirteen years, Rose must have been especially shocked at his "Irish" wife, who faced the challenge of adapting to yet another unfamiliar landscape, along with integrating into a new clan and taking up a new way of life.

Had she been Tagish, Kate's sister-in-law would have identified herself through her mother, Hannah Stiles, a plain-faced woman born in Vermont, married in Illinois, and transported to the West by her husband, Augustus Perry Carmack, who took up farming in the hills west of San Jose following the California gold rush. But like virtually all women of the dominant culture, Rose was defined primarily through her husband, James Watson. They had married in 1869, the year the Transcontinental Railroad was completed, heralding the official settlement of the West. Rose

Rose and James Watson in 1887. (Yukon Archives, James Albert Johnson fonds, 82/341 #5)

(officially, Hannah Rosella) was then fourteen; her husband, James Watson, was thirty-eight. Rose's mother had died six years earlier, when Rose was eight years old. Her father had remarried and moved with his new wife to San Benito Country, where they had a daughter, born four months before Rose married. When

Rose's father died suddenly, she and James had taken eleven-year-old George into their home.

To the extent that it had infected George Carmack, gold fever came not from his father but from Rose's husband James, who at age eighteen had traveled with his parents and six siblings in a train of sixty-four ox-teams bound for California, where gold had been discovered at Sutter Creek. Prospecting along the American River and on Mormon Island, James's father had found enough gold to set himself up in ranching on the coastal side of the mountains, while James found work as a freighter, running his wagon from Marysville to the mines. When the rush was over, he followed the rest of his family to Monterrey County, drawn by fertile soils and an abundance of water. There, he met and married Rose Carmack.[1]

In 1884, the year before George Carmack went looking for gold in Alaska, Rose and James moved inland to San Benito County, created a decade earlier out of the eastern portion of Monterrey County. They settled along Tres Pinos Creek, where James's father, mother, and several of his brothers had relocated shortly after the railroad was extended there. Five miles south of Hollister, the San Benito County seat, Tres Pinos was a small but prosperous trading center for livestock, hay, and grain. The Watsons were typical of those who settled in the area, 49ers who stayed on to work the fertile soils in the mild climate of the hills between the Sierra Nevada and the coast.

Between the Gabilan Mountains to the west and California's Central Valley to the east, the Mutsune Indians had once occupied the lands that became San Benito County. They lived a mostly nomadic lifestyle, much like the one Kate had known, except that the Mutsune had hunted mule deer, antelope, and elk instead of moose and caribou, and for shelter, they had built huts of willows and tall native grasses instead of alder and birch. By the time Kate arrived, there had already been much intermarriage between the Spanish and the Mutsune and the Americans, who in the early days of California's history had been known to give up their citizenship in order to marry a Mexican national. In terms of race, there were certainly worse places she could have landed.

She first came to San Benito County at the end of the dry season, as sunsets cast golden light over brown, rolling hills. In those days, Southern Pacific trains pulled right into the Tres Pinos, a little western-style town with boardwalks and false fronts and hitching posts and troughs to water the horses. Along the town's one main block were six saloons.[2] To get to the ranch belonging to Rose and James Watson, the Carmacks traveled five miles south by carriage to Paicines,[3] where there was a blacksmith shop and a big livery stable that hosted occasional community dances. From Paicines, the carriage took them over Panoche Road, which veered to the southeast toward the New Idria quicksilver mine and then onto Cottonwood Road, which forked past the cemetery and ran alongside Cottonwood Creek. All along Cottonwood Road were small ranches like the one owned by James and Rose Watson, quarter-sections fenced in for cattle, hogs, turkeys, and hay.

No one in the Cottonwood section was getting rich, but the setting was idyllic, the farms nestled in a peaceful little valley cradled on either side by low hills. Except for the bells of freighters running horse teams from Tres Pinos to New Idria, it was quiet; in the evening, Kate heard frogs, crickets, and hoot owls. Besides the familiar cottonwoods and willows, there were palm trees and big spreading oaks and pepper trees, imported by the Spaniards, while along Tres Pinos Creek grew fragrant eucalyptus, imported more recently to replace dwindling hardwoods.[4] Among the sedges and stem thistles were jackrabbits, red-legged frogs, bobcats, and deer, plus the occasional rattlesnake, weasel, skunk, raccoon, ground squirrel, and elk. There were herons and egrets, and nesting rails and eagles, both golden and bald, these familiar to Kate from the Alaska coast near Chilkoot and Dyea. And there were crows, a smaller version of the ravens Kate knew from home.

Skilled as she was at adapting, Kate soon came to appreciate the quiet beauty of the ranch country, though it was utterly foreign, as was life on a ranch. Her seasonal rounds were replaced by daily farm chores dictated by cycles of planting and harvest. As she had depended on the help of the Crows during her first marriage, she relied on George and his clan for help in adjusting. Frugal and industrious—those were the terms used to describe the Watsons of San Benito County. Rose, James, and her widowed sister-in-law Ellen Watson were founding members of the Paicines Baptist Church; Rose was the church's first treasurer. For the first time, Kate attended regular Sunday church services, where women dressed in their best frocks sang from hymnals and the clergy felt no obligation to dispense medicines or take in orphaned children.

Of all the Watsons, the one most liked by everyone, including Kate, was James's younger brother, Jake, a confirmed bachelor who lived with his mother on the ranch adjacent to Rose and James. A tall, quiet, kind man, Jake was the one people called on for help, whether it was for shearing sheep or doctoring a cow.[5] James Watson, Kate's brother-in-law, was sixty-eight years old; his health was failing, and his assets were few; though he owned his house free and clear, his pasture lands were worth only $200. Plain-faced like her mother, his wife, Rose, had always been childless, but she loved children and was called Aunt Rose even by those outside the large Watson clan. She took a quick liking to Graphie Grace.

Though she and George had been big news in Seattle and San Francisco, Kate folded into the community of San Benito County with little fuss. Under the domed sky, there were hills to roam and streams to follow. As evening fell and again when day dawned, the quiet swelled with the warbling of birds and the croaking of frogs, a reminder of Jim's animal helper. In winter, the wet season came, though that particular year it brought not as much rain as was needed.

Tule fog rolled in thick from the coast, hanging low to the ground for weeks at a stretch, not unlike the ice fog that settled over the Klondike Valley when temperatures dipped to forty below. It was Kate's first winter without snow. For her Tagish family, it was time for snaring hares and trapping weasels and repairing snowshoes and nets. It was time for stitching mukluks and parkas, and for attending potlatches, where each clan thanked the other for helping when loved ones died. Instead, Kate spent this winter learning the ways of the ranch and sewing with fabric instead of skins.

Jim and Charlie had gone home to retrieve their wives and children so that they, too, could experience these places beyond imagining: Seattle, San Francisco, and even tiny Tres Pinos. On January 24, 1899, Kate, George, and Graphie met up with them at the Commercial Hotel in San Francisco. "They are infatuated with the town, and have spent all their time since their arrival in sightseeing," wrote one reporter, describing a phenomenon that went both ways. "Along Market Street yesterday afternoon the pudgy little Indian children and their mothers were the cynosure of all eyes . . . They came here to enjoy themselves and do not intend to let the mere matter of a thousand or two stand in their way."[6]

Kate's visiting relatives rode cable cars, visited the caged grizzly bear at Golden Gate Park, strolled through Chinatown, and gazed up at the big Nob Hill mansions. They shopped, acquiring clothes, toys, and fancy goods unavailable back home. Though San Francisco was huge—the eighth largest city in America—there were others they knew there, traders and prospectors from the Yukon: Jack McQuesten and his Koyukon wife, Jennie, had settled in Berkley; Gordon Bettles of the Showman House and his Koyukon wife, Sophie, came and went from the city; Clarence and Ethel Berry, who had made a fortune on El Dorado Creek, had returned to the Bay Area to invest in oil fields, as would Howard Hamilton Hart, the prospector who had shared a cabin with Kate and George during Starvation Winter.

While in San Francisco, Kate and her relatives sat for portraits at the new Vaughn & Keith Studio. In hers, Kate wears a high-collared dress of crisp, black crinoline with tiny pleats at the bodice and cuffs. Beneath a tidy bow at the neckline hangs a necklace fashioned of flattened gold nuggets; on both wrists she wears gold bangles, and on her fingers, gold rings, including

Studio portrait of George Carmack, Kate Carmack, and Graphie Grace Carmack in California, 1898. This was Carmack's first trip Outside since 1885. His rheumatism bothered him and when he reached Seattle the first thing he bought was a cane. (Yukon Archives, James Albert Johnson fonds, 82/341, #22)

one that serves as a wedding band. Clasped at her waist is a belt with a large, filigreed gold buckle. Curled tightly, her dark hair is arranged in a neat bun on top of her head. Her features are soft, her lips full, her face a perfect oval. Her gaze is straightforward and determined, contributing to an overall regal appearance, with only her large, worn hands to betray the labors of the life she'd left behind.

The formal pose represents the greater posing required of Kate outside of Alaska and the Yukon. In one sense, this was a form of adaptation, a skill at which Kate excelled. But as author Sherrill Grace points out, it was also mimicry of the dominant culture, "an unstable, uncontrollable practice; it can backfire on the mimic to betray him or her."[7]

At some point, George brought his Tagish relatives to the Watson ranch at Tres Pinos; there are stories of how Jim and Charlie horrified Rose by shooting gophers to be cooked up for supper.[8] In March 1899, the Carmacks left California for the long journey back to Bonanza Creek, with the goal of arriving in time for spring clean-up. They stopped first in Seattle, where George used proceeds from the Bonanza Creek claims to establish the Carmack Gold and Copper Mining Company, dedicated to exploring the potential mineral wealth of the Cascade Mountains. He also invested in Microbane Medical Company, its chief product being a tonic guaranteed, if used properly, to cure baldness. In addition, he paid $8,000 for a duplex and single-family home on a double lot on 3rd Avenue in Seattle, and he shipped a crate of Washington apples back to California for Rose and James to enjoy.

On March 26, Jim, Charlie, and their families boarded a steamer bound for Skagway and Dyea; their arrival would be delayed when the steamer struck a dangerous reef along the Alaska coast, and all ninety-six passengers had to be rescued by a lighthouse tender and transported to Juneau.

In the company of three hundred other Klondikers and on a boat loaded with four hundred tons of freight, Kate, George, and Graphie left Seattle a week after Jim and Charlie's departure.[9] Their journey would be shorter than it had been on the way out—thanks to the construction of the White Pass & Yukon Railroad, passengers could now travel through Skagway instead of St. Michael, without the burden of packing themselves and their luggage over the Chilkoot Trail.

Disembarking in Skagway, Kate found the seasonal camp from which the L'ukaax̱.ádi had hunted mountain goats and dried salmon and picked berries transformed into a boomtown with a reputation for lawlessness, owing mostly to the activities of a gang headed by outlaw and conman Soapy Smith, who had found the town perfect for fleecing Cheechakos fresh off the boats, one of his favorite schemes being to charge $5 apiece for telegrams to be sent to folks back home—over a wire that went no farther than the alley behind his saloon.

Soapy's reign of terror ended with his death in a shootout in July 1898, but at the time of Kate's arrival plenty of bawdy houses and gambling halls and saloons remained in Skagway. Much of the frenzy to reach Dawson had died down, the creeks having long ago been staked. Still, there were optimists. If a wanderer like George Carmack and his Indian relatives could stumble on gold, why couldn't anyone? There must be other Klondikes in the vast northern wilderness, waiting to be discovered—or so thought the optimists.

And though the challenges were still many, access to the North was improving, with a crew funded by London investors laying rail through the White Pass, remaking the trail that Skookum Jim had, with reluctance, shown to William Moore back in 1887. At first, the White Pass Trail had been thought suitable for horses, though hundreds, if not thousands, ended up dying there before the railroad went through, with conditions being so awful that prospectors swore they had seen horses purposely throw themselves over cliffs.

With the railroad, the boomtowns of Dyea and Bennett—neither of which Kate had seen in their heyday—were becoming irrelevant, and packing over the Chilkoot Trail was all but over. There were still 250 people living at Dyea, including some of Kate's Tagish relatives, but one by one, the buildings that had gone up there were being dismantled and hauled off to Skagway.[10] The Chilkoot Trail—and with it, the traditional trading patterns that had motivated Kate's family to arrange her marriage to George—were becoming irrelevant. No longer could Kate's relatives earn packers' wages to purchase the trading goods—kettles, guns, sugar, cloth—to which they had quickly become accustomed.

Having watched the migration of tens of thousands of stampeders pass through Dyea, Kate's family made plans to relocate to Todezáané, on the shores of Lake Bennett, where the caribou came through. The railroad would stop there on the route between Skagway and Whitehorse, which meant new jobs to replace their wages from packing, and stores where they could buy luxuries like tea, sugar, and canned goods.

In the spring of 1899, however, the railroad reached only from Skagway to the summit of the White Pass; to reach Dawson from there, you had to travel on foot down the mountain and then by dogsled over the frozen rivers in winter or by small boat and then by steamer after the ice went out. April was a dicey month for overland travel, so Kate and her family likely visited her family while waiting for break-up.[11] Kate told her family of the sights she'd seen in Seattle and San Francisco—lights that came on with the press of a button, cobbled streets, fine homes, and new-fangled bicycles.

In many ways, Kate was the same woman she had always been, though more confident, having adapted to circumstances more extraordinary than she could fully describe. What the future held, however, she couldn't say. George had no desire to stay in the North. He'd arranged for his brother-in-law, German immigrant Julius Huttman, to work the claims at Bonanza. After this spring clean-up, or maybe the next, he planned to sell out and settle Outside, dividing his time between California, where he'd purchased 160 acres from Huttman, and Seattle.

Dawson was another place that had greatly changed since Kate's departure the previous summer. There had been two big fires, one of which had destroyed the Opera House and a bank, leaving only a big twisted metal box where the money had been.[12] Most of the tents had been folded up and stashed away, including the big white circus tent belonging to Mary Hitchcock and Edith Van Buren, the socialites who had arrived in Dawson as Kate was preparing to leave on her first voyage beyond Alaska and the Yukon. Terrified at the thought of having to winter in the North, Hitchcock and Van Buren had caught one of the last steamers before freeze-up, traveling upriver to Lake Bennett and then trekking on foot to the White Pass summit in order to catch the train to Skagway. It was not a journey they wished to repeat.

The wealthy heiresses had hoped to leave Dawson bearing proof that they could do what Kate had already done with her sewing: make their own money. "I just want to show my family that I know how to do something," said Van Buren, "and it would be a proud moment for me to carry home a bag of my own earnings—and I want it all in gold dust, too."[13] But their plans to open a movie theater in Dawson had failed when their animatoscope suffered from a lack of carbide and leaking gasbags, and though Hitchcock had grubstaked a hundred miners, it was too soon to tell whether her investment would pay out. In New York, she was already being lauded as a true adventurer and explorer of the North; in addition to the book she had published, she was in much demand for lectures.[14] She maintained that women who ventured north would be "most chivalrously treated," although she also warned, "there is no use in taking a cargo of things there unless you know just what to take."[15]

When Kate arrived in Dawson in the spring of 1899, two of the Tagish "Nantuck Boys," Jim and Dawson, were still in the jailhouse. As they awaited execution, their health was failing. In February, both Frank and Joe had died of pulmonary troubles. Bishop Bompas had written to Canadian officials in Ottawa, urging that the sentences of the remaining Nantuck Boys be commuted and that they be released to the custody of the Anglican mission. By putting them to death, he argued, violence in the Yukon would only increase, as their clans would seek retribution. He also pointed out that the Native people of the Yukon had been remarkably hospitable given the sudden influx of newcomers, especially since their land had been taken from them and several had been shot at and otherwise harmed by the prospectors. But his pleas were ignored—the verdict held, and the hanging of the two surviving Tagish men, though postponed for procedural reasons, was still anticipated.[16]

On a happier note, Kate was finally able to reunite with her niece, Mary Wilson, who had grown into a thin, pretty, and well-mannered eight-year-old. Though hardy and active, Selina Bompas was seventy years old. Vexed by a lack of hired help, she ceded to the bishop's request that she downsize their household. "The Indian women make so much now by working for the white men that they do not care to go to service, and I found it impossible to get any girl to help me on any terms!" she wrote. "Our elder girls have been leaving us one by one, and the Bishop wishes to give up the charge of Indian children, which has been a pretty heavy charge for the last twenty-five years."[17]

At Bonanza, Kate watched over Mary and Graphie Grace while George, Jim, and Charlie oversaw spring clean-up on the Bonanza Creek claims. The fever pitch along the creeks had slowed considerably, with miners leaving the Klondike by the boatload for Nome, where gold was said to be so plentiful that you could sift it from the sands on the beaches. Though no rush would match the Klondike in terms of sheer excitement, Nome attracted plenty of disappointed Klondikers who hoped this time they'd get lucky—some 8,000 left Dawson in 1899, either for the goldfields of Nome or a return to the lives they'd left behind.[18]

Kate and George had no reason to be tempted by Nome—the spring clean-up on their claims yielded another $125,000 in gold dust. Once Julius Huttman had been schooled in how the gravels were worked, Kate's husband gave him power of attorney to handle all activity, except sale, on his two claims and also on Jim's. Carrying $15,000 in gold, George, Kate, Graphie, and Mary Wilson left Dawson on June 20, 1899, aboard a sternwheeler bound for Skagway, where they boarded the *Humboldt* for Seattle, Kate preferring this route over the longer journey down the Yukon to St. Michael. They arrived in Seattle on July 3, checking into the Hotel Seattle in time for the girls to enjoy Independence Day festivities in the city while they awaited the arrival of the rest of their gold dust, which had been shipped on the *Roanoke* from St. Michael.[19]

This time, Kate knew what to expect in the city. But things quickly went bad. Interest in the wealthiest Indian woman in the world had never truly subsided, and she ended up giving the papers plenty to talk about. Though highly speculative and exaggerated, the stories were based on police reports and clearly have some element of truth. Most curious because it was picked up a San Francisco reporter but was not mentioned at all in the big *Seattle Daily Times*, the first incident happened only days after

Kate's arrival in the city. Summoned by buzzer to the Carmacks' hotel room shortly after George had gone upstairs, the following was reported:

> A bellboy answered it and came downstairs with a white face and bulging eyes. He had seen Mrs. Carmack doing her husband up, and he was satisfied that there was murder in the air. The clerk ran up and ran down again and called, "Police!" Two officers were hurried down from headquarters. They pounced upon Mrs. Carmack, and that terminated the most exciting fight the hotel has seen in a long time.[20]

The paper reported that George was in "a terrible condition," with his cheek cut open (but no knife found), finger marks on his throat, and his pants "nearly cut off of him." He was put to bed, and "no one was allowed to see him." The reporter speculated that George's "big, powerful Indian wife" (Kate stood only to George's shoulder) feared that "Mr. Carmack would desert her and take a white woman in her place," adding,

> Those who are not acquainted with Indian life in Alaska cannot appreciate the feelings of Indian women in such matters. Carmack, according to the hotel people, has not given his wife cause for jealousy. Possibly he may have left her for a time while looking around the city, but there is nothing to show that he has slighted her in the least.[21]

The "efforts of secrecy" noted by the reporter regarding this incident make it hard to determine what actually happened. There are no records of George commenting on it to anyone, even when it would have been to his advantage during subsequent legal battles with Kate. Was he embarrassed? Had he first turned on his wife? Had she reason for anger? Was alcohol involved? And where were the girls when all this was happening? None of these questions would ever be answered.

The incident revealed a side of Kate—a fierce temper and lack of restraint—that is documented only one other time, a mere two weeks later. In this next—and last—ugly incident, alcohol was most definitely involved. Throughout Alaska and the Yukon, the introduction of liquor had been an ongoing difficulty for Natives.[22] As booze turned up at potlatches, leaders like L'unáat had begged for its sale to be banned, though they overlooked the brewing of hoochinoo, ostensibly for trade with inland groups.[23] Canadian authorities did end up banning the sale of alcohol to Natives, but access was still easy, especially for hooch. Among both miners and Natives in the North, binge drinking was a problem. Jim and Charlie were both known for drinking to excess but not Kate, although by her own admission she did have a fondness for port wine.

Having been quietly asked to leave the Seattle Hotel after the July 6 incident, the Carmacks checked into different lodgings, where they waited for the arrival of the *Topeka*, which docked on July 21, with Jim, Charlie, Jim's wife Mary, and their daughter Daisy aboard.[24]

Four days later, George went with some businessmen "down the [Puget] Sound" to investigate some investments. When Kate went to visit Jim and his wife at their hotel, she found them drinking with "a number of gamblers" who had smuggled a gallon of booze into the room for the purpose of getting Jim drunk. "So much for the debasing tendencies of great wealth and the firewater of the white man," noted a reporter for the *Seattle Post-Intelligencer*:

> Before the supply of liquor was shut off, Mrs. Carmack and her sister-in-law had ceased to discuss Klondike cooking receipts, sub-Arctic management of servants and the utility of polar bear skins for crazy quilts and strayed into areas less profitable for argument . . . Mrs. Carmack, remembering the valorous deeds of forefathers made a swift grab for her sister's scalp lock.[25]

According to this account—a prime example of how Native people were marginalized by stereotypes—Jim kicked Kate out of the room, at which point "the exiled Mrs. Carmack crooning a wild and warlike melody and punctuating the pauses in the tempo with bits of Indian profanity, started out on a hunt for her absent spouse." According to newspaper reports, Kate was arrested while "executing an aboriginal Yukon war dance" on the second floor of the Seattle Hotel. Both she and Jim were hauled off to jail.[26]

In the company of "several white men of more or less shady reputation" at the bar of the Seattle Hotel, Charlie kept drinking. A police officer suggested he return to his room, but Charlie ignored him. Hours later, he appeared of his own volition at the police station, saying he'd been robbed. As it turned out, Charlie's valuables were right where he'd left them, in the hotel safe—twenty-seven gold rings, two gold watches, five gold nugget scarf pins, a diamond stud pin, two gold nugget chains, and $400 in cash.[27]

The night Kate spent in jail was sobering, in every sense of the word. Hauled into court the next day, she was fined $3.60. She refused to say who had furnished the alcohol.[28] The incident was a reckoning: Never again would Kate make the news for bad conduct.

George was furious, although when he wrote to Rose of the incident he made no mention of Kate's night in jail, saying only that Jim and Charlie had gotten drunk and ended up in the "cooler." He also complained that the papers had not told the truth. "I feel like takeing an ax and smashing something," he wrote. He told Rose not to worry about him and not to mind what she saw in the papers. "I don't drink and I don't care what the rest does," he said—a bit of a stretcher since, according to fellow prospectors and by his own admission elsewhere, George Carmack had been known to tie one on with the rest.

While avoiding the specifics of Kate's embarrassing encounter with the law, George did tell his sister, "If Kate's trunks were here I would ship her back to Dyea mighty quick she is getting so unreasonable I am simply to good to her that's all."[29]

CHAPTER FIFTEEN

SIMPLY A MISERY

WITHOUT EXCUSING KATE'S BEHAVIOR in these unfortunate incidents, it's worth noting that the pressures on her were mounting. Her journey home had been brief, and George had plans to relocate permanently to places where she would be required to mimic the behaviors expected of her by her husband and everyone else.[1]

After George's anger cooled, the Carmacks, including Mary Wilson, proceeded to San Francisco and then to San Benito County. A strict Baptist, Rose stood for no drinking, which allowed for the return of calm to Kate's life in a place where the demands and expectations were more measured than in Seattle or San Francisco—ranch chores, church, sewing, and caring for the girls. She settled in for another winter in California, with Mary and Graphie Grace attending one of the country schools along Cottonwood Road and George's sister happy to dote on the two of them.

Despite the trouble in Seattle, Kate understood that she was *'anyAdi* now—a town child, a noblewoman—not only because she was the daughter of a Deisheetaan chief but also because she was rich. As *'anyAdi,* she had an obligation to be generous and knowledgeable. She had a duty to carry herself with a certain dignity—no more flying into a rage or sleeping off a drinking binge in jail.[2] Never mind what had happened in July—all over San Benito County, she would come to be known as a lady.

In September, George got word that a deal he had initiated during their stay in Seattle had been inked—he had purchased an interest in a lawsuit, taking a quit claim deed on a Seattle property valued at more than $200,000 from owners who had exhausted their funds to litigate its disputed title. Even his own attorney called it "a bold speculation on Carmack's part."[3] In what would prove an ironic twist, the land interest George had purchased was rooted in an ugly divorce and contested remarriage.

The century drew to a close. In San Francisco, every available officer was on duty, alert to the throng gathered along Market Street to welcome the New Year. Tin horns shrilled and cowbells clanged. Inspired by alcohol, grown men hooted and howled, strong-arming evergreen boughs waved by fellow revelers at their female companions. At midnight, the ruckus dimmed as a lone bugler stepped from the crowd and blew the long mournful notes of taps,[4] a farewell to the nineteenth century. The newspaper offered a glowing report of the overall prospects of the new century: "Prosperity oozing from every one of the country's pores, with new gold fields looming up all over the north, and money in every one's hands and more to back it in every pocket."[5]

A hundred miles to the south of the city, where the Calaveras fault line jagged off the San Andreas Fault, it was only the burrowing owls that hooted, and when cowbells clanked, it was around the necks of the few cattle that roamed the Watson ranch. Three winters had passed since Jim had found the gold foretold in his encounters with Wealth Woman. Back in the Yukon, Kate might have welcomed the New Year by plodding across a frozen lake, the skin soles of her boots rustling in the snow, her breath barely visible in the star-scattered night. She would have taught Graphie and Mary how you had to check your muskrat snares early in the day, while it was still dark, and how after you skinned them you tossed the carcasses to the dogs, except the heads—those you burned.[6] Instead, the moist California air prickled her skin as she watched the fog rolling east from the ocean while neighboring ranchers eyed the skies, anxious for rain—but not too much—before the dry heat of summer fell over the California hills.

For Kate, there would be no more famine, no more winter camping in brush shelters, no more hauling fifty-pound packs up a mountain to earn the wages to buy dolls and clothes for Graphie. As befitting a woman of wealth, she wore gold jewelry and dressed in fine clothes and stayed in fancy hotels when she and George visited San Francisco. Still, she was not entirely at ease. Her family was far away. She was ill-equipped to teach her daughter the right ways to behave in a place where she barely understood them herself. And could she really count on George's wealth, when it was Jim's connections with Wealth Woman that accounted for their fortune?

For his part, George was ready to be done with the North; every time he went back, his rheumatism acted up. And even in the California hills, there was talk of how the Yukon was changing. The local paper published a letter from Charley Sairs, a San Benito County resident who had gone north to Dawson, encouraged no doubt by George Carmack's luck. "Every time I think of Hollister and all the old boys," Sairs wrote to a friend back home, "my mouth waters for the chicken dinners at your hospitable mountain ranch. I have been 'up against it' but will come out all right. This is a hard country on a man, it tells on his constitution."

Dawson had burned again, Charley said. This time, he predicted, it would not be rebuilt. "It will be deserted by spring, for everybody is going to Nome. Lots go out over the ice every day now. I shall go myself by the first boat. Like the others, I intend to rock out gold on the beach and then come home in the fall. Dawson has seen its best days. Like all mining camps it rolled 'em high and it will die easy." Charley wrote that he had five mines he was trying to sell, but he said you couldn't sell a $20 piece for $15 in Dawson.[7]

From California, George began to divest himself of his ties with the Klondike. He mortgaged his interest in No. 1 below Discovery to Howard Hamilton Hart. That left two claims to be worked: George's Discovery claim and Jim's No. 1 above. Regardless of how much gold was left, the Carmacks had plenty of money—newspapers estimated their wealth at $300,000 to $400,000. In addition to his Seattle investments, George also bought into the Farmers Hay Company of San Benito County that spring. Unfortunately, the year started out poorly for hay, all fog and no rain, with local creeks slowing to a trickle.[8] He also had the 160 acres he'd purchased from Huttman, down the road from Rose and James.

In the first week in April 1900, during the Moon of the Coming-Back Swans, George Carmack left Tres Pinos by train, headed north for one last spring clean-up. For reasons that remain unclear, Kate stayed behind with Rose, James, and the girls. Maybe she had begun to feel settled in California. Maybe she was concerned about leaving the girls. Or maybe after the embarrassment of the previous summer, George refused to take her. A small piece in the Hollister paper mentioned his departure, noting that he expected to be gone several months. The day after he left, a hard rain fell, the way Kate knew it did when someone was sad about leaving a place.[9]

Later, when George Carmack began making headlines again, out-of-town papers would put a dramatic spin on the moment of his departure. "Mrs. Carmack last saw her husband April last, when she and her child accompanied him to the depot," one reporter wrote. "She expected that she was to go with him on his journey, but as the train pulled out, Carmack grasped her hand, shook it, jumped on one of the moving cars and was gone."[10]

As the seasons turned from spring to summer, Kate waited for her husband's return. She was invited to a wedding in Tulare, where the Carmacks had relatives. The invitation, addressed to Mr. and Mrs. Geo. W. Carmack, would one day be filed in court among other evidence that George and Kate really had been husband and wife.

By one estimate, George's "clean-up" that year was his best ever, yielding $400,000 in gold.[11] In the wee hours of the morning on July 3, he left Dawson City, arriving in Seattle on July 15 and in San Francisco on July 25, an easy day's journey by train from Tres Pinos. But he did not continue on to the ranch. Instead, he mailed a letter to Rose:

> I suppose you think it strange that I do not come straight home. But the fact is and I might as well tell you first as last I cant never live with Kate again it is simply a misery. I don't know whether you ever noticed or not but I am not happy with her. You may blame me as you may but I will make no excuses. You may tell her so if you like . . . There are no use for her to try to see me because she can't find me . . . as soon as Kate leaves I will come and see you.[12]

Rose was shocked. She and James (who was ailing) traveled by train to Gilroy, where they met with George face-to-face. When they returned to the ranch on Cottonwood Road, they gave Kate the news: Her husband was not coming back. He had sold everything in Dawson. He would not come to talk with her himself. What he wanted was for her to leave Graphie (and presumably Mary) with Rose and travel alone to Seattle, where Jim and Charlie were staying. There, Kate could meet with George's lawyers, and they would fix things.

The situation was incomprehensible. Only two years had passed since George had bragged to reporters of how he would sail with her and Graphie across the Atlantic to the exposition in Paris. There had been trouble in Seattle, to be sure, but that was behind them. Every indication from her husband when he'd left was that he would return. In his desk at the ranch, he'd left his watch, several shares of Carmack mining stock and Microbane Medical stock, plus notes regarding money owed to him by his neighbors. While away—until May, anyhow—he'd written letters from Dawson, addressed to Kate Carmack. How could he have all at once decided that life with her was so unbearable? And why did he refuse to come and tell her himself?

A letter was written on Kate's behalf, not by Rose but by one of her Tres Pinos neighbors. Addressed to "Mr. Jim, and Charley

Tirgress [Tagish], Seattle Hotell," the letter explains Kate's predicament: though in California, her husband refused to come to see her and, according to Rose, Kate would never see him again. "I don't like to go to Seattle to my home by myself all alone," Kate says in the letter. "I got a nice home . . . I wish you would come and see me. I cry myself sick." She talks about wanting to see Susy, meaning Susie George, daughter of L'unáat and Aagé, who sometimes acted as an interpreter for Jim. "I can talk good inglish to Susy," Kate says. "Love to you all."[13]

Somehow, the letter never got mailed, leaving Kate alone to sort through what to do next.

Rose wrote to George—not complaining; she seems never to have complained—of the difficulties he'd left her to handle. Kate refused to leave. James was in failing health; to get proper medical care, he needed to move into town. No doubt sensing the stress in the household, Mary begged to be allowed to return to Mrs. Bompas.

In his reply from Seattle, where he'd traveled on business, George admitted he might be selfish, but he said he couldn't help it. He urged Rose to spare no expense to keep James comfortable while he lived and to spare no expense with regard to his final resting place once he was gone. Beyond that, the bulk of his letter deals with how busy he was and how he needed Rose to tend to some unfinished business he'd left in California.

His immediate concern was divesting himself of his partners, Jim and Charlie, effectively dissolving the family collective. "Thank goodness they go back north tomorrow and I am done with them," he wrote, noting that Jim had gotten himself a night in the station house after another drunken spree. "It seems like the more I save for them the more they want. I sold my interest in the Klondike to Jim. I sold it cheap just to get rid of them."

The deal wasn't as generous as George made it out to be. He traded his share in the Discovery Claim and Jim's claim at No. 1 above, both of which had been extensively worked, for Jim and Charlie's share ($20,000) of the real estate the three of them had purchased in Seattle. For the remaining claim, No. 1 below, the claim in which he'd promised Jim half an interest, he took $10,000 from Jim—but six months earlier, he'd mortgaged this very same claim to Howard Hamilton Hart, leaving Jim with a share that was potentially worthless.

The Seattle property George planned to mortgage to Rose so that "if Kate wants to get to much she wont get nothing."[14] He also asked his sister to empty his desk of its contents. If anything was missing, Rose was to "go after her [Kate] about it tell her that I sent for them and if she don't give them to you, I will have her arrested for stealing."[15]

After giving these instructions, George wrote another letter, this one addressed to "my little niece Mary." He told her he'd heard about her wanting to go back to Mrs. Bompas:

> Now Mary I think you are very ungratefull for what I have done for you. I do not want Graphie to be rude to you but you must remember that Graphie has more right in the house than you have . . . I saw your Father in Dawson and I asked him to write to you and send you something but he did not do it. He don't seem to want to do any thing for you so you see I have got to take care of you and you can't go back to Mrs. Bompas. If you cant be a good girl I will have to send you to the Sisters School but I think you can be good if you try. Now kiss Aunt Rosa and Graphie and I will be always your uncle George Carmack.[16]

Having no alternative, Mary stayed in California, while Uncle George kept his resolve to stay away from San Benito County. In his stead, a stranger arrived. She called herself Mrs. Mary St. Clair; George called her "that fuzzy-headed blond woman" or "fuzzy wuzzy." She had traveled all the way from Dawson to inform Kate that at the Palace Hotel in San Francisco, George Carmack was living with another woman.[17]

Until the arrival of Mary St. Clair, neither Kate nor Rose had a clue about this other woman, who'd left Dawson on July 3 in the company of George Washington Carmack: Marguerite Saftig, also known as Marguerite Laimee, Marguerite LeGrand, and, to the Northwest Mounted Police, as Bridget or Biddy McCarthy. The daughter of parents who had emigrated from France to San Francisco, Marguerite was a short, stocky woman with a large mouth and a formidable gaze. She had arrived in Dawson in July of 1898 in the company of Frenchman Joseph LeGrand, a "macque," or pimp, with whom she had traveled from the silver camps of Idaho to the gold mines of South Africa and the gold fields of Australia. In Dawson, she ran a cigar shop, a common front for prostitutes.

George Carmack's propensity to play loose with the facts was nothing compared to Marguerite's disregard for the truth. In clinical terms, she appears to have been a pathological liar: brazen, manipulative, determined to get her way, and oblivious to the gross contradictions in her various stories.[18] She had a violent temper and was not a person to be crossed.[19] But she was also charming and affectionate, especially with George Carmack.

Like Rose and Kate, Marguerite had married young, at age fourteen. Shortly afterward, while in Spokane, she attempted to divorce her husband, but the case was never resolved. After working the sex trade in the silver mining districts of Idaho, she traveled the world with Joe LeGrand, moving from gold camp to gold camp; later, she would say that LeGrand had followed her all over the world because he wanted to marry her.[20]

When she and LeGrand landed in Dawson City, Marguerite found that the sex industry there operated much as in other mining camps, with a hierarchy among the women. At the top were the dance hall girls, those who performed on stage and also those who danced with miners for the price of a drink. Not all of these women exchanged sex for cash, but a good many of them did. Outside of the dance halls, there were upscale brothels run by madams; in these, the gold miners showed a preference for French women.[21]

With cigar stores as a front for their illicit activities, women like Marguerite were in the middle of the social structure of the demi-world. In the business she ran first at the Green Tree Hotel and later (after the Green Tree burned in a fire blamed on a prostitute) at the corner of Second and Queen, Marguerite appears to have worked independently of LeGrand, setting her own fees, conditions, and hours. Despite what Marguerite would later claim, none of the "cigar store owners" in Dawson were especially wealthy; few had assets totaling more than $400.[22] But at least they weren't splitting their receipts with a madam or a pimp, and on the social scale they were above the common prostitutes who worked out of the Lousetown cribs.

The Northwest Canadian Mounted Police checked in regularly with Marguerite (or Biddy, as they knew her), as they did with all prostitutes in Dawson City. Following an outbreak of venereal disease in the fall of 1899,[23] the Yukon Council had ordered that Dawson prostitutes submit to monthly examinations and display certificates of health in their places of business, be they brothels or cribs or cigar stores. Even after the federal government put a stop to this practice on the grounds that it effectively legitimized prostitution, many women continued to display the certificates of health, which had proven good for business.[24]

George Carmack entered Marguerite's life at an opportune time. In Dawson, pressure was mounting to stop the practice of solicitation from venues like her cigar store. It didn't help that the new century had begun with yet another fire started inadvertently by a prostitute, this one wiping out a whole city block between 2nd and 3rd avenues.[25] Now three for three in their association with Dawson's big fires,[26] women like Marguerite were facing increasing calls to move their trade outside the city limits.[27]

If Marguerite had learned anything traveling from gold camp to gold camp, it was to assess your options before your hand was forced. Nome was one possibility; plenty of women in the trade were headed that way. But by all accounts, Nome was a mess. Claim-jumping was rampant—almost every claim had two owners, and some had half a dozen—which explained why one out of every three newcomers was flat broke. Nome was also much seamier than Dawson, full of thieves and murderers and lacking in opportunity, according to one prostitute who'd worked both towns.[28]

And while Dawson's glory was fading, the town was far from washed up. Each time it rose from the ashes, it became a little more sophisticated. By 1900, there were more horses than dogs in the streets, and shops with real plate glass windows displayed a tantalizing array of goods. And though there might be more miners leaving than coming, across muddy Queen Street from Marguerite's storefront, the doors of the Canadian National Bank swung all day long with the comings and goings of miners depositing gold.

When she met George Carmack in the spring of 1900, Marguerite was twenty-six years old. She liked to say that the two of them became acquainted at a dinner party hosted by Mr. and Mrs. Joe Collins. But the only Mr. and Mrs. Collins who resided in the area were at Bonanza Creek, working their American Gulch claims, not exactly well-situated for fine entertaining.[29] There was also the small problem of women like Marguerite not being welcome in the homes of Dawson's more respectable families, not unless they married and abandoned their wanton ways, and sometimes not even then.

However they met, whatever they did in the days and nights spent together—activities, then as now, best left to the imagination—Marguerite acquired a clear and sudden sense of direction. She wasted no time. By July, she'd packed up and said goodbye to the Klondike, leaving not for Nome, and not with Joseph LeGrand, but in the company of Kate's husband.

CHAPTER SIXTEEN

NOWHERE TO TURN

THEFT, EXTORTION, KIDNAPPING, and intent to murder—the intrigue associated with Kate's abandonment escalated quickly. Turn-of-the-century Victorian fascinations were ignited by idea of this woman spurned, an Indian no less, and her stakes in an unlikely fortune in gold.

Autumn of 1900 was indeed a desperate season for Kate. Adding to the trauma of George's refusal to return was an eye ailment that would plague her for the next two years, causing intense pain and a sensation she described as something like a skin growing over her eyes. At home in the Yukon, she might have gathered and dried the red buttons of "eye medicine moss" to grind into a powder that she could mix with warm water as a wash to soothe her eyes.[1] But there was no moss of any kind in the San Benito ranch country where George had deserted her.

Though it's impossible to know for certain, Kate may have been suffering an immunologic response to the tuberculosis pathogen, to which she would surely have been exposed. Of the waves of post contact diseases that struck Natives of the Yukon and Alaska in the nineteenth century—smallpox, syphilis, typhoid, measles, scarlet fever, influenza—tuberculosis hung on the longest, a slow-building but persistent epidemic that would not peak until well into the 1900s.[2] The disease was yet another negative effect of the gold rush, with many of the would-be prospectors either carriers of TB or actively symptomatic—at the end of the nineteenth century, an estimated 70 to 90 percent of the urban population in Europe and the United States was infected.[3] The rheumatism George suffered may also have been a manifestation of tuberculosis, a disease that killed many of his friends, including Arthur Harper and Joe LaDue, who died of tuberculosis in 1898 and 1901, respectively.[4]

Only as recently as 1882 had a physician discovered that the cause of tuberculosis was bacterial as opposed to hereditary. Beyond the sanatoriums where the wealthy could hope for a recovery brought on by rest and a change of climate, physicians were at a loss when it came to treating the disease, which was easily mistaken for other disorders. In some individuals, tuberculosis manifested as phlyctenular keratoconjunctivitis (PKC), resulting in symptoms such as those Kate suffered—redness, pain, and tearing of the eyes. In the worst cases, the result was corneal scarring and blindness.[5]

Whatever the source of Kate's crippling eye pain,[6] she relied on treatment from a doctor of magnetism. Magnetism, also called "animal magnetism," had developed from the practices of the eighteenth century German doctor Franz Mesmer, who touted a technique in which the healer sat facing his patient, their knees touching, and ran his hands above the afflicted parts of the body to stimulate fluids that could overcome whatever external influences were disrupting the individual's health and wellbeing.[7] By the time Kate was treated for her eye ailment, the practice developed by Mesmer had evolved significantly, and generally the term *hypnosis* was favored over the *magnetism*. But Dr. L. A. Steward of San Benito County, who addressed Kate's eye pain, still called herself a doctor of magnetism. Through what she termed the "Afflications of Vital Magnatism," Steward believed Kate's condition required no medication; instead, she "doctored" Kate's eyes and "Sciattica Nerves"[8] using hypnosis.

The methods of a hypnotist in those days were in some ways similar to what Kate might have expected from an Indian doctor, or shaman. Though helpless to curb the epidemics that devastated Native groups throughout Alaska and the Yukon, shamans were still called upon to treat other ailments that failed to respond to traditional medicines. When summoned to treat an illness, they would typically bring woven mats along with animal bones, rattles, and other objects that represented their helper spirits. They might lay their hands on the head of the afflicted person, much as Dr. Steward would have laid hands on Kate to transfer of her "mesmeric aura." And not unlike a hypnotist, a shaman would sometimes speak directly to an illness in order to make peace with it.[9]

Despite Dr. Steward's treatments, Kate continued to suffer, and her distress became even worse when Rose turned her out of the house. Increasingly, James needed medical care, prompting the Watsons to make a temporary move to Hollister, the county seat of San Benito. The girls could come along, Rose made clear, but Kate was not welcome. All in all, Rose's stressful life would be greatly simplified if Kate would only do as George asked—leave the girls in California and go back to the Yukon without a fight.

What Rose didn't count on was Kate's determination to remain with the girls, and the way in which Rose's own friends, neighbors, and family would rally to her sister-in-law's side. With their help, Kate found lodging in Hollister, a little cottage next door to the house that Rose had rented. More than anything, Kate wanted her girls back.[10] She believed Rose was teaching them "queer things," including stories about Kate getting drunk and packing a revolver with the intent of killing George.[11]

To live on, Kate had $500 that her husband had sent with the idea that she would leave San Benito County and never return. Of this sum, Kate deposited $240 with the Farmers Exchange, a retail establishment not unlike a trading post, and $180 in the Bank of Hollister.[12] At the urging of Mary St. Clair, the "fuzzy blonde" from Dawson City, Kate put a wobbly signature to papers that authorized a local judge with dubious credentials to represent her in a suit for divorce from George Carmack on the grounds of desertion and adultery. The suit sought custody of Graphie Grace and a division of community property that included an estimated value of $1 million for the Bonanza Creek claims, $20,000 in bank deposits, $30,000 in Seattle real estate, 160 acres in San Benito County, the Farmers Hay Company stock, promissory notes, and an unknown sum in cash.[13]

The motives of Mrs. St. Clair in helping to initiate this suit for divorce remain unclear. According to at least one of Kate's California friends, Mary St. Clair said that once Kate and George were divorced, she (Mrs. St. Clair) would bring her own suit for $75,000 against George Carmack for breach of promise to marry, a contention that sheds yet another light on Kate's jealous rage the previous summer.[14] Adamant though she was in her resolve to punish George Carmack, the details of Mary St. Clair's motives never emerged. Perhaps George had taken up with her first, before he met Marguerite. Had he promised marriage without Mary St. Clair knowing that he already had a wife, she may in fact have had legal grounds to sue him when he failed to make good on his promise.

In San Francisco, the newspaper alluded to another motive that involved a theft from George's lover, Marguerite:

> Also from the north, all the way from Dawson, came a strange lady, who took the affairs of Mrs. Carmack in her own hands and proceeded to assist her in compelling George Carmack to giving one-half of his property to his wife. What the motive of the lady from Dawson was, she told no one, and the only clew is that she has a grievance against a certain woman in Seattle named in the complaint for divorce as a correspondent. It is alleged by the lady from Dawson that a diamond was stolen from her by this Seattle person, which shows they have met before, and there may be other reasons than that of the missing diamond which prompt her to make a 6,000-mile trip for the purposes of taking such an active interest in fighting the battles of a lonely Indian who does not even realize what it was all about.[15]

Whatever the motives behind Kate's lawsuit, it infuriated her husband.[16] In response, he hired a man to spy on Kate and her supporters in San Benito County. "He knows every move that is made," George wrote to his sister. "He pumps every one and he pumps them good and dry . . . he is very careful."[17]

George's spy may have been discreet, but the newsmen were not. "Sensational Suit" read the headlines. "Klondike Miner Millionaire Opposes Divorce." In actuality, what George Carmack opposed was not the divorce itself but the fact that through her divorce complaint, Kate had demanded custody of their daughter and half of the Carmack wealth.[18] Her divorce complaint alleged that George and Marguerite had lived in Dawson as husband and wife from May 9 until July 3 (1900) and that they had traveled together to San Francisco, where they continued to share a residence at the corner of Filbert and Taylor, where George "lavished upon the Saftig female jewels of unknown value and habitually squanders upon her from $50 to $100 per day."[19]

Besides the news items that named the new lover whom he'd been trying to keep secret, George had other troubles. "The Indians Jim and Charley is down on me to kill," he wrote to Rose. "That [is] what I get for being honest with them. It seems like the more you do for some people the more you get it in the neck."[20] With the help of his attorneys, George was preparing a countersuit for divorce, in which he planned to charge Kate with infidelity.[21]

As affidavits were being gathered, L. A. Steward, the doctor of magnetism, again visited Kate, this time in Hollister. Finding her unable to go out due to the pain in her eyes, head, neck, and back, Steward stabled her horse and moved in with her, assuring her she would remain until Kate got her children back. Kate worried over what the doctor would charge. Indian doctors required payment up front, though this was considered a gift to the shaman's helping spirits and not to the shaman herself—an article of clothing, especially a handkerchief, was a common form of compensation, as were silver coins.

The doctor of magnetism took over Kate's correspondence, writing on her behalf to John Durst, a San Francisco attorney

Kate had met through mutual friends, people she and George had known in the Klondike. George's desertion caused her great anguish, Kate said in this letter, which had been compounded when Rose took the girls. If George was going to leave her, she at least wanted him to come like a man and tell her so, and arrange their separation between the two of them. "I get crazy in my head," wrote Steward on Kate's behalf, adding that if Rose didn't return the girls, she might do "something bad." To the letter, Steward added this postscript:

> This American In. Lady has sent for me to assist her in her present trouble. I think Mr. Carmack can arrange things more agreeable, and had better do so. He Lady and wife has been realy very sick, and she has made good warm friends here among the people of this town and neighborhood and she has been a lady. Everyone speakes in her favor and she was very much pleased at it. But it seems from what I gather restrictions has become overbearing regarding enough to live on. And she don't understand what it all means—although she keeps cooler than I would under the circumstances—and she should have her child if she wants it. She is just as nice and capable of rearing it as her sister-in-law.[22]

In his reply to Kate's letter, Durst wrote that he had known since September that George Carmack was living with another woman in San Francisco; recently, he had also been informed of George's pending suit against Kate for divorce.[23] "While my acquaintance with you and your husband is very slight," Durst wrote, "I think the charge that you have not been true to him is absolutely false."

Kate would have to fight such accusations, the attorney warned, or she would stand to lose all the property and her child. "You cannot expect him voluntarily to do what is right by you, or to go back to you," Durst advised. "What you must do is protect yourself."[24] Durst would become Kate's strongest and most capable advocate. He wrote to the publisher of the San Benito newspaper, and the two of them concurred that it would be best if she were to drop the suit for divorce initiated at the urging of the mysterious Mary St. Clair. Instead, they decided, Kate should contest George's suit for divorce with the help of a more reputable attorney.[25]

As the legal wrangling heated up, George became increasingly belligerent. One item that fueled his anger was a full-page story on page two of the October 21, 1900, Sunday edition of the *San Francisco Call*. "The Romance of Indian Kate Who Showed the Gold of the Klondike to George Carmack," read the headline. The piece features a photo of Kate in a dark belted dress and a tidy, flat-topped hat adorned with dotted fabric and three feathers. On her lap is Graphie Grace, hair braided, wearing a simple hat and a belted satin dress with dark collar and ruffles, along with high-topped boots. At the bottom of the page is a photo of a white clapboard house; "The Carmack San Benito home" reads the caption.

But the focal point of the piece is a large pen-and-ink drawing of a dark-haired Indian woman tending to a pale, ailing man covered in blankets, an illustration that accompanies the "true story" of "real gold," and "an Indian maiden, faithful and true, who showed the gold to her paleface lover that she might win him forever to her heart."

Though admitting that Kate's telling of her story "has not been clear, for she does not speak English well," the writer appears to have had no qualms about filling in around the edges, prefacing his tale with this disclaimer: "From as nearly as the romance of her life can be made, from the simple statements of fact which she has given, it is this."[26] Kate's "simple statements of fact" were these: Her family had found George Carmack starving and weak.[27] They helped him recover, and as his wife, Kate had continued to care for him as they traveled throughout the Yukon and Alaska, gathering food and sewing his clothes and nursing him when he was sick.

From this straightforward version of events, the writer spun a story of how George Carmack, with a prospector's ingenuity, set out to acquire from the Indians of the North the secret of where gold might be found. But these Indians, with "the reticence of wisdom rather than the dumbness of stupidity" knew exactly what would happen if the white men found gold: "their wild forests and streams would be destroyed, and their fish and game ruined, and so they kept their secret."[28] In his "long and weary" hunt for gold, the article says, George witnessed the deaths of two of his companions. When he himself lay desperate and dying, covered only by ragged furs, he had the good fortune to be found by "Indian Kate, then round-faced, bronzy, brown, and laughing."[29]

"This is the only part of the story which she [Kate] tells with clearness," the writer interjects, "and upon the telling and dwelling upon it has come to mean all of her life, for she has not grown mentally in the least from what she was as a wild forest child with the simple wants a natural life creates."[30] While the image of "wild forest child" plays nicely into the stereotypes of the day, the fact was that Kate would have had little reason to elaborate. She and her family had acted as they knew they should, helping a man who was hungry and sick. What more needed to be said?

Quite a lot, apparently, to satisfy the reading public—when Kate came upon George in his distress, his face "drawn, white and hard," the writer says, she knew instantly that he was "the ideal for which she had waited," having "scorned all the advances of the brown-faced men of her tribe" as she "sigh[ed] in her heart for the companionship of one of the tall, strong, active men of the south."[31] By rubbing two sticks and adding a bit of pitch pine and bark, she started a roaring fire, the writer explains, in order to save the man who would become her true love. She removed her own fur parka, "warm with the heat of her body," and covered him with it.

Her own people were short on food, so there was no sense in her taking George to their camp, and besides, the medicine of the Indian doctor might prove too strong for him. So she sacrificed her own food to nourish him, raiding the cache in her village under the cover of darkness. She built him a shelter of pine boughs next to a large rock that would soak up heat from the fire to warm him. For months she visited him in this shelter she'd made, shyly bringing him food. When spring came and he had recovered, "with all her womanly arts she persuaded him [to stay], for she had grown to love the life she had saved."[32]

After their Indian marriage, this romanticized Kate reasoned that she would lose her husband unless she defied the warnings of her brother and told him the secret of where he could find gold. So it was that she led George Carmack to the rippling creek where there were riches beyond measure. Having saved his life and led him to his fortune, she then followed him to "the land of the sun," where she was "proud to be seen with her big handsome white husband."[33]

In her present troubles, the writer maintained, Kate's only solace was her bicycle, "on which she takes solitary rides through the mountains of the coast range." Though Rose tried to get her to leave, she hung about the house in Hollister because Graphie was there, leaving only at nighttime. "The child, too, with that peculiar unhappy disposition which often shows in persons of mixed race," the writer says, "cares little for her mother who adores her."[34]

The paper promised a sensational divorce suit that would be "good reading for those who are interested in mysterious ladies, loving Indian girls, and tons of gold."[35] And George Carmack vowed to give it to them. When he learned that Kate had filed for dismissal of her lawsuit, he refused to let the matter drop. "I wont dismiss mine untill every thing is settled," he wrote to Rose. "What business is it to them what state rooms I ocupied and what Hotels I stoped at and who I stoped with. I considered my self a free man and I could do what I please and I don't care how many letters they got, and if there is another woman in the case it will be one that I will not be ashamed of and one that they cant hold a candle to if I should produce her."[36]

It was the first time George had hinted in his letters to Rose that there was another woman behind his sudden decision to abandon his wife. What he failed to mention was that on October 30, 1900, five days before sending the letter, he and Marguerite Saftig Laimee, aka Marguerite LeGrand, aka Biddy McCarthy, had been married in a private ceremony in Olympia, Washington. Given that George was already married and Marguerite's divorce from her first husband had never been finalized, the legitimacy of their union would later be called into question. However genuine their love may have been, the whirlwind courtship and marriage seemed a determined move on the part of Marguerite to secure George's affections—and his assets.

During the month of November, George barraged Rose with letters in which he made multiple requests. He wanted her to send his shotgun and his safe deposit box key. He wanted her to retrieve his box of nuggets from the bank and send it to him by express. He wanted the mortgage and note from Charley Watson. He wanted her to get a note from Jake Watson that set up terms of interest in exchange for George paying one of his bills. He wanted his stock certificates. He wanted to know how Frank Curtis, the handyman whose child Rose was raising, stood with regard to the dispute between George and Kate. He wanted to know whether his neighbor was "as thick as ever" with Kate,[37] asking, "Does Dr. [George] Mankins come around and tell his troubles to you any more [?] I wish he would tell some of them to me out where no one could hear him."[38]

He warned Rose not to confide in their brother-in-law Julius Huttman, to whom he had granted power of attorney over his mining claims: "I wouldn't trust him as far as I could throw a streetcar," George wrote.[39] Informed that public sentiment was against him in San Benito County, he said, "I wonder what that public consists of. I don't think a Dago scavenger would hawl them in a gut cart through the streets after dark."[40]

He also fumed over Kate. The judge would find her "no fit subject to raise a child," and besides, he claimed, she was only pretending to want Graphie to spite George and Rose and to get more money from him.[41] "If she should take her to Alaska I will informe the Canadian Police," he wrote, "and the first time she gets intoxicated and makes any trouble they will take the child away from her, I know that as soon as she reaches her people they wont do a thing but get on a big drunk and the whole caboodle will get arrested because I will have the police posted and they have very little love for Indians up there."[42]

Though Rose's husband was near death, George still refused to return to San Benito County. "I could not get in town without every body knowing it and there are some of them just mean enough to set Kate after me and kick up a row so she could get some kind of a holt on me again and cause me more trouble."[43] He began using a private seal, an "M," on his letters, and he began numbering the missives. On some he added a postscript instructing Rose not to repeat any part of the letter to anyone, and to destroy it when she was done reading—instructions that Rose ignored.

Assuring her he had the advice of the best lawyers in Seattle, Vancouver, and San Francisco, George brushed off Rose's warning that photos of him, presumably with his new wife, were going to be introduced into the case.[44] In preliminary proceedings, he denied any income beyond $200 per month from the hotel he had purchased. He denied that he had ever been married to Kate. He denied that Graphie Grace was his child.[45] He vowed that he would not allow the divorce suit to be withdrawn unless Kate signed an agreement that released him from all obligations to her.[46]

In response to Kate's "wailing over the custody of her two children," Dr. Steward ushered her into Superior Court, where kidnapping charges were filed against Rose Watson for keeping Graphie Grace and Mary. The demand was that the girls be returned and damages of $10,000 be rendered.[47] This legal maneuver got Rose's attention: she allowed Graphie and Mary to return to Kate.

Weary of the lawyers and the courthouse and the papers, Kate and the girls planned to leave town with a stranger who was coming from Gilroy to get her. It was a plot to kidnap and kill Kate, wrote one of the neighbors to George.[48]

Coupled with her eye ailment and her husband's continued absence, the various people who took an interest in her situation taxed Kate's skills at adapting and negotiating. She grew increasingly desperate. Corresponding with John Durst, the president of the Bank of Hollister wrote, "I will say in confidence she has some bad advisers among her so called friends, and she does not know her mind from one moment to another . . . she [Kate] has no idea of money or accounts, and no doubt is honest in what she says. I have felt sorry for her, and have endeavored to assist her, but it is hard to make her understand."[49]

Writing from San Francisco, Durst urged Kate to have patience with the workings of the courts and not worry herself into sickness. On November 28, 1900, a motion filed on her behalf for substitution of attorneys was affirmed by the Superior Court in San Benito County, effecting the dismissal of the initial suit for divorce. Local newspaper publisher A. D. Shaw and a reputable Hollister attorney would serve as Kate's new counsel, working in cooperation with John Durst.[50]

In early December, Shaw traveled to San Francisco, where he met with George Carmack and his attorneys; in a letter to Rose, George admitted that Shaw appeared "very Gentlmanly and reasonable."[51] George wanted Rose to ask Kate, if Kate would talk to her, what she had done with the $500 he had sent, which he felt should have been enough for her and the girls to live on for a year. Two days later, he wrote again, urging Rose to be wary of contact with Kate. "So it seems that Kate is trying to make friends with you. Lookout I think that someone sends her to see and hear what she can, or else to try and get hold of some of my letters, they have been trying all kinds of schemes to get me to write to her."[52]

George's warning reached Rose as she was grieving the death of her husband. On receiving news of her loss, George wrote with his sympathies, noting how much it hurt him not to have been there before James died and how trying it was for him to not be able to attend the funeral. In order to "propitiate for my enforced neglect," he reiterated his offer to have a tombstone made for James, bearing whatever inscription Rose desired.[53]

But George's own situation was what most consumed him. With days of his brother-in-law's death, he had all but forgotten his sister's grief. He wrote again, asking for Rose to send by registered mail his stock certificates, the Carmack Gold and Copper Mining Stock and the Microbane Medical. Also, he advised, "if you see any of your friends whose hair is falling out, or if they have dandruff, the Microbane will cure it without fail, and it will grow hair on bald heads if directions are carefully followed. You need not be afraid to recomend it."[54] On the day James was buried, George sent his sister copies of some of the letters he had received from people in Hollister, all of them pleading for him to return to Kate. "Read them over," he told his grieving sister, "and see what you think of your neighbors."[55]

CHAPTER SEVENTEEN

All They Once Possessed

When John Durst wrote in December 1900 that his wife had returned from Nanaimo and was staying at the Franklin Hotel in San Francisco, Kate took the girls there to visit. The change of scene did her good; in a letter dictated to one of her reputable friends, she said she was happier in the city.[1]

Three days before Christmas, a friend of George Carmack reported seeing Kate and the girls at the Commercial Hotel in San Francisco; according to this friend, Kate had "a pretty good jag on" and the girls were trying to get her to go home—though if in fact, as George himself suspected, Kate were staying with the Dursts, it seems odd that she would have risked their disapproval by getting drunk. When George's friend asked Kate why she didn't take George's proposed settlement of $2,500, she purportedly answered that she wanted $100,000, the same amount that one of her more self-serving "friends" had demanded in a letter she wrote to John Durst.[2]

When Kate returned to Hollister in mid-January, Durst advised her to stay away from those who were meddling in her situation. He also said she should put no confidence in Rose

Watson. He asked Kate to be patient while a new suit was filed on her behalf, for separate maintenance. By the end of January, George had dropped the idea of reaching some sort of settlement with Kate in favor of a new strategy. "The whole thing hangs on the marriage," he wrote to Rose, "and I don't see how they can prove that, I never introduced Kate as my wife to any one that I know of, I never even told you that she was my lawful wife and you never asked me, because I had very good reasons for it, but I found out enough last spring to justify me in a separation, and no one knows about it here and I don't want to expose the whole thing unless I have to but the way they are trying to graft money out of me I think I will have to show the whole thing up."[3]

George then went public, reassuring reporters that he was not leaving Kate because she was an Indian. In fact, he said, "I did my utmost to form her after she commenced carousing in Dawson by bringing her to Seattle. Everyone in Seattle knows the result. I could not stop stories of her jamborees, much as I grieved over their appearances, because they were true. I stood it as long as I could, and then the separation came."[4]

Other than the incidents in Seattle during July 1899, there was no documentation to support George's claims of Kate's "carousing in Dawson" and "jamborees." But no matter—there had been no civil contract, George pointed out, and when it came to marriage by the customs of Kate's people, he had no idea what that meant. He told reporters that Kate had refused "the fair amount of money" that he had offered as a settlement. Furthermore, he called "ridiculous" Kate's version of the Klondike discovery, which was that Jim and Charlie had discovered the gold while dragging a moose up a riverbank, though later in life, George would tell this same version of the discovery himself.[5]

Deposed to testify under oath in the suit for maintenance, George was not so bold in his assertions about Kate, instead walking a fine line with regard to their relationship. Yes, he had lived with Kate as his "klootch" (Native wife) from 1887 to 1900. During those years, he had cared for her as a man ordinarily cared for his wife. When they traveled, he admitted to having registered at hotels as "Mr. and Mrs. Carmack." The last letter he had written to her, on May 19, 1900, from Dawson, was addressed "Mrs. Carmack."[6] Yet in the same deposition, Carmack also said he was never married to Kate and he did not consider her to be his wife. Overall, his admissions were damaging, the wife of attorney John Durst assured Kate in a letter. "Mr. Durst says it is going to be a nice little legal battle but he expects to win," she wrote. "Don't be discouraged. Brighter days are coming for you."[7]

Kate and the girls spent the last two weeks of February at the Windsor Hotel in San Francisco while her own deposition was taken. Once she had been given a chance to explain how she had been wronged, Kate had every reason, from the Tagish perspective, to expect swift justice. Upon her return to Hollister, she began (with the help of friends) writing to Durst, wanting to know when a settlement would be reached, as she was out of money. "She has evidently no clear conception of the proceedings that have been taken," wrote newspaper publisher A.D. Shaw. "Something must be done for her very quick, as she has not anything left, and is anxious to compromise."[8]

Upon receipt of Shaw's letter, Durst wrote to Skookum Jim, who was in Dawson City, explaining how George had abandoned Kate and how Rose had also turned her out. "She is now destitute and has nothing to live upon," Durst wrote. To settle the suit for maintenance would take six months to a year, he explained, and until then Kate needed a few hundred dollars so that she and the girls would not suffer.

Responsible as always for his sister, Jim sent money. Kate paid her bills, and Graphie got a new bicycle.

George continued to needle Rose about his financial affairs in San Benito County. She was to tell Mr. Fredson that George would take no less for his Fredson Hay Company stock than what he had paid for it; he also demanded interest on his investment. He wanted to know whether there was any chance of getting any money for the personal notes that were owed him; even a cow or a horse would be better than nothing, he said, explaining—without apology—that he was too busy to settle these matters himself.[9]

The legal proceedings dragged on. From the Tagish perspective, justice was straightforward: If someone wronged you, you gave him a chance to make things right. If he failed to do so, you took whatever action was needed to settle the score, and after that, normal relationships would resume. That George Carmack had taken another wife was not, from Kate's point of view, so egregious—Aagé, after all, had been one of three wives of L'unáat. The problem was that George refused any contact with Kate. As for the money, what mattered was not so much how much Kate got from their mutual assets but some sort of compensation for wrongdoing so that order would be restored, which in Kate's case meant returning to a larger family group.[10]

Months after her deposition, Kate was still waiting for a decision while John Durst grappled with the argument that she and George had never truly been husband and wife. With no legally recognized documentation of their marriage, Durst needed to prove that Kate and George had a duly recognized common law relationship in which Kate's ability to support herself and Graphie would be found disproportionate to the large fortune George intended to keep for himself.[11] In Canada, where Kate and George began living as husband and wife, only two years were needed for such a relationship to be considered a common law marriage.[12] During his deposition, George Carmack had admitted to living with Kate for fourteen years. But owing to the ongoing border dispute between Alaska and Canada—it would not be settled until 1903—there may have been uncertainty over whether Canadian common law applied in this case.

Frank Curtis, who kept up the ranch for Rose, tried to get Kate to go to the courthouse and sign a paper accepting a $2,500 settlement from George.[13] She was unsure what to do, especially since she had recently learned that George had deeded their 160 acres in San Benito County to his new wife, Marguerite. A friend wrote to Durst on her behalf: "'Have you heard from Mr. Durst?' is the question Mrs. Carmack asks me so often . . . Do you realize what these long months of waiting mean to the poor woman who cannot read, and has reason to be suspicious of every one?"[14] [15]

At the urging of another friend, Kate solicited the help of yet another attorney in Hollister.[16] While he and John Durst debated the question of how best to proceed, Kate took matters into her own hands. In the company of a woman from Hollister, she and the girls traveled to Seattle, having been summoned by Jim, who planned to arrive there within the month. "As the festive George and his new wife are in the Washington metropolis, interesting developments may be looked for," predicted the *Hollister Free Lance*. But when Kate arrived in Seattle, George left town to check on his mining interests in the Cascades.[17]

Kate longed to take Mary and Graphie Grace, who'd fallen ill in Seattle, back to the Yukon. Her idea was to travel north with Charlie, who was already in the city; after a month at home they would return to Seattle with Jim. But Charlie wasn't sure this was a good plan. Kate's legal situation was complex and neither of them fully understood it. They decided she and the girls should wait in Seattle until Jim arrived and then follow his advice.

Kate would be foolish to settle for a paltry sum, advised a divorce expert consulted by Durst.[18] The matter of where she and George had entered into a contract of marriage was crucial, he noted, and it would be helpful to know whether there was any truth to the claim that Kate had helped George survive in the wilderness or that she had led him to gold, as the "somewhat sensational and romantic" account published in the *San Francisco Call* had suggested.[19]

For her part, Kate cared about none of these details. Nearly seven months had passed since her deposition in San Francisco. She was out of money. Her eyes still hurt. She was alone in the city, far from home. And when Jim finally arrived, he bore bad news: their only surviving sister, Kooyáy, mother of Dawson Charlie and Patsy Henderson, was ill.

This was all the reason Kate needed. With the girls, she sailed north with Jim. As the ship ploughed along the rocky coastline of British Columbia and Alaska's Inside Passage, the burdens she'd been carrying fell away, replaced by the familiarity of landscape, of language, of thinking, of acting. As the ship chugged north, the ocean waters turning from emerald to teal, swirled with silt from glacial streams that tumbled down the mountains to the sea, her excitement mounted: home. She was almost home.

Arriving in Skagway, Kate, Jim, and the girls boarded the train that now ran all the way from Skagway to Whitehorse, where a full-fledged town had sprung up near the treacherous rapids of Miles Canyon. The train carried them through forests of hemlock and Sitka spruce, winding through high alpine meadows to White Pass, then descending to Bennett, already a ghost town, and on to Nadashaa Héeni, the narrows between Nares Lake and Lake Bennett.

There, on the north side of Nares Lake, near where people from Atlin, Teslin, Lake La Barge, and Little Salmon River had traditionally gather to trade, the White Pass and Yukon Railroad had platted a town they called Caribou Crossing, although the caribou were no longer plentiful there, the herd having been decimated by hunters, both Native and white, to feed the tens of thousands who stampeded north in pursuit of Klondike gold. In this newly platted town, Kate and Jim and the girls returned to a place that was old and familiar and yet also new.

The absence of caribou at Caribou Crossing was among the many abrupt changes in subsistence patterns that were playing out across Alaska and the Yukon, including each of the places Kate had lived—Tagish Lake, Chilkoot village (now all but abandoned), Forty Mile, Fort Selkirk, the Klondike. As a result, the *Klondike Nugget*, a Dawson newspaper, was predicting doom for the indigenous people of the Yukon:

> Civilization will ultimately wipe the Indians out of existence. This is the whole story in a nutshell, and it is apparent that the Indians themselves have a very well defined notion that such will prove to be the case. They see the land, which they considered their own, taken away from them without even their permission being asked. The game, upon which they have been accustomed to depend very largely for subsistence, is being driven back into the mountains, and when the game has all disappeared the Indians see nothing ahead for

> them but extinction . . . Formerly the Indians owned all the ground, all the fish and all the game. Now they own nothing . . . How they could lose all they once possessed and get nothing in return is something they cannot comprehend.[20]

Kate's family had done what they could to keep ahead of the changes. Through the marriages of Aagé and Kate, they'd allied themselves with the prospectors, though ultimately neither Sed Wilson nor George Carmack had behaved as expected. Many in the family had moved to Dyea at the height of the gold rush to participate in the cash-based economy as packers. Although those opportunities proved short-lived, the changes to their way of life were long-lasting—the populations of salmon and moose and caribou were depleted, the fur trade disrupted, and their fall hunting camp transformed into a railroad town.

Where to go? What to do? Jim took the initiative, building a two-story log home near his family's old camping site along the narrows that connect Nares Lake with Bennett Lake; he'd begun construction even before the railroad reached Caribou Crossing, bringing lumber by train from Skagway to Lake Bennett and then by raft across the length of Lake Bennett to the narrows.[21] There, in what had been the traditional lands of his people, he now had access to stores and transportation to Seattle and Dawson, the two places he visited most, aside from his traditional hunting and trapping spots.

Jim wasn't the only one who saw potential in the new railroad town. With the completion of the White Pass & Yukon tracks, Bishop Bompas seized the chance to establish a mission in the southern part of the diocese, an ambition that had taken hold after he visited Lake Bennett in the summer of 1899.[22] The town of Bennett, as it turned out, and Atlin to the west, were both in British Columbia, beyond the boundaries of the Selkirk diocese. But in the new railroad town of Caribou Crossing, the bishop recognized an opportunity to minister to the Tagish people, who had until then existed beyond the reach of the Anglicans, or any other church, for that matter. According to Bompas, a mission at Caribou Crossing would be "one of the last links of the chain of the Church Missionary Society stations which girdle the world."[23]

In August 1900, the bishop and his wife traveled upriver to Whitehorse and then to Caribou Crossing, arriving there at about the same time as Kate and the girls.[24] Aside from the station house, the NWMP post, and a few Tagish families camped on the far side of the lake, where Jim was building his house, they found only a small hotel and a tent that served as a roadhouse. The roadhouse proprietor, a friendly Scotsman, advised them that for living quarters they might purchase a bunkhouse built by the Canadian Development Company to house workers during the railroad construction on the south side of the lake near the railroad bridge.

Shabby and overrun by mice and squirrels, the roadhouse smelled of whiskey and tobacco, but it was an improvement over the tent the missionaries had brought as back-up housing for winter. Selina hired a Tagish woman to scrub the floors and a Tagish boy to gather up and dump in the lake the whiskey bottles that littered the yard. "One had to shut one's eyes to the internal aspect of things, and to dwell on its possibilities and surroundings," Selina wrote to her friends. "But in this the mountains were helpful, and anyone who has lived long among mountains will bear witness to their calming, soothing influence." Selina also appreciated the climate at Caribou Crossing, milder by far than Forty Mile, and the fact that she was now by her estimation 1,500 miles closer to home, with regular mail service and even newspaper delivery, thanks to the railroad.[25]

With the arrival of the missionaries, more of the Tagish began moving from Marsh Lake to the new railroad town, a development that the bishop and his wife took as a sign of interest in their mission, although it was likely the result of Jim building his house there. Selina wrote:

> Tents sprang up along the lake a short distance from us. Several families with numerous children and dogs appeared as occupants, and, thus, a good prospect of occupation for us was rapidly provided. The Bishop's medicine-chest was soon

> brought into requisition, for an Indian is apt to look upon all "yaltis" (praying men) as more or less "medicine men;" we have to treat all manner of complaints, real and imaginary, describable and indescribable . . . The children (the nucleus of our school yet to be) were in and out of the Mission all day. We loved the dear little dark-eyed gipsies, full of fun and mischief. It has always been a wonder to find how soon they get into our hearts, and take such deep root there that one is ready to join in that most thrilling of all cries, an Indian mourner's wail, when a child is taken from among them.[26]

Because they were part of her *shagóon*, her past and the essence of who she was, Kate enjoyed the calming, soothing effects of the mountains in a deeper way than Selina Bompas ever could. She walked among the plants she'd learned about from her mother—the arctic aster, the soapberry, and the lingonberry—breathing air scented with arctic sage, spruce needles, and ancient dust ground by glaciers. She laughed and cried and told stories among the people who knew her best, the Dak̲l'aweidí and the Deisheetaan, all of whom were family in one way or another.

Kate arrived home in time to attend one of the last great Tlingit potlatches, held on the coast in the old tradition. From deep into the Interior and as far down the coast as Sitka, two thousand people were invited to attend the feast to honor an Eagle/Wolf chief who was dying. The potlatch host was tall, handsome George Shotridge, son of Kohklux, now chief of his father's Chilkat clan. On the first floor of a forty-foot house that Shotridge had built especially for the event, there was dancing to the old songs, while on the second floor, clan treasures were displayed.[27] In addition to traditional foods, the guests enjoyed canned grapes, canned peaches, candies, cakes, and copious amounts of pilot bread—the thick, hard crackers that were a processed food staple in the North. After this last great fete, the dying chief declared, "The Indians shall be good and live as the whiteman, and peace shall reign among the tribes."[28]

CHAPTER EIGHTEEN

A HIGH STANDARD

THOUGH HER HOMECOMING GAVE KATE much to celebrate, she still suffered from the pain in her eyes, and Kooyáy, her only surviving sister, was still ailing. A letter was written on Kate's behalf to John Durst, asking that he send her trunk, with the shipping charges to be refunded to him. "The poor woman has hardly anything that I can tell and needs the trunk badly," wrote H. M. Wooldridge. "Her sister is sick and she can't leave. But she expects to come out in the spring."[1]

Along the lake, to the east of the Carcross Bridge, Jim had a small cabin built for Kate and the girls. The low hills and high plains deserts of San Benito County seemed far away—and indeed they were. Each morning, Kate looked out on the emerald waters of Lake Bennett, once overrun with the boats of miners clamoring to reach the Klondike, now trafficked mainly by grayling and trout. From the craggy hillsides came the shrill cries of marmots. Across the lake, sands fanned out in dunes formed of deposits carried from an ancient lake bed.

Where the long lakes now named Nare and Bennett met, Animal Mother had once anchored a moose hide swing over four low mountains: Facing the Water, Wind Blowing the Forehead, Caribou Mountain, and Gopher Mountain. In Tagish, the names are as beautiful as the landforms—*Taaghahi, Metaatl'e Schech'ee, Medzih Dzel, Chiih Dzele*. A big bull moose was the first to walk the line that fastened the hide, like a tightrope. Reaching the swing, he sang a story-song about his achievement, then fell through the hide to wander the earth. Cow moose, calf, caribou, sheep, wolf, and rabbit—all of them followed, taking turns on the swing and singing their stories. Then Animal Mother rolled up her moose hide and shooed the animals off, scattering them across the land.[2] The place where she'd strung her swing was called *Todezáané*, "Blowing All the Time," a valley between the four mountains where Shaaw Tláa's family had traditionally hunted caribou and hung meat to dry for the winter. Like the Tagish clans, the caribou traveled with the seasons, and Animal Mother's valley was a place they had often returned to until they were overhunted during the rush for gold. Now *Todezáané* was known as Caribou Crossing, soon to be renamed "Carcross."[3]

Graphie, Mary, and Jim's daughter Daisy joined five Indian children brought from Moosehide to attend the newly opened mission school, overseen by thin, dour-faced Miss Ellis, an Anglican missionary. At first, classes were held on the same side of the lake as the train station, in a newly built house furnished with bedsteads, tables, benches, and chairs built by the Bishop and two Tagish boys from saw-cut lumber and wooden boxes scavenged from the lakeshore—litter left from the rush to the Klondike. But only weeks after lessons began, the Bishop recognized a serious flaw with the new schoolhouse: it lay on the opposite side of the railroad bridge from where Graphie, Mary, and the other local children were living.

"The children thought nothing of the dangers of crossing that bridge," Selina Bompas wrote. "They would run across for their five cents' worth of candy even when a train was in sight rounding the corner on the line from Bennett; they would skip fearless over one, two, three of the sleepers which lay so far apart that one could see the blue waters of the lake flowing."[4] In the interests of safety, the Bishop arranged a trade with the Northwest

Mounted Police: the new schoolhouse for the NWMP barracks on the south side of the lake.

Dleit K'áchk'w arrived, the month of little snow, and then *Shaanáx̲ Dís K̲ukaxeit*, the Digging Moon. Early in January 1901, during a church service inside the Carcross bunkhouse turned mission house, Bishop Bompas baptized Kate and Graphie Grace Carmack into the Anglican Church.[5] Having attended the Paicines Baptist Church with Rose, Kate understood church in a way others in her family could not—spiritual benefits aside, membership was part of belonging, of fitting in, of acceptance—a way of easing your way between cultures.

As the long days returned, in the month of *K'óox Dísi*, it was time for the women to set out muskrat traps. *Kahaakw.ish* arrived, the month of the hooligan spawning on the coast, and then *Kayaaní Dísi*, when the ice went out and the snow melted and green shoots of wild celery and salmonberry were gathered.[6] From the south came flocks of Green-winged Teal, American Widgeon, Northern Pintail, and Trumpeter swans that stopped to rest at the Natasaheen River on the way to their breeding grounds.

Kate had planned to leave in the spring, to return to Seattle and then to California to take up her role as plaintiff in the suit for separate maintenance, a petition that if found in her favor would entitle her and Graphie to a share of the Carmack fortune. By legal standards, if she had ever been married to George Carmack, she still was: she had withdrawn her suit for divorce, and by virtue of the fact that he had already married Marguerite and was now claiming never to have married Kate in the first place, George's suit for divorce made no sense. From a legal and economic standpoint, it was foolish for Kate not to follow through with the proceedings, especially given what George had said in his deposition about living with her as his wife and the role her family had played in his subsequent wealth. But didn't she have real wealth, the kind she'd known from birth, right there at Caribou Crossing?

From a young age, Kate had been equipped to make choices under the most difficult of circumstances. She'd known how to adjust to life among the Tlingit and how to cope when her husband and daughter succumbed to disease. She'd known how to maintain the new alliances her family made through her, even when her husband knew nothing of how to behave, even when she'd longed for home. As they wandered, she'd known when to let go and when to hold her ground.

There had been confusion and troubles, to be sure, especially once gold became part of her life. She'd made mistakes. But in the end, she was still Shaaw Tláa, a Wolf, of the Dakl'aweidí, the Killer Whale nation, daughter of Gus'dutéen, who was the daughter of Húnx̱u.aat, whose people came from Tahltan, the flat place now called Telegraph Creek. The place where she came from, the people who had formed her—this was who she was at her essence, her *yaahei.*

She knew where her wealth was—not in Seattle or California, not in George Carmack's bank accounts, or his hotel, or his Microbane Medical stock. It was right there in the Yukon, with Jim and Graphie and Mary and all of her family. Among Animal Mother's mountains, she knew the right ways to act, surrounded by those who loved her always, the Daḵl'aweidí and the Deisheetaan.

Kate stayed where she was. Foregoing streetcars and restaurants and fancy hotels and depositions and legal wrangling, she opted for the place she called home.

To protect himself and his gold, Jim hired a bodyguard, a former Mountie who had recently married Louise George, daughter of L'unáat and Aagé. Kate, of course, needed no such protection. Having no money, she relied on Jim for support. The results of his encounters with Wealth Woman continued to play out, though never with such effect as they had in the Klondike. When he received word that gold had been found in the hills surrounding the new Alaskan community of Fairbanks, Jim grubstaked his brother-in-law, a white prospector who was married to his wife's sister. But as it turned out, news of the Fairbanks riches had been greatly exaggerated. Thousands of claims had been illegally staked, and many miners left before enough gold was found in neighboring creeks to justify them coming. Jim's grubstake went south—regrettably, his brother-in-law informed him, he'd lost $7,000 of the investment.[7]

But Jim's Dawson claims were still paying. When his house was finished, he furnished it with brass beds and other fine furniture bought in Seattle. While he mostly did what he loved best—hunting, fishing, trapping—Wealth Woman with her golden stick was never far from his mind. In the summer of 1902, in the Ruby Range east of Kluane Lake, he and Charlie found gold again, at Bullion Creek in what would become known as the Kluane district.[8] When four prospectors showed up in Whitehorse with forty-three ounces of gold they had collected from the creek in only nine days, a new rush was on.

Considering what had happened in the Klondike, hopes were high. After the ground froze, Jim hired a four-horse team to haul a boiler 175 miles from Whitehorse to be used in thawing the ground for drift mining, with the drivers cutting a road as they went. At ninety feet, Jim's crew hit bedrock, but the water rushed in so fast the pumps couldn't keep up. It was rumored the entire venture cost him $100,000, a loss he and others would attribute to his failure on that long-ago night on the shores of Lake Bennett to catch up with Wealth Woman and perform the proper ritual.[9] Overall, two thousand claims were staked in the Kluane district, and though a few yielded a respectable $2 a pan, overall the rush proved small and short-lived,[10] with only $40,000 in gold taken from the creeks.[11]

Though he no longer actively worked his Klondike claims, Jim's lease arrangement with a dredging company entitled him to half of the gold the company recovered. All over the Klondike, corporations backed by investors like the Guggenheims were snatching up claims once held by individuals. The eyesore of tailings piled up by placer miners using flumes and sluice boxes was nothing compared to the wholesale remaking of the landscape by hydraulics and dredges. Through hoses, water was blasted at the hillsides surrounding the Bonanza Creek cabin where Kate once lived, and from the big dredges that floated the creeks, worked gravel was piled in mounds that snaked alongside the waters. Large-scale mining came even to Caribou Crossing, in the form of the Conrad silver mines in the mountains ten miles south of town.

As Kate's eyes healed, she took up sewing again. Out of dark blue fabric, she made a ceremonial robe for Jim, decorated with scarlet bands and nearly three thousand hand-sewn pearl buttons.[12] Adapted from the Tlingit, the making of these types of robes, also called "button blankets," signifies a special relationship between the maker of the robe and the person who would wear it. Together, Kate and Jim had shared the difficulties—and the pleasures—of the wealth that reconfigured their world. It had all started with packing over the Chilkoot Trail, and so for the back of Jim's robe, Kate stitched a border in the shape of a pack.

From the smaller items she sewed and sold to tourists who came through on the train, Kate made "quite a bit of money," according to Mary Wilson. "I think I like Kate better than Graphie does," she wrote to "Aunt Rose" in 1906. "But Graphie doesn't get so mad now as she used to." With Mary's help, Kate also maintained contact with Jake Watson, George's tall, unmarried brother-in-law, who though without wealth had always enjoyed a reputation for kindness.[13] None of their letters survive, so the nature of their correspondence remains unknown.

Remarkably, Kate appeared to hold no grudge against William and Selina Bompas, despite the fact that following Aagé's death, they had taken Mary, whom Kate by rights should have raised. Well into their seventies, the bishop and his wife enjoyed Carcross, and Selina especially was loved and respected there.[14] "Two septuagenarians of grace and broad culture," a visiting church official said of the missionaries, adding that despite "circumstances the average citizen of the Empire would feel to be past endurance," the Bishop and his wife were "as happy as [they were] heroic. She, accomplished far beyond the standard one meets with in London drawing-rooms, unless among the most cultured circles; he, a fine scholar, steeped in Hebrew and Syrian lore, as well as in the commoner studies of the clergy, live on, love on, labour on in this vast expanse, little trodden but by the Indians for whom they live and will die."[15]

Graphie, Mary, and Daisy were among the students William Bompas taught each morning, a task he enjoyed even though he likened his efforts to "writing in sand."[16] In 1903, he had petitioned the Canadian government for help in establishing a permanent boarding school in Carcross. Under the terms of an earlier agreement forged between the government and the church regarding the education of the Indians, the government would pay for construction of schools, and the church would staff them, with ongoing expenses to be covered by the government on a per capita basis.

But there simply weren't enough students in Carcross to fill a boarding school. In order for the venture to be fully funded, children from as far north as Dawson would have to be taken from their families and raised at the school. As Bompas saw it, this was a benefit—the removal of children from the influence of their families and culture would enhance their moral education. In particular, Anglican officials wished for the "best and most influential Indians" to set an example by sending their children away to school.[17]

For the purposes of "moral education"—and proving to the government the need for a bigger facility—Graphie and Mary likely boarded at the mission school, even though Kate and other relatives lived in the same town. In the early days of such schools, Native families often assumed that their children would benefit from such an arrangement, learning to read and write and behave as outsiders expected. In his will, Skookum Jim summed up this thinking, charging his executors with making sure his daughter, Daisy, was "brought up in a manner to enable her to take her place among white people with whom she has been associated in childhood."[18]

Like Daisy, Mary and Graphie had spent significantly more time among white people than they had with their Tagish relatives, a divide that would only intensify as they grew older. In 1904, Graphie moved to Whitehorse to live with Isaac Stringer, in line to replace Bompas as the Anglican bishop of the diocese,

Carcross School, 1903. In the back row, second from right, is Graphie, age 10. To her right is Mary Wilson, age 12. (Yukon Archives, Anglican Church fonds, 86/61, #587)

and his wife Sadie, a pleasant, round-faced woman who for years would serve as something of a surrogate mother to Graphie. After four years at a mission on Herschel Island, where Sadie did her baking in an oven she constructed herself from old biscuit tins and her bathing with a sponge in a zinc tub only large enough to stand in, the Stringers arrived in Whitehorse in the midst of a labor shortage due to the Kluane gold strike. Enter Graphie Grace, who at age eleven helped with ironing and served as a companion for the Stringers' daughter Rowena, who was three years younger than Graphie. In Whitehorse, Graphie also attended public school, a privilege not available to most Native children and, occasionally, Isaac Stringer took her and Rowena to the movies.

Through another arrangement made by Bishop Bompas, fourteen-year-old Mary Wilson was also taken from Kate, transported from Carcross to Dawson to help Reverend Reed and his wife with housekeeping. Never was there any suggestion that Kate was less than capable of raising Graphie and Mary; rather, there was an overriding assumption that to live with the missionaries would better prepare the girls for womanhood. For her part, Kate's interactions with the Anglicans continued to be amiable, including her help in cleaning the Carcross rectory in anticipation of the Stringers' move from Whitehorse to Carcross once Bishop Bompas had officially retired.

By June 1906, the transfer of the bishop's duties was all but complete. Bompas was suffering the effects of age. Following a bout of scurvy, he had lost all sense of taste and smell, and his voice and eyesight were failing. "Courage, courage," he would whisper to himself as he went about his duties. As Stringer prepared to assume the role of bishop, thirteen-year-old Graphie was back in Carcross. One calm, sunny Friday in June, in the company of her friend Annie, she ran away from the mission school. For students at the mission school, it was hardly a singular escapade. Selina Bompas shared this perspective:

> [A pupil might be] merry as a grig at times, but if he catches sight of his father or any friend going hunting, the hunger for freedom comes upon him—he will start to run after the hunters, and if caught and sent back to school he will cry and yell until the whole camp is roused, and tearful, sympathizing mothers rush in to know why the Mission folk are killing their darling? The girls are equally resentful of restraint, and look upon a closed door or window as their natural enemy. These spasmodic fits of intolerance of confinement cease after a year or so, but we have always to remember that fresh air is an Indian's natural food—he was born and bred in the woods and has early been used to such extremes of temperature as would make a white child shudder.[19]

With the night air only a little chilly, Graphie and Annie stayed out all night. The next day, the local police found them near a stream and returned them to Carcross, delivering Graphie to her mother and Annie to the care of Bishop Bompas, who was packing for a trip downriver. To complete the transfer of his duties, Bompas handed over the diocese account books to Isaac Stringer; then, after his 8:30 prayers, he drew a bath for Annie in the storeroom. When she'd finished bathing, he returned to the storeroom, which was also his study, to complete his Sunday sermon. As he leaned against a box, he fell forward, unconscious.

Panicked, Annie called for help. When Stringer arrived, Graphie's distraught friend was cradling the bishop's head in her lap. Checking for vital signs, Stringer found that the elder man's seventy-two years had come to an end. At first, Selina could not fathom it; she asked Stringer to recite the prayer for the sick even after her husband's heart had clearly stopped beating. In Carcross, flags were lowered to half-mast. In the robes he had worn for everyday worship, the bishop was buried at the local cemetery. Skookum Jim was one of the pallbearers.

Graphie and Annie were told that through the trouble they caused by running away, they had shortened the bishop's life. "Annie has been very good since," wrote Stringer, "and I hear Graphie wants to come back to school but she will have to eat humble pie before I let her back."[20]

Whereas Bompas had been a churlish, reluctant administrator, Stringer brought new energy to the role of bishop. He made plans for a "white school" in Carcross[21] while continuing to pursue the residential school application, which had been initially turned down. Already the problems with forcing Native children into boarding schools were becoming evident. "My belief is that the attempt to elevate the Indian by separating the child from his parents and educating him as a white man has turned out to be a deplorable failure," wrote Frank Oliver, Canada's Minister of the Interior. "The mutual love between a parent and child is the strongest influence for the betterment of the world, and when that influence is absolutely cut apart or is deliberately intended to be cut apart, as in the situation of the Indian children in industrial schools, the means defeats the purpose itself."[22]

After years of Graphie going off to live with the missionaries, Kate's relationship with her daughter was already damaged. All that Kate and her Tagish relatives would have taught Graphie—the story-songs of her clan, the right ways of behaving, the skills that would make her a productive member of the community—these she had little opportunity to learn. Like her mother, she was strong-willed, and the two of them butted heads. From a young age—she'd been only five when the gold made her parents wealthy beyond reckoning—she had gotten whatever she wanted: pretty boots, pale-faced dolls, a new bicycle. Kate took some comfort in knowing that the missionaries had at least equipped Graphie with the skills she herself lacked—mostly notably, the ability to read and write. But as Graphie approached puberty, who would see to her seclusion? Who would make a brush shelter and a fire to warm her, and prepare her first drink with beads in the water, a drink that was spilled twice before it was given to her, to make sure she would not grow up to be greedy?[23]

Graphie had no interest in puberty seclusion. After the death of William Bompas, she returned to the Stringers to help with the children and the chores. The family relocated to Dawson City, chosen by the newly appointed bishop as a location better suited for the church's headquarters than Carcross. Graphie was hundreds of miles from her mother, but at least she was in a place that Kate knew and with people she trusted. Among the women of Dawson, Sadie Stringer proved unique in her respect for Native people, defying the town's class-conscious women by entertaining the Native wives of village pastors at social events in her home, where they were treated as equals.[24]

More typical of the era were the attitudes of the two men Jim relied on for help in managing his affairs. One was Percy Peele, who had arrived in the Yukon with his young family from British Columbia at the height of the gold rush. From his initial post as a Canadian Customs Official at Log Cabin, not far from the Chilkoot summit, Peele transferred to Lake Bennett and then to Carcross, where his daughter, Vivian, became friends with Jim's daughter Daisy, as well as with Graphie and Mary. Jim's other advisor was Willard Phelps, a deacon of the Anglican Church. Enticed by Klondike gold, Phelps had come to the Yukon via the long and arduous overland route through Canada. Like many others, he never made it to Dawson. From his office in Whitehorse, he served as Jim's attorney, drafting several wills on his behalf.

Whatever their good intentions, Phelps and Peele lacked Sadie Stringer's determination to rise above contemporary prejudices. In their correspondence, Phelps wrote that Jim was "a good Indian about the only one I ever knew." Of Jim's daughter Daisy, Peele wrote to Phelps that she was "like most Indians, a thankless individual."[25] Phelps concurred, writing to Peele "you know how ungrateful Indians are,"[26] and adding that Daisy "is an Indian and one cannot expect a high standard."[27]

In the first will Phelps drafted for Jim, in 1904, $5,000 went to Jim's wife and the remainder of his fortune to Daisy. If Daisy were to die before reaching age twenty-one, $1,000 of Jim's estate would go to Susie George, and the remainder would be divided equally between Kate and three other relatives.[28] Notably excluded was Jim's nephew Charlie, who had acquired a unique privilege that allowed him to drink legally. Under Canada's Indian Act, which became law in 1876 and was amended in subsequent years, Natives were forbidden from exercising the usual rights of citizens, though as the wife of white man, Kate had been excluded from this edict. Through an attorney, Charlie applied for Canadian citizenship, using the name Charlie Henderson, though in Carcross he was known as Dawson Charlie,[29] to distinguish him from Tagish Charlie, a Deisheetaan of the Crow Moiety.[30]

By an act of parliament, Charlie got his wish: he was excluded from the provisions of the Indian Act. As "a man of considerable means,"[31] he acquired the right to vote and the right to buy alcohol, the same as any white man. Noting that he shunned the "Indian mode of life," the *Whitehorse Daily Evening News* described him as "intelligent, capable, temperate in habits, and a good citizen."[32] But Charlie's temperance proved short-lived, and his legal right to drink was revoked only two years after he had acquired it.

Jim also did his share of drinking. Through stories that emphasized his jovial nature, his indulgence became the stuff of legend. As he labored at the "King's Woodpile" in Dawson, chopping wood for the NWMP as punishment for drinking, it was said that one of the Mounties asked how many times he'd been arrested. "One thousand times," answered Jim. "What's the matter? You jealous?"[33] And when the NWMP came to Carcross to enforce the ban on Native drinking by confiscating all the liquor from the Caribou Hotel and dumping it in the river, Jim was said to have paddled out in his canoe and dipped his cup in the water to enjoy the free booze.[34]

Good-natured or not, drinking took its toll on families. Charlie's wife left him, and so did Jim's.[35] In 1905, Jim changed his will to exclude her, appointing Bishop Stringer and Percy Peele guardians of his daughter and setting up a $20,000 trust account for Daisy's expenses, funded by a $65,000 windfall he received from selling his Klondike claims to the dredging corporation that had been leasing them. It was Daisy's teacher at the mission school who suggested the trust fund to Jim, noting that his health was not sound and "some of the crowd" were taking advantage of him.[36]

There are both written reports and oral accounts of Jim and Charlie's fondness for liquor, but there are no such records of Kate having indulged to excess either in California or upon her return to the Yukon. Her acceptance into the Anglican Church also suggests that she steered clear of alcohol, as church officials refrained from baptizing those who drank to excess. While Kate admitted to having enjoyed port wine during her visits to San Francisco, if she drank at all in Carcross it must have been discreetly, as ladies of the era sometimes did, sometimes relying on bottled medicines with a high alcohol content in order to do so.[37]

Even after losing the legal right, Charlie continued drinking to excess, a worry to Kate and all who loved him. During the dark morning hours of Christmas Day, 1908, he disappeared. Two days later, Jim discovered his body ten feet underwater in the narrows between Nares Lake and Lake Bennett, a stretch of water that remains ice-free for most of the winter. Though some among the Tagish suspected foul play, the NWMP ruled Charlie's death an accident, the result of slipping from the bridge while under the influence of alcohol. In a news item regarding his death, he was remembered as "very profligate with his money, being inordinately found [sic] of drink and an easy mark for unscrupulous white men for whom he constituted an easy source of revenue."[38] Aside from the Caribou Hotel in Carcross, conveyed to his estranged wife upon his death, the bulk of his fortune was gone.[39]

Charlie's wife sold the hotel to a white couple, Edwin and Bessie Gideon. To the extent to that such relationships were possible in post–gold rush communities, Bessie and Kate became friends. In Carcross, where the population was half white and half Native, the segregation of the Tagish on a 160-acre reserve established by the government in 1905 had less effect than in towns like Dawson and Whitehorse, where the white majority favored enforcement of curfews designed to keep Natives off the streets after five o'clock in the winter and seven o'clock in the summer.[40]

The year that began with mourning her nephew's death continued badly for Kate. The Stringers departed Dawson for a furlough Outside, leaving Graphie in the care of a Mrs. Joe Wilson, an arrangement that, as always, would have included her helping with household chores. Within months, Graphie received a far more enticing offer—her father wanted to bring her to Seattle, where his role in the Klondike discovery was to be lauded in the opening of the Alaska-Yukon-Pacific Exposition (AYPE) in the spring of 1909.[41] For what was billed as the World's Most Beautiful Fair, George had commissioned the fabrication of a telegraph key fashioned from twenty-two of the gold nuggets he'd taken from Bonanza Creek, a key that the president of the United States would use to telegraph the message that would officially open the fair.

For sixteen-year-old Graphie, it was an opportunity not to be missed—leaving the quiet, isolated town of Dawson for the excitement and glamour of a city. And it was only a visit. Neither she nor anyone else informed Kate of her plans; later, Kate would speak of how a stranger packed Graphie's belongings and took her from Dawson without her mother's knowledge or permission.[42]

Three weeks before the opening of the Alaska-Yukon-Pacific Exposition, Bishop Stringer spent a day in Seattle, where he had supper with George and Marguerite Carmack. "They were kind in every way," Stringer wrote to his wife. "Graphie Carmack was just as usual . . . I made no reference to her coming out from Dawson in the way she did."[43] Graphie had a piano, but did not play. She showed off her three dogs, two hounds and a spaniel, and Stringer gave her the gift of a handheld mirror. "They seem to keep pretty much to themselves," the bishop wrote of the Carmacks,[44] noting that only rarely did Graphie see her cousin Mary Wilson, who was also in Seattle, nor did Graphie appear to have any other friends.

Rousing patriotic tunes played by military bands entertained the crowd of 80,000 that turned out for the opening ceremony of the Alaska-Yukon-Pacific Exposition (AYPE) on June 1, 1909. At precisely noon, President Taft used the telegraph key made from George Carmack's gold to tap out a welcome. When the message reached the fairgrounds, a gong sounded five times. Amid the sharp retorts of a twenty-one gun salute, the American flag was unfurled, and the exposition was officially launched. Seattle had good reason to celebrate. In only a decade, more than $175 million in gold from Alaska and the Yukon had passed through the assaying office there.[45]

Along the AYPE's Paystreak amusement corridor, Graphie took in the most popular exhibits, including an "authentic" village of live Igorrote people transported from the Philippines. In a paper-maché igloo, she witnessed one hundred "Alaskan Siberians—Eskimos," clothed in fur parkas despite the summer heat.[46]

For a short while, George was famous again, and this time it wasn't for leaving his wife. With some derision, the *Dawson Daily News* reported the "fanciful picture" he related to the Seattle papers on the occasion of the exposition: "In long mushes over winter trails when Indian hunters found caribou scarce, there was always an abundance of nature's rought [sic] fare to fall to Mr. Carmack's rifle. In the summer he fished in the streams and trapped game so successfully that his Indian companions came to look upon him as one specially favored by the Mother Earth."[47] When asked why he had not returned to the North since 1900, George blamed not his changing of wives but his rheumatism. "It seemed to me that the north was jealous of the treasure secret and resented my laying it bare to the world. I have said good-bye to the north; I shall never go back again."[48]

It was another promise George Carmack would fail to keep.

CHAPTER NINETEEN

A LIGHT LEFT ON

GRAPHIE'S ORIGINAL INTENT HAD BEEN TO VISIT her father for a month and then return home. But she stayed on, and complications arose: she became pregnant. The father of her child was Marguerite's brother, Jacob Saftig, a stout thirty-one-year-old. In June 1910, he and seventeen-year-old Graphie Grace Carmack were married in a small ceremony at the Seattle home of George and Marguerite. Graphie wore a gown of white messaline and carried a shower of white roses.[1] Kate was not in attendance, nor would she ever meet her grandson, Ernest, who was born in October 1910. Graphie gave her son Jim's name, Keish.

This was the end result of Graphie's "moral education"—that she would marry into the clan of her father's second wife. From the Tagish point of view, it wasn't so much the marriage but the distance and the foreign ways of thinking that set things off-kilter for Kate. She would never again see her daughter. "For any mother this separation and loss would be a terrible blow," notes author Sherrill Grace, "but the race, class, and matrilineal cultural context for this loss made Kate's experience extreme."[2] The only contact she would have was the occasional letter—Graphie

At the Carmack home in Seattle, circa 1910. Seated in the front is George Carmack. In the middle row, far left, is Marguerite's mother, and to her left, Marguerite. In the back row, far left, is Graphie's husband (and Marguerite's brother) Jacob Saftig, and to his left, Graphie. (Yukon Archives, James Albert Johnson fonds, 82/341, #32)

liked to get letters well enough, but she was bad about writing them.[3]

Through Graphie's marriage to Jacob, Kate would eventually have three grandchildren; they would grow up first in Seattle and then in California, and Kate would meet none of them. Her granddaughter, Marguerite, would know nothing of what it meant to be Wolf, of the Dakl'aweidí, the Killer Whale nation. She would not know her mother as Aagé, daughter of Shaaw Tláa, daughter of Gus'dutéen, daughter of Húnx̱u.aat, whose people came from Tahltan, the flat place. She would never learn the song of remembrance from the time her clanspeople went under a glacier.

Lacking contact with Graphie's children, Kate cut up the fur coat in her trunk and made parkas for her niece's children, whom she called her grandchildren.[4] She told her stories to Angela Sidney, daughter of Tagish and Maria John, and she was "just like my husband's mother" to Kitty Smith, wife of Kooyáy's son Billy, helping to deliver Kitty's baby while they were "way out hunting."[5]

While seasonal rounds were no longer what they had been, Kate still traveled to fish camp and fall camp and also to visit friends and relatives. In July 1910, Isaac and Sadie Stringer called on her in Atlin, British Columbia, a place known as "Little Switzerland" because of the snowy peaks that border the blue-green waters of Atlin Lake, the traditional lands of the Tahltan, who along with the Tagish traced their origins to the three Dak̲l'aweidí sisters from Angoon; in one way or another, Kate would have been related to virtually every Native person who lived there. By this time, people had taken to calling her "Kate Carmacks," the *s* added because of the town of Carmacks, which had sprung near the site of George's unsuccessful trading post.

Before visiting Kate, Bishop Stringer gave a presentation in Atlin about his harrowing brush with death the previous year during an attempt to return to Dawson City after a visit to Hershel Island, the far northern outpost where he had established a mission. With only two blankets for warmth, little wood for a fire, and only the occasional ptarmigan or rabbit to sustain them, he and his traveling companion had been forced to slice up their sealskin boots and chew on the leather for sustenance. "Palatable," Stringer wrote in his journal during the four days that they ate their boots for breakfast, lunch, and dinner—though the leather uppers, he noted, were not as good as the soles. When they finally found their way back to civilization, Stringer and his companion discovered that the newspapers had already declared them dead. From then on, the missionary who'd been something of a surrogate father to Kate's daughter became known as The Bishop Who Ate His Boots.

In 1911, Kate met George's wife, Marguerite, for the first time. She came through Carcross on the train, on a trip that appears to have involved disposing of a half-lot she'd acquired in Dawson before she met George.[6] With Marguerite was Kate's new son-in-law, Jacob. The two of them offered Kate money, but she refused it—she wanted no Carmack money, she told them, though she did accept some clothing and one of Marguerite's hats as gifts.[7] That same year, the Deisheetaan clan house on Six Mile River, where Kate had grown up, was torn down. Raising foxes for their pelts was becoming popular, and one of Kate's relatives used the scrap lumber to build a fox farm.[8] The following year, the Tagish Dak̲l'aweidí clan house was demolished, because "the old people were all gone."[9]

Visitors regularly came through Carcross, a tourist stop on what the White Pass & Yukon Railroad promoted as "The Scenic Route . . . of the World." By railroad, passengers could travel in "luxurious railroad coaches" from Skagway to Whitehorse, with transfer to "palatial steamboats" that took them to Dawson.[10] Among the favorite tourist souvenirs were hand-sewn items, miniature moccasins and mittens crafted by Native women, including Kate.

More impressive by far than those hand-sewn trinkets was an elaborately decorated cape Kate stitched. Her most artistic and enduring achievement, the cape was fashioned using elements from the three cultures through which she had navigated: the Tagish, the Tlingit, and the Anglo-American. To construct the cape, she relied on Tagish methods, beginning with the snaring of dark-furred gophers in simple wire loops. Small holes were dug to the side of gopher burrows for placing spring-poles; in the span of three days, a person might set a hundred snares, all of which had to be checked regularly.[11] After fleshing dozens and dozens of skins with a stone scraper, a person would wash the pelts and dry them on wooden stretchers, then soften them by hand.[12]

Though gopher pelts are lightweight and warm, they are also thin and delicate, so it was with great care that Kate stitched them together,[13] shaping the furs into a wrap designed like the ones she'd seen in Seattle and San Francisco—fastened with a rounded white ermine collar, her cape hangs over the shoulders in gentle folds to the hips. But what makes this cape unique is the beadwork Kate added to the ermine-trimmed red felt borders that she stitched along the bottom and side edges. During a period in which European-influenced floral designs were used by most Yukon beaders, Kate's work puts an elaborate, personal, and even fantastical spin on designs that are more traditionally Tagish. Like Tlingit art, her beaded images are highly figurative and narrative in form, though she relied on none of the stylized patterns used on the coast. Instead, her beadwork is highly original, incorporating images that, taken in sum, appear to represent various aspects of her life as it unfolded among and between cultures.[14]

Along the front edges of the cape, Kate beaded chains of bells, paired by color, white and gold. Along the bottom are more figurative shapes, each distinct from the other, no two precisely alike. On a strip of felt sewn up the back of the cape, she stitched a series of images that appear to form a narrative of her life that can be read, bottom to top, like a totem pole. At the base is a stylized, three-toed frog like the one associated with Jim's Wealth Woman encounters, beaded of white, green, and gold diamond shapes. Next is an elaborate and fanciful creature with white limbs curled at the ends, two striped black wings, a head of stacked triangles that phase from mostly black to pure white, and a heart-shaped tail—a mysterious image that hints of love with the heart-shaped tail, though this might also signify the beaver, crest of her father's clan, and also, in the triangles that form the creature's head, a transition from the present world to the world of the cloud people.

Above this unusual creature is a black-bodied bird with striped wings, its claws wrapped around a golden stick reminiscent of the one used by Wealth Woman to point Jim toward the Klondike. Blue triangles drip from the bird's wingtips, suggesting water or tears. Atop this bird is a branch with five leaves, three white and two gold, possibly representing Kate and her siblings, she and Jim among the living, and their three closest sisters—Aagé, Kooyáy, and Nadagáat Tláa—who had passed on. Topping the entire panel, a second bird rises like a phoenix, looking in the opposite direction of the first, white-bodied with colorful wings, each undergirded with two sharp triangles that suggest power and resilience in contrast to the dripping wings of the dark bird beneath.

With no explanation from Kate, the meaning behind these beaded images remains a mystery, much as her life, with its twists and turns, must have seemed in some ways to her. Sewn of delicate skins and embellished as it was, the cape was meant to be worn only on special occasions such as the 1912 memorial potlatch hosted by the Wolf moiety to honor the Crows for their help when Dawson Charlie died. During the three years following Charlie's death, Kate and other Dak̲l'aweidí had been preparing for the potlatch—trapping furs, tanning hides, sewing ceremonial clothing and gifts, and gathering and drying meat and fish to feed the guests.

As the wealthiest man in Carcross, Jim hosted the potlatch. For food and gifts, he contributed $2,000 plus a hundred blankets, with Patsy Henderson contributing $500 plus fifty blankets, and their cousin Tagish John putting up another hundred blankets. The blankets were cut into strips so each guest would have a piece to take home along with gifts of cash. No white people were invited to the potlatch, but Matthew Watson, who owned the general store in Carcross, invited himself in order to take pictures, one of which he sold as a postcard.[15]

From all over the region—Atlin, Whitehorse, Champagne, Aishihik, and Marsh Lake—guests traveled by river and on foot to attend. As they approached the Carcross Indian Reserve, they shot their rifles into the air to announce their arrival, then streamed into Charlie's old house and Jim's big two-story home for the celebration. Jim, Kate, and others took turns making speeches about their ancestors, dancing, singing, and showing off headdresses, carvings, and fancy clothes.

For two weeks, Kate and her Dak̲l'aweidí relatives fed the guests. After the Crows finished setting the marker and building the fence around Charlie's grave, the potlatch ended with a big feast featuring Charlie's favorite foods. Like other guests, Kate ate and drank at the potlatch not only for herself but for her dead ancestors—Charlie; her mother; her father; her brother, Tlákwshaan, and sister, Tusáxał, who died in epidemics along the coast; her sister Nadagáat Tláa, who died in the blizzard on the Chilkoot Trail; her sister Aagé, who died at Forty Mile; and Kate's first husband, Kult'ús, and their daughter.

The feast culminated with Jim and other high-ranking hosts making solemn speeches of thanks to the Crows for all they had done. Then the children were honored, receiving prized clan names and dancing while wrapped in calico cloth, which was then given away. Finally, Jim called the names of the guests one by one, bestowing gifts as he expressed his thanks for their help after Charlie's death. Though Kate had little of value, she contributed to the treasure trove of gifts that had been piled in Charlie's house for the guests to admire. By the end, all were satisfied—the host clan, the guests, even Charlie's spirit—as their ancestors were remembered and the bonds within their moieties were renewed.[16]

Not long after the festivities, Jim left Carcross on an extended journey that would include a stop in Seattle to share some big news with, of all people, Kate's former husband—news of a big gold strike at Silver Creek, near Atlin. Upon receiving a letter from Tahltan Chief Charley Johnson informing him of the discovery, Jim went straight to Atlin, arriving on Christmas Day. After assessing the situation, he set out over the 220-mile winter trail to Telegraph Creek, then followed the Stäkéen River to Wrangell to catch the next steamer to Seattle so that George Carmack would be among the first to know.

At least that's what Jim told George. As Jim suspected, his former brother-in-law still had the gold bug; in fact, in his excitement, he appears to have forgotten completely how only a few years earlier, Jim had been "down on him to kill." Going back on his vow never to return to the North, George set out for Atlin in the company of Graphie's husband and two prospector friends. When they arrived, a small stampede was on, and this time, the Indians were ready—along the trails, they were selling moose meat for 25 cents a pound and snowshoes for $14 a pair, and they'd engaged the services of an attorney to represent them in selling $300 claims along the box canyons and waterfalls of Silver Creek.

One of George's partners, a veteran of the Nome gold rush, became immediately suspicious: the country didn't look right for gold. He panned all day at Silver Creek but found only one small nugget, which he threw back. Try the Jennings River, the Carmack party was told, but still they found nothing. George's partner gave up, selling his $300 outfit for $50 and returning to Seattle. He declared to reporters that the whole thing was a hoax concocted by the Indians. "A worse looking place could not have been picked for a fake stampede," he said. "Still, those Indians were pretty cute. They made a pile of money out of the moose meat and the snowshoes and the deposits on the sale of the claims."[17]

Even Skookum Jim had been fooled, George's partner maintained. But there remains the question of why Jim would have traveled so far and long to track down George Carmack with news of another Bonanza; surely he felt no great love for him after George treated Kate so badly.[18] And beyond this singular event, there's no indication that Jim and George every reconciled. If the rush was indeed an elaborate, well-orchestrated hoax, it would have been the ultimate payback, a way for Jim to settle the score with George Carmack. To pull off such a ruse, so complete that George's friends believed that Jim's own relatives had suckered him in, was an accomplishment worthy of a known jokester like Jim, and a prank utterly suited for a man like George, easily seduced by the potential for profit, whether in a product deemed to cure baldness or in another rumored Bonanza. Even after his partner left, George wasn't about to admit he'd been duped; he prospected around Teslin Lake all that summer and got nothing for his troubles.

After the small frenzy over Atlin gold faded, Jim spent the better part of the next two years among his Tahltan relatives. Traveling overland to Telegraph Creek and by boat to Liard and

Teslin, he hunted and trapped and did a little prospecting here and there in the back country. He was gone from Carcross for so long that his attorney feared he had died, for Jim had long been suffering from a chronic kidney ailment, Bright's disease.

His health failing, Jim finally decided he'd better go home. He snowshoed along an old trading route, his only companion the big dog that pulled his toboggan. As the condition grew worse, he had to be taken by dog team to Teslin and then to Tagish, where his cousin Tagish John and son Johnny were staying. "I'm glad to be back," Jim told them. "I'm a sick man, and I want to die in my hometown."[19]

Jim left his faithful dog with his cousin while eighteen-year-old Johnny drove him by dog team to Carcross. The weather that winter was brutal, with temperatures dipping to sixty below zero. Kate was happy to see Jim, though it was clear his health had turned for the worse. After visiting his family, Jim traveled by train to Whitehorse, where he was admitted to the hospital.[20] Given his condition, his legal advisors revisited the terms of his will. When Jim told them he wanted to make some adjustments, they suggested he add a clause stipulating that upon Daisy's death, whatever was left in the trust he'd set up for her be used for the benefit of the Yukon Indians.[21] He also bequeathed $1,000 to Kate.

Having passed the age of maturity, Jim's daughter, Daisy, had moved from Seattle to California where, to the dismay of her guardians, she had taken up acting in motion pictures. Informed of her father's illness, she arranged to meet him in Seattle, where he was planning to travel in hopes of restoring his health, but before that could happen Bishop Stringer sent a telegram advising that Daisy had better come north at once if she wanted to see her father while he was still alive.[22]

She rushed to the hospital in Whitehorse, where as a Native, Jim was kept in a separate ward from the white patients.[23] Shortly afterwards, Jim was discharged from the hospital so that he could return home to die. In Carcross, Kate helped care for him, as did Daisy and a number of relatives who journeyed from Teslin and Telegraph Creek. While there was much concern over what would become of Jim's money after his death, he in fact had few assets beyond the $20,000 that was locked into Daisy's trust fund. Still, tensions over his money escalated to the point that Daisy wrote to her guardian requesting police protection "against the hostility of the Indians."[24]

To Kate's great sorrow, Jim died on July 11, 1916. At his request, he was buried in a fancy casket, wearing the new suit he had picked out. In the papers, there was nothing about how he had packed 165 pounds of bacon over the Chilkoot Pass, or how he had fought off a bear, or how he had followed the cries of Wealth Woman's child. There was nothing about his frog helper, or his visions of the golden-haired woman, or the house he'd had built for Kate, or the potlatch he'd hosted in memory of Charlie. There was nothing about the $20,000 he'd left in trust for his daughter, or how about how that trust fund would be appropriated for the betterment of the Yukon Indians after her death. Instead, his obituaries were a rehashing of how Skookum Jim Mason had discovered gold and then squandered his share.

"The Discoverer of the Klondike Died a Pauper," read one headline. "He got plenty of excitement out of his gold, the first great strike in Alaska's most sensational gold field," the article stated, "but he didn't get much happiness." The reporter repeated the story of the gold coins thrown from the Seattle Hotel, though in this version, it was made to seem as if the spree had been all Jim's doing. Details of extensive shopping Jim and his wife had done in Seattle were also included.

> They bought silks and satins and soda pop and lingerie and jewelry and canned salmon and print cloth and eggs and canned fruit and candy. Anything in gaudy colors or good to eat won their gold and they never asked the price . . . The hotel room began to take on the appearance of a madhouse. In the midst of this confusion of food, drink, finery, and frippery, Skookum Jim and his squaw delved and puttered, unpacking, tasting, trying on, excited as children.[25]

So it was that Outsiders remembered Kate's brother, a man who had earned exceptional admiration and respect among his own people.

Daisy stayed a few weeks in Carcross and then returned to Seattle to marry. Despite the acrimony between her and her Tagish relatives, she had at one time expressed an interest in wedding someone local. Inquiries had been made of an eligible bachelor of the Wolf clan, but his response was, "Who wants to marry a white lady anyway? She acts white lady too much."[26]

Of the children born to Gus'dutéen and Kaachgaawáa, Kate was the only one left. In difficult times, Jim had always been there to help. He had intended to also provide for her after his death. But every penny of his fortune was tied up in the trust that would benefit Daisy and, eventually, the Yukon Indians. Of the $1,000 he'd bequeathed to her, Kate received nothing.

As executor of Jim's estate, Bishop Stringer did not see fit for Kate to continue living in Jim's house and using his belongings. When she learned that Stringer had agreed to sell everything in the house for $72 to a man in Carcross, Kate began to sell Jim's belongings herself, believing the bishop had no right to dispose of her brother's personal possessions.

Stringer was not pleased. In April 1917, Kate wrote him a letter, with the help of a local resident. In a more desperate tone than she had ever taken with George, she pleaded for the bishop to deal with her directly:

> Mr. Townsend and the police are coming to my place, kicking the door at night, at bedtime. They threaten to put me in jail if I [won't leave] my brother's house and if I take anything from the house. They say that you are selling everything. You should have explained just how things were . . . If they have business with me, they should come in the daytime . . . I need money to buy wood with, and clothing, too. You might at least let me have a few things or the empty old house to spend the rest of my days in. Instead they keep me out of my brother's house. I feel like committing suicide. I

> will if those people don't stop abusing me. Please answer at once. I want to know the truth.[27]

After some back and forth, it was agreed that Kate could have the $72 in proceeds that would come from the sale of Jim's belongings, to be doled out to her at the rate of $5 per month. "I think she ought to get this little help," wrote the Bishop to Daisy, "even though she is not perfect."[28] On Kate's imperfections, he failed to elaborate.

Carcross storekeeper Matthew Watson added to his own coffers by selling postcards that featured Kate, now in her fifties. In the photo, her hand rests on the head of a black dog that stares intently at her free hand, as a dog will do when it has been favored with treats. She wears no gold rings or bracelets, only a plain, tidy skirt and blouse, her waist too large by far for the glittering belt she wore in her San Francisco portrait twenty years earlier. Parted neatly, her hair is pulled back in a bun. Though noticeably aged, her face still radiates beauty, and her smile is broader than in any other photo of her.[29] "Kate Carmack, wife of discoverer of the Klondike," reads the inscription on the postcard.

With the prospect of Jim's house being sold, Kate retreated to a small, white clapboard home, sparsely furnished with a rusty stove, mirror, and chair. On her wall hung colored lithographs of the King and Queen of England, and beside them, pictures of two Native men.[30] Along with the $5 per month Kate received from the sale of Jim's furnishings, the government provided a small subsidy intended for those who had no other means of support, primarily the old and the indigent.[31] Occasionally, Graphie Grace also sent money.[32]

Every now and again, Kate received out-of-town guests. One was Charlotte Cameron, an intrepid traveler and author who had made two trips around the world. In 1919, she stopped in Carcross, where she visited Matthew Watson's General Store with the intent of buying a moose hide table covering like the ones at the Caribou Hotel. In the store, a Tagish family pointed to her hat with its stiff feather and showed her the buckskin shirts, pouches, and baskets they had brought to barter.

After the family left, the storekeeper explained to Cameron that for his Tagish customers, shopping was something of a ritual. They would linger in the store, choosing and paying for items one at a time, until nearly the whole day was spent. They had a special fondness for sweets: candy, chocolate, and preserves. He also spoke of how the men would take two wives—an older woman experienced at sewing moccasins, snaring birds, making mats, and tanning skins, and also a younger woman. The storekeeper also shared his views on the potlatch tradition, officially banned under Canada's Indian Act, noting that "many a chief has found himself reduced to penury."

Cameron judged Carcross to be a dull little settlement of log cabins, a place where you had to be sure to stay on the boardwalks or sand would ooze into your shoes. At the hotel, someone suggested she combat boredom by paying a visit to Kate Carmack. Plagued by mosquitoes that descended on her ankles from the high rushes and weeds, Cameron proceeded along the dusty road around the shore of Lake Bennett toward the Indian reserve. By inquiring, she found Kate's little house, weeds growing alongside the door. When Cameron knocked, several big dogs rushed out to greet her.

"Even today she is comely, although dressed in ragged cotton," Cameron wrote of her meeting with Kate. "Her straight, thick, black hair was parted over a broad forehead. Her eyes were large, kindly, and dark. She appeared pleased to meet me, and shook hands." Kate showed off to Cameron the portraits in which she wore her gold nugget belt and necklace. She pointed out her daughter and husband, noting that she no longer saw George because he was living with his "white wife" in Seattle. Graphie kept promising to visit, Kate said, but she never came. When Cameron asked if she missed big cities and fine meals, Kate admitted her fondness for San Francisco and port wine.[33] Before she left, Cameron pressed upon Kate an impromptu gift, a large blue silk handkerchief decorated with white flowers. "Come again, come again," Kate urged.[34]

Another of Kate's visitors was a prominent Seattle attorney who had known Kate, George, Jim, and Charlie during the height

Kate Carmack, Carcross, 1919, the year of Charlotte Cameron's visit. Matthew Watson sold this image on a postcard. (Yukon Archives, Anglican Church of Canada General Synod Archives fonds, 78/67, #174)

of the gold rush. He claimed that Kate confirmed to him what he understood to be the real truth about the discovery of gold in the Klondike—that she herself found the first nugget.[35] Charlotte Cameron also mentions Kate finding gold nuggets in her dishpan, although in her book about her travels in Alaska, she deems this a "romantic version" of the Klondike discovery and gives no indication that Kate in any way substantiated or endorsed the idea.[36]

Not surprisingly, given her cultural perspective, Cameron emphasized the riches-to-rags aspect of Kate's story. But that wasn't how Kate defined herself. As a Tagish elder, her wisdom and experience were valued. She knew about the weather, the land, the animals, the people, and the spirit powers of the universe. She knew about the future because she knew about the past. Like all elders, she was drawing close to "old peoples' mountain," meaning that she was getting ready to begin life all over again.[37]

In 1920, the people of Carcross were stricken with the Spanish influenza, a killer strain of the flu that first appeared in February of 1918 in San Sebastian, a sunny tourist town on the northern coast of Spain.[38] Within months, the disease swept through Europe, China, India, Japan, portions of Central and South America, and the Caribbean. One-fifth of the flu's victims suffered only a mild form of the illness. For the other 80 percent, the sickness took one of two courses, both of which ended nearly always in death. In some, the virus went immediately to the lungs, which filled with fluid. Delirious with fever, these victims succumbed within days, sometimes hours, dying of what amounted to suffocation. For others, the illness started like any flu, with the usual fever, chills, and aches. Four or five days later, infection set in, with bacteria spreading inside the lungs, resulting in pneumonia and, ultimately, death.[39]

Before it was over, the world discovered firsthand what the Tagish and Tlingit already knew far too well—the alarming effects of a virus against which entire populations had few defenses. No one would ever be able to say for certain how many deaths resulted from the Spanish influenza; estimates range from 20 to 100 million. In contrast, 9.2 million died in World War I combat.[40]

In the remote communities of the North, the Spanish flu arrived late, but it was as virulent as ever. Whole villages were wiped out and hundreds of children were orphaned. Carcross was one of the last places hit, with the disease picking up where the gold rush left off, destroying families and altering traditional ways of knowing and being.

Kate had weathered the sickness that took her first husband and her daughter. She had evaded death by tuberculosis. She had survived the mumps, which routinely killed those who lacked immunity. But in the middle of a March so cold and snowy that the trains had quit running, Kate fell ill with the Spanish flu. At first, it seemed to take the milder course—aches, pains, chills, headache, fever. Then she took a turn for the worse. As she grew weak, her breathing labored, she found it hard to get out of bed. Her family, the few that remained, took care of her, the way she'd taken care of Jim and so many others who had passed on. Though she clung to life, she did not fear death, knowing that her spirit would be reborn.[41]

After ten days of sickness, the disease overcame her. After a lifetime of adapting and relating and honoring the ways that sustained her, Kate set off on her final journey, from life into death, on March 29, 1920. Seeing that Kate's light was left on, her cousin Tagish John began to weep[42]—a light left on illuminated the way for the dead as they departed life.

At the time of her death, all that remained of Kate's material wealth were a pair of sealskin gloves and a gold watch engraved with her initials.[43] Even as outsiders lamented all she had lost, she herself had long recognized the real gain she'd achieved by returning to the family and the land that she loved; despite pressures to the contrary, she had neither defied her own people nor exiled herself from them. And though others insisted on framing her as a woman stripped of wealth, she understood the capricious nature of fortune, as demonstrated by the Wealth Woman of legend; as opposed to riches, she measured herself against the actions she knew to be right.

She was a good woman, the Tagish people say of her still—a good woman, who came from good people.[44]

EPILOGUE

AT THE TIME OF KATE'S DEATH, there were few people left in Carcross to sing mourning songs and feed her favorite foods to her spirit and make the smoke that united the living humans with spirits.[1] Two days after Kate died of the Spanish flu, her cousin Tagish John also succumbed. The disease went straight to his lungs, and he died in the arms of his son Johnny, who was trying to feed him an orange.[2] Because he had begun hiring out as a guide for big game hunters seeking trophy kills in the Yukon, Johnny had the money to pay for a proper funeral and headstone for his father.[3] Kate's grave was marked with only a slab of plywood, her name scrawled in charcoal.[4]

Responding to an inquiry regarding the money bequeathed to Kate in Jim's will, Jim's attorney informed Graphie Grace of her mother's death. She traveled north to collect Kate's photographs and gold watch—the only time she would return to place of her people, the Dak̲l'aweidí.[5]

In 1922, George Carmack's death brought Kate back to court, posthumously. He died in Vancouver, British Columbia, where he had traveled with Marguerite to address a local chapter of the Yukon Order of Pioneers (YOP). The speech was a proud moment for George, who had been excluded from an earlier reunion of Klondike pioneers hosted by his old friend Howard Hamilton Hart, who'd helped found the YOP,[6] by design, a fraternal organization of white men; those whose ancestors had been there for centuries were excluded, as were women.

Hart and Carmack had been friendly enough when they shared a cabin during Starvation Winter and again in the early months of 1900, when Hart mortgaged Carmack's claim at No. 1 below Discovery. But later that year, when Carmack abandoned Kate and sold No. 1 below to Jim after he'd mortgaged it to Hart, tensions arose. George wrote to Rose that he suspected Hart, along with their half-brother Julius Huttman, of conspiring against him.

In August 1901, Hart left the Klondike, boarding the steamship *Islander* with a satchel that contained $40,000 in gold. After the ship's departure from Skagway, the passengers settled in their beds, only to be awakened abruptly when the ship struck an iceberg. In the scramble for lifeboats, one man jumped while clutching his suitcase filled with gold, missing the boat (literally) and drowning (also literally) under the weight of his fortune.

Hart was wiser. He abandoned his satchel of gold and leapt into the last lifeboat, avoiding the fate of the sixty-seven passengers who drowned.[7] By investing in oil wells in Bakersfield, California, he acquired a second fortune that enabled him, among other pursuits, to host a lavish Klondike reunion in San Francisco in 1911. But when the newspapers printed the guest list for the upscale affair, George Carmack's name was notably missing.[8]

Redeemed by the invitation of the Vancouver YOP "igloo," George read to the twenty men assembled there from the memoir he'd been working on with George T. Snow, a version of the Klondike discovery in which he omitted Kate altogether and claimed sole credit for finding the gold, as he had begun doing after leaving Kate—speaking to a reporter in 1904, George claimed he'd never had any Indian relatives; Jim and Charlie had been hired to pack for him, nothing more, and that was how they happened to be at Bonanza Creek on the day gold was found.[9]

Following George's speech, the members of the Vancouver igloo passed a resolution that proclaimed him the true discoverer of gold in the Klondike. Six days later, George Carmack died of pneumonia at Roycroft Hospital in Vancouver, with Marguerite at his side.[10] Services were held in Seattle, where George was buried. Marguerite, who called herself George's constant companion, did not bother to set a monument over his grave, a project that would be accomplished by the Yukon Order of Pioneers in 1975.

Following his death came four years of legal wrangling over the Carmack estate. The trouble began with Marguerite's terse communication to Rose regarding her brother's death—she sent only a two-word telegram, reading "George dead."[11] In turn, Graphie learned of her father's death in the newspaper; Marguerite would later claim she had no idea where Graphie and her husband were living.

The language of George's will, written in 1914, was simple enough: his property was to be divided according to the laws of the state of Washington. Marguerite filed to have herself appointed executrix of the Carmack estate and declared herself the sole heir to what remained of the fortune, which she estimated at $1,500.[12] In response, Rose and Graphie hired legal counsel to demand that a third-party administrator be appointed to determine the rightful heirs and the true value of what remained of the Carmack fortune. Among the attorneys employed was one to represent the estate of Kate Carmack, making a claim to the money on the grounds that she and George had never divorced.

Judge King Dykeman, who had gone himself to the Klondike in 1898, presided over the Superior Court proceedings. As an interim measure, Dykeman granted Marguerite's request for $350 in monthly maintenance, but at the same time he removed her as executrix and appointed a third-party administrator. Graphie, Rose, and the attorney for the estate of Kate Carmack appealed the maintenance award on the grounds that Marguerite's marriage to George was "pretended and illegal," leaving Kate and Graphie as the only true heirs to the Carmack fortune. The complaint alleged that in "a common design, plan and scheme to obtain control of the wealth and property of George Washington Carmack and Kate Mason Carmack his wife," Marguerite was willfully and maliciously withholding facts from the court.[13]

A year and a half after George's death, Dykeman ruled in favor of Graphie, Rose, and the attorney for Kate's estate. He found that from 1887 to 1900, George had presented Kate to the world as his wife, and that he had likewise acknowledged Graphie Grace as their daughter. In his ruling, the judge named Kate and Graphie along with Jim, Charlie, and George Carmack as having made the "very valuable" discovery of gold at Bonanza Creek. He also concluded that the assets of George Carmack were substantially greater than Marguerite had let on. From the sketchy information that Marguerite had been compelled to provide, the judge estimated the value of the estate at $140,000, maybe more—a substantial sum compared to Marguerite's $1,500 estimate.[14]

Included in the judge's finding of facts were Carmack's hasty courtship with Marguerite and his abandonment of Kate in California. In addition, Dykeman noted that Kate's suit for separate maintenance, filed by John Durst in San Francisco, had never been dismissed. The court also gave no credence to Marguerite's claim that she had left the Klondike with $55,000 in cash that she kept on her person, earned in little more than a year from the proceeds of "selling cigars" in Dawson.[15] "The many contradictions in her testimony, her apparent effort to conceal the facts, her reluctance to testify, her suppression of evidence, her demeanor upon the witness stand, and the improbability of her testimony, all convince the court of its incredibility," wrote the judge in his findings.[16]

Ordered to turn over to a third-party administrator all property acquired in her twenty-two years of marriage to George Carmack, Marguerite appealed to the Supreme Court of the state of Washington. As in Dykeman's courtroom, her testimony was evasive and contradictory. When she met George Carmack, she said, he had no money; in fact, he was "in the hole." Everything they owned, she claimed, had been purchased with $60,000 in cash she brought out of Dawson from her cigar store earnings.[17] "Mr. Carmack used all my money," she said; every bank deposit he ever made to the time of his death, she maintained, was from monies he obtained from her—she allowed him to do this, she said, because she did not want him to have to look small. Of Graphie and Jacob, Marguerite said, "Carmack had not spoke to either one of them for over a year. He did not want to have anything to do with them." In fact, Marguerite claimed, Graphie was not George Carmack's daughter at all.[18]

Like Dykeman, the judge who oversaw the case for the Supreme Court of Washington was unimpressed with Marguerite's testimony. "What appears to be remarkable is that she remembers the details of things that occurred in 1901; but when it comes to business affairs she does not remember anything," he noted.[19] Marguerite urged her brother, Jacob, husband of Graphie, to convince his wife to settle out of court for $5,000. In response, Graphie took her children and moved in with Rose and Frank Curtis, whom Rose had married in 1906.

After three years of legal battles, an out-of-court settlement was finally reached. Of an estate that Marguerite had initially claimed was worth $1,500, Graphie got $45,000, half of which went to pay her attorneys. Another $17,500 went to pay the administrator and his attorney, along with the attorney for the estate of Kate Carmack. After paying her attorneys, Marguerite was left with $100,000.[20] By the time of her death in 1942, she had lost most of this fortune by sinking it into three mines in Placer County, California. The $2,500 left after her final debts were paid went to her niece. To drive home the point that her brother had botched the $5,000 settlement offer with Graphie Grace, Marguerite left him five dollars.[21]

The children of the Klondike prospectors who married Native women met with varying degrees of happiness. Graphie Grace married three times; within a year, her second husband managed to spend most of her $45,000 settlement.[22] Her cousin Daisy, Jim's daughter, died young, as her guardians had predicted she would, having spent much of her forty-four years in and out of hospitals and marriages. Per her request, she was buried in the Carcross cemetery next to her father.

After Bishop Stringer's mention of her being in Seattle in 1909, there is no trace of what became of Kate's niece Mary Wilson; she was not among the guests at Graphie's 1910 wedding. Jennie Harper's son Walter, born a few weeks before Graphie Grace, achieved fame as the first to officially summit Mount McKinley, the tallest peak in North America, as part of a team organized by Archdeacon Hudson Stuck, for whom Walter served as an interpreter. Prior to the expedition, Walter had never climbed a mountain.[23] Following his achievement, tragedy struck—newly married, Walter and his wife drowned when the *Princess Sophia* sank off the coast of Alaska in 1918.

Those who stayed on the land that had always sustained them fared better than those who left. Kate's cousin Johnny Johns pulled his children out the Choutla Residential School at Carcross, where students would suffer "strappings" if they dared to speak their own language. In order to open his own business, Johnny gave up his rights under the Indian Act, and as a world-famous big game guide, he hired relatives from as far away as Dawson to work for him. From the trophy hunters who came only for capes and head mounts, he made sure to always salvage meat to distribute among his people. When the Alaska-Canada Highway was hastily built as a security measure during World War II, Johnny was hired to show US soldiers where the road should be built. Because jack pines grew where the ground was good, he directed the crew from jack pine to jack pine; when new orders came to make the road crooked so it wouldn't be an easy target for bombing, he routed it past the pretty lakes where he liked to fish.[24]

Johnny's sister Angela had always been fond of her cousin Kate Carmack. Toward the end of a long life in which she went to great efforts to make sure the heritage of her people was documented, Angela was honored by the Order of Canada for helping to preserve Tagish culture and language.[25]

As wife of Mountie turned hunting guide Tom Dickson, Kate's niece Louise, daughter of Aagé and L'unáat, earned the admiration of guests at the lodge she ran with her husband at Kluane Lake. Of striking beauty, Louise used her rifle to put meat on the table for her large family—caribou, Dahl sheep, moose, geese. She trapped furbearers and tanned hides. She sewed mittens of caribou skin that she beaded and embroidered. She helped her husband with his trap lines, and while he was out trapping on his own, she twice delivered own babies.[26]

The virtues of an Indian wife were many, Tom Dickson maintained: No corsets; no high-heels; no running to the store to see the latest in fashion; no idle gossip. Louise was always healthy, he said, and so were their children, who were well trained. "Last of all," Dickson said, "the Indian woman can be trusted better than the white woman."[27] Eventually, Tom and his wife separated. With her sons, Louise raised mink during the years that fur farming was popular in the Yukon. She married again, to another hunting guide, and when she died she left 146 living descendants.[28]

For years, the White Pass & Yukon Railroad paid Kate's nephew Patsy Henderson five dollars a week to tell the story of how gold was found in the Klondike. In some of Patsy's accounts, Jim found the first nugget; in others, Charlie found it. No stranger to the ways of the white man, Patsy eventually demanded a raise from the railroad company. "The price of flour going up, bacon's going up, sugar go up," he told his boss. "And now even the price of bullshit going up, cause from now on I gotta have $7.50."[29]

Near the site of George's short-lived trading post, the town of Carmacks was formed; today, it has some five hundred residents, many from the Little Salmon/Carmacks First Nations. The Klondike Highway passes through town, connecting Skagway with Dawson City. Near the end of that highway, on the banks of Bonanza Creek, interpretive signs placed by Parks Canada have been updated, giving Skookum Jim—not George Carmack—credit for finding the gold that started the rush to the Klondike.

Ernest Saftig, the grandson Kate never met, visited the Yukon when he was eighty years old. "The physical resemblance to Kate, Carmack's Tagish Indian wife, is pronounced," noted a reporter for the *Whitehorse Star*, adding that Saftig displayed "a lot of Kate's legendary spunk."[30] In an odd twist, Saftig was good friends with John Wayne, the actor who played cowboy hero against countless Indians in Western movies.

As part of the Klondike Gold Rush Centennial celebration in 1996, a plaque was added to Kate's gravesite, the wooden plank having been replaced with a proper granite monument that bears the name by which she was known during the latter part of her life—Kate Carmacks—along with the inscription "Gold I Bring to Crown Him Again." The centennial plaque reads "With Respect and in Honour of Your Discovery, and with Gratitude for Your Legacy—To all First Nations & to all Yukoners."

No one will ever know for certain exactly how much gold came out of the Klondike. From the claims filed by George Carmack and his Tagish relatives, the only real wealth that remains is in the trust set up by Skookum Jim. Many years after Jim's death, Native leaders asked the trustees to redirect the funds away from the Anglican residential schools, which ended up causing much heartache for Native students and their families. In a purpose closer to Jim's intent, the trust monies now help fund the Skookum Jim Friendship Centre in Whitehorse, the oldest Native organization in the Yukon, with the mission of bettering the spiritual, emotional, physical, and mental well being of the First Nations people of the region. Among the Centre's programs is one that would have surely pleased Kate—Women of Wisdom workshops that teach the old ways of healing, grieving, and reconciliation. The interest earned from the trust fund also helps the Centre to recognize Yukon First Nations leaders who serve their communities.

Despite the onslaught of change precipitated by colonial interests in the North, the Tagish people have never forgotten the importance of *haa shagóon*—their ancestors and their destiny. In 1973, Tagish leaders were among the first to present to the Canadian prime minister a document titled "Together Today for Our Children Tomorrow," an indictment of the Indian Act and a blueprint for the future. In 2008, the Carcross-Tagish First Nations became one of eleven Canadian bands to sign the Yukon Land Claims and Self-Governance Agreement, giving them independence from the Indian Act.

To maintain their self-reliance and self-determination, the Carcross-Tagish First Nations have implemented taxation as a modern form of the potlatch system of redistributing wealth, and they have instituted a clan-based governance structure. To achieve economic stability, they operate a corporation with the express mission of putting people before profits. And in a modern twist on the trails that were once so vital to their way of life, Tagish youth have transformed a road built in 1910 by Sam McGee, an outsider immortalized in a Robert Service poem, into an epic biking and hiking trail.

Purchased by Johnny Johns from Jim's estate after Kate's death and gifted to the Dak̲l'aweidí as a clan house, Skookum Jim's home has been moved from the Indian Reserve to the center of Carcross Commons, as part of a program that repatriates indigenous arts into the community.[31] Upstairs are exhibits that showcase the history of the Tagish people.

"When we showed all these guests into the Yukon," says Justin Ferbey of the Carcross Tagish Management Corporation, "there was one thing we never considered: that you were all going to stay so long."[32] Now that these "guests" have settled in the region, Ferbey says, the Carcross-Tagish First Nations hope that the land where the animals danced will become a destination where visitors come to recreate and to live.

As they continue to adapt, Kate's people affirm their ancient ties to the land. "We who are Tagish and we who are Tlingit, our heritage has grown roots into the earth since olden times," proclaims an elders' statement on the Carcross-Tagish First Nation website. "Therefore we are part of the earth and the water."[33]

ACKNOWLEDGMENTS

So many people helped with the research and crafting of this book that it feels impossible to adequately thank them all. First and foremost, my father, Louis Lehmann, acted as my unpaid and ever-willing research assistant, using his research and genealogy skills and resources to hunt down the most obscure information. Due in part to his efforts, I was able to communicate with descendants of almost every one of Kate's key associates in this story, many of whom had done meticulous research that they shared with me. Among them are T. J. Murray of the (Sophie) Bettles family; Ed Jones, descendent of Joe LaDue and author of *All That Glitters: The Life and Times of Joe Ladue*; Craig George, whose Aunt Lillian Johnson Corbitt, as a boarder of Rose (Carmack) Curtis, acquired a number of her personal belongings after her death; James McQuiston, descendent of Jack McQuesten and author of *Captain Jack: Father of the Yukon*; Cindi Long, whose great-aunt was married to Howard Hamilton Hart; Phyllis Fast, descendent of Arthur and Jennie Harper, to whom I'm especially grateful for reminding me of the Athabaskan syntactical reliance on verbs over nouns, and also her cousins Jan Harper-Haines and Ethel Pronesti; Neil Knudsen, whose great-aunt was married to the foster son of Rose (Carmack) Curtis; and Jeff Blystone, a Carmack descendent.

For their help with archival research, my thanks go to Donna Darbyshire at the Yukon Archives, who also connected me with author lian goodall, who was researching the life of Kate's daughter; Laura Mann, who welcomed me at the Dawson Museum and shares my enthusiasm for this project; Sheila Praeder of the San Benito County Historical Society, who spent a whole day helping me pore over old newspapers and other source material; and Gary Lundell at the University of Washington Special Collections, who helped me access the entire collection of George W. Carmack papers. Effusive thanks go to author and research extraordinaire lian goodall of Whitehorse, who helped with procuring many of the documents referenced within these pages and also took pity on me (and my dog), inviting us to stay two nights in her home when I was only a stranger on a research adventure with nowhere to sleep.

For assistance with Tlingit spellings, *gunalchéesh* to X̲'unei Lance Twitchell and also to the Sealaska Heritage Institute as well to Thomas Thornton and Keri Edwards for their scholarship. Thanks go also to John Ritter of the Yukon Native Language Centre for his advice on Tagish spellings. Any errors in language and spelling are my own. For pronunciations, I encourage readers to access print and audio resources at the Sealaska Heritage website (Tlingit: www.sealaskaheritage.org) and the Yukon Native Language Centre website (Tagish: www.ynlc.ca).

Others who offered invaluable information, assistance, and encouragement include Yukon historian and author Michael Gates; *Anchorage Dispatch News* editor Mike Dunham; Cynthia Von Halle of the Klondike Gold Rush National Historical Park; Jay Moynahan, who searched his databases for information on Marguerite Laimee; Sallie Calhoun, who took me on a tour of her Paicines Ranch, which operates much as such ranches did at the turn of the century; Delores Smith, who shared the documentary she produced on Kate's brother, Jim; and author Dan Henry, who has written extensively about Tlingit history and insisted that I tell Kate's story.

I owe a great deal to the readers who graciously read an early version of the manuscript and helped me shape the focus and vision of the story: author M. J. Kirchhoff (*Clondyke; Dyea, Alaska*), whose sharp eye for detail and documentation of local history is unparalleled; author Lael Morgan (*Goodtime Girls; Wanton West*, and more), whose editorial judgment I much admire; author David Neufeld (*Chilkoot Trail: Heritage Route to the Klondike*), who directed me to the work of Richard White and others; author lian goodall (*William Lyon McKenzie King; Photographing Greatness*), who reminded me (many times!) to keep Kate front and center in the narrative; two astute readers who also happen to be family, author Chris Lehmann (*Rich People Things; Revolt of the Mass Cult*) and my father, Louis Lehmann; and finally—and especially—author and anthropologist Julie Cruikshank (*Life Lived Like a Story, Reading Voices, The Social Life of Stories*, and more), whose body of work has made this book possible.

Of those who are no longer with us, I'm grateful to Catharine McClellan for her extensive ethnographic survey of Southern Yukon Territory; to Alaska's iconic statesman James Wickersham for gathering documents—in 1938, when he was nearly blind and in failing health—with the intent of telling Kate's story; and to James Albert Johnson for retrieving the Wickersham papers and leaving them to the University of Washington Special Collections.

Most of all, I want to thank the elders and others of the Carcross-Tagish First Nations and Tlingit clans: Inez Larson, great-granddaughter of Kate's sister Aagé; X̱'unei Lance Twitchell, who shared the Tl'anaxéedáḵw story as told by Seidayaa Elizabeth Nyman, of the Yanyeidí clan in Aatlein (Atlin); Justin Ferbey, who arranged an open forum for me in Carcross; Robin Lovelace-Smith, an amazing artist and spokesperson for her clan; Doris MacLean, matron of the Carcross-Tagish Dakl'aweidí; and especially elders Annie Auston and Ida Calmagene, who invited me into their homes and shared their stories; Ida even took me (literally) to the mountaintop, where she showed me all around the land as she knows it.

A special *gùnèlchīsh* to Angela Sidney and Mrs. Billy Smith, both deceased, whose love and respect for their Aunt Kate is evident in the oral histories they shared in *Life Lived Like a Story* and other publications. Without their openness and passion for preserving the culture and heritage of the Tagish-Tlingit clans, Kate's story could not be told.

Together, we are a band of voices bringing forward perspectives on a life and an era that have been too often overlooked. Any errors in compiling and conveying this narrative, however, are solely mine.

ENDNOTES

PREFACE

1 George W. Carmack papers, University of Washington Archives.

2 Pierre Berton, *The Klondike Fever* (New York: Carroll and Graf, 1958), 441–443.

3 "Tagish," http://www.ynlc.ca/languages/tg/tg.html, accessed May 22, 2015.

4 *The Chicago Manual of Style*, 16th edition, section 8.37 (Chicago: University of Chicago Press, 2010), 402.

5 "Tagish," http://www.ynlc.ca/languages/tg/tg.html, accessed May 22, 2015.

CHAPTER ONE

1 "Ten Tons of Gold from the Frozen North," *Tacoma Daily News* (August 31, 1898): 4. Another source, "Returning Adventurers," *New York Times* (August 31, 1898) makes "a conservative estimate" of $1.5 million in gold carried on the Roanoke.

2 In *The Reckless Decade* (Chicago: University of Chicago Press, 2002), H. W. Brands discusses the frontier as the area (both geographical and psychological) where the predictable and unpredictable meet; he also quotes from the 1890 US Census Report: "Up to and including 1890 the country had a frontier of settlement, but at present the unsettled area has been so broken into by isolated bodies of settlement that there can hardly be said to be a frontier line," 23.

3 Virgil Moore, "George W. Carmack," *The Klondike News* (April 1, 1898).

4 Terrence Cole, Introduction to *Two Women in the Klondike* by Mary E. Hitchcock (University of Alaska Press, 2005), ix–x.

5 The sternwheeler was the riverboat version of the steamship, with a steam-driven paddle at the stern.

6 Mary E. Hitchcock, *Two Women in the Klondike* (University of Alaska Press, 2005), 33.

7 Karan Smith, "Gold in the Veins," *The Yukon News* (August 26, 1998).

8 "Threw Money at the Crowd: Returned Klondiker and His Alaska Wife Amuse the People of Seattle," *The Reading Eagle* (November 30, 1898), 13. As with many of the events in Kate's life, alternate versions of this story have circulated. In this book, the author relies wherever possible on primary and/or multiple sources.

9 Rayna Green, "The Pocahontas Perplex: The Image of Indian Women in American Culture," *Massachusetts Review* 27, no. 4 (1975).

10 Ibid.

11 "Ten Tons of Gold from the Frozen North."

12 George Carmack, letter to Rose Watson, June 20, 1897.

13 "How the Klondike Was Discovered," *Omaha World Herald* (September 11, 1898), reprinted from *The San Francisco Examiner.*

14 James Albert Johnson, *George Carmack* (Vancouver: Whitecap Boos, 2001), 115–116.

15 William Ogilvie, *Early Days on the Yukon* (New York: Arno Press, reprinted 1974), 133.

16 Thomas F. Thornton, *Klondike Gold Rush National Historical Park Ethnographic Overview and Assessment,* Final Report (August 2004).

17 "Million and a Half," *The San Juan Islander* (September 8, 1898), 1.

18 Lisa Mighetto and Marcia Montgomery, *Hard Drive to the Klondike* (Seattle: University of Washington Press, 2002), 64–66.

19 Pierre Berton, *The Klondike Fever* (New York: Carroll and Graf, 1958), 127–128.

20 H. W. Brands, *The Reckless Decade* (Chicago: The University of Chicago Press, 1995), 197.

21 Brands, 79.

CHAPTER TWO

1 Bradley J. Birzer, "Reflections on New West History by a Conservative Thinker," http://www.theimaginativeconservative.org/2012/08/reflections-on-new-western-history-of.html; "Richard White and

the New Western History," http://www.washington.edu/research/showcase/1990a.html; John Whitehead, "How Have Americans Viewed the Frontier?" http://www.loc.gov/rr/european/mofc/whitehead.html. My thanks to David Neufeld for directing me to these sources.

2 Until outsiders came, no one indigenous to the Americas would have called herself "Indian." Therefore, wherever possible, I distinguish affiliation by band and tribe: Tagish, Chilkoot, Chilkat, etc. For collective references, no single term satisfies. In this context, I've opted for "Indian," in part to distinguish between other Native groups, such as the Aleut and Inuit/Inupiat; in part to overcome the problem of conflicting verbiage in the United States (Native American) versus Canada (First Nations); and also because among the people to whom it may apply, the term "Indian" is returning to favor over other options, since more recent terms (Native American, etc.) have, like "Indian," been imposed from without.

3 Angela Sidney in *Life Lived Like a Story*, by Julie Cruikshank in collaboration with Angela Sidney, Kitty Smith, and Annie Ned (University of Nebraska Press, 1990), 44.

4 Angela Sidney, *Haa Shagóon* (Whitehorse, Yukon: Council for Yukon Indians and the Government of Yukon, 1983), xiii–xv. This volume is an excellent resource for understanding the complexities of Tagish-Tlingit naming.

5 Sidney, *Life Lived Like a Story*, 75–78.

6 1865 appears as her birth year on the US Census of 1900; 1859 is given as her birth year in testimony she gave before the Alaska Boundary Tribunal (1903); 1857 is the birth year assumed by the 1911 Canadian census, in which her age is listed as 54.

7 Julie Cruikshank, *Dan Dha Ts'edenintth'e: Reading Voices* (Vancouver: Douglas and McIntyre, 1991), 37.

8 Through marriages and trading alliances, the Tagish became "Tlingitized," acquiring customs of the Chilkoot and other coastal clans and learning their language. Today, many of Shaaw Tláa's descendants refer to themselves as "Tagish-Tlingit."

9 Millions of years ago, the Yukon followed a direct course to the ocean, flowing south to the Pacific. But tectonic changes forced the river north and then west in a course of nearly 2,000 miles to the Bering Sea. From Kate's childhood home, *downriver* on the Yukon means north, or *up* on a map, a geographical rendering little used by the Tagish before the rush to the Klondike began.

10 Catharine McClellan, *My Old People Say: An Ethnographic Survey of Southern Yukon Territory* (Ottawa: National Museums of Canada, 1975) 356–358. Traveling along the coast of Alaska in 1793, British explorer George Vancouver noted, "In all the commercial transactions the women took a very principal part, and proved themselves by no means unequal to the task. Nor did it appear that either in these or in any other respect they were inferior to the men; on the contrary, it should rather seem that they are looked up to as the superior sex, for they appeared in general to keep the men in awe, and under their subjection" (Thornton, 41, quoting Vancouver 1901 IV: 254–255 and deLaguna 1983:81).

11 Catharine McClellan, *My Old People Say*, 355–356. An excellent resource on Tagish culture published in two parts with consecutive page numbering; part 2 begins with page 325 and includes the index for both volumes.

12 Ibid, 165.

13 Ibid, 214.

14 McClellan, *My Old People Say*, Part 1, 77.

15 In terms of social organization, the term "headman" is more appropriate than "chief" for a leader of the Tlingit or the Tagish. But as the term "chief" was the one used by the outsiders, Tlingit leaders like Koh'klux also referred to themselves in that way.

16 Davidson, 178.

17 Davidson, 179.

18 Michael Gates, *History Hunting in the Yukon* (British Columbia: Harbour Publishing, 2010), 29.

19 Eliza Scidmore, *Alaska: Its Southern Coast and Sitkan Archipelago* (Boston: D. Lothrop, 1885), 115–116. Though Beardslee suggests Koh'klux did not earn his scar until nine years later, George Davidson (Gates, 29) describes him as "carrying a bullet-hole in his cheek."

20 Frederick W. Seward, *Reminiscences of a War-Time Statesman and Diplomat*. New York: Putnam, 1916, p. 387.

21 Ibid, 388.

22 Ibid.

23 Ibid, 389. A full decade later, still vexed by what happened that day, he peppered visiting naturalist John Muir about how exactly George Davidson had managed to turn daylight into darkness. See John Muir's *Travels in Alaska*, New York: Modern Library, 2002, 129. Convinced of Davidson's authority over the heavens, Kohklux

revealed to him the various passages to the Interior secreted and guarded by the Tlingit. Having never before put pen to paper, the Tlingit headman spent two full days sketching two maps, one drawn with the help of his wives, which detailed every footpath, camp, settlement, and food cache between his village and the ill-fated Hudson Bay fort. Davidson reciprocated with a representation of how the eclipse had appeared through his telescope, and he impressed Koh'klux by transcribing the Tlingit names for various landmarks named by the chief. See also *The Report of the Superintendent of the United States Coast Survey Showing the Progress of the Survey during the Year 1869*. Cruikshank, *Reading Voices*, 114–117; Washington: Government Printing Office, 1872, 56–57.

24 Cruikshank, Julie, in collaboration with Angela Sidney, Kitty Smith, and Annie Ned. *Life Lived Like a Story*. Lincoln: University of Nebraska Press, 1995, 114–117.

25 Thornton, 110.

26 Thornton, 119.

27 Thornton, 120.

28 Kitty Smith, "The First Time They Knew Koch'en, White Man," in *Life Lived Like a Story*, as told to Julie Cruikshank (University of Nebraska Press, 1995). For a more complete understanding of the functions of story and song among the Tagish, see Cruikshank's *The Social Life of Stories* (Lincoln: University of Nebraska Press, 2000).

29 Terrence Cole, Foreword to *Along Alaska's Great River* by Frederick Schwatka (Anchorage: Alaska Northwest Publishing, reprint 1983), 7.

30 Frederick Schwatka, *Along Alaska's Great River* (Alaska Northwest Publishing, reprint 1983), 32–34.

31 Ibid, 36 and 44.

CHAPTER THREE

1 Thornton, 91–92.

2 Thornton, 69–71. The terms here are from the Chilkoot Tlingit.

3 McClellan, *My Old People Say*, 193–195.

4 Ibid, 355–357.

5 Ibid, 201.

6 Rab Wilkie and the Skookum Jim Friendship Centre, *Skookum Jim: Native and Non-Native Stories and Views* (Heritage Branch,

Government of Yukon, 1992), 124. Cruikshank, *Reading Voices*, 129, names the trading partner as the brother of Shaaw Tláa's mother. It's possible that each of the sisters would have married Deisheetaan chiefs, one on the coast and one in the interior.

7 Thornton, 95–96.

8 McClellan, *Part of the Land, Part of the Water*, 206–207, explains the details of marriage arrangements.

9 The Tagish spelling is Lunaát'l, but because of his historical importance on the coast, the Tlingit spelling L'unáat is used here. There is some confusion regarding Aagé's intended husband and the man she actually married. In a few accounts, their names are switched. But a large body of evidence confirms that she and L'unáat, second chief of the Chilkoot, were in fact married. The two girls who were born to them, Susie George and Louise George Dickson, claimed Aagé and L'unáat as their parents; in some English renderings, Aagé and L'unáat were known as Jennie and George Thlunaut.

10 Cruikshank, *Reading Voices*, 129.

11 Aurel Krause, *To the Chukchi Peninsula and to the Tlingit Indians, 1881/82* (University of Alaska Press, 1993), 123.

12 Richard White, *The Middle Ground* (Cambridge University Press, 2011), xiii. White's analysis of the complex interactions between various Indian groups, the French, and the British in the *pays d'en haut* (the Great Lakes Region) challenges popular thinking about the frontier, including stereotypes of the pioneer hero and the obstructive and/or romanticized Indian. In the years following his book's release, the term "middle ground" has been used as it is here, as a broader metaphor that encapsulates the complexities of relationships along the frontier.

13 Though it's not known for certain where on the coast Kult'ús and Shaaw Tláa settled, in all likelihood it was in the vicinity of Chilkoot village or, for a time, in the newly resurrected Deishu Hit community, known by 1882 as Haines Mission. In *Life Lived Like a Story* (37), Shaaw Tláa's niece Angela Sidney tells how the original Deisheetaan woman from Angoon, a village far to the south, fell in love with a chief's son in the northern part of the Alaska Panhandle and raised three daughters in the Taku River area near Juneau. One of the daughters married a Tagish man, moving inland. But some Deisheetaan remained on the coast. They had their own village, Deishu Hit, in the present-day site of Haines, although Thornton (50) reports that no Indians lived there

during the contact period prior to the Mission being established. While none of the other coastal villages is specifically linked to the Deisheetaan, Thornton's source recalls (46) that there was substantial travel between Klukwan and Deishu and then upriver to Chilkoot and Dyea, a seasonal fish camp and jumping-off point for the Chilkoot Trail, the most direct route between the Tagish clans and the coast. Shaaw Tláa's oldest brother was buried at Dyea, and since her sister Aagé married L'unáat, a clan leader from Chilkoot, it's likely that she and her other sisters also married there.

14 Carrie Willard and Mrs. Eva McClintock, editor, *Life in Alaska: Letters of Mrs. Eugene S. Willard* (Philadelphia: Presbyterian Board of Publication, 1884), 13.

15 "Cinnamon bears" are brown-colored black bears.

16 Willard, 85.

17 Willard, location 1073, Kindle edition.

18 Ibid, 120.

19 Krause, 125. Another reason given for the name "Stick" was that the Tagish and their inland neighbors decorated themselves with feathers stuck in their hair and through nose piercings.

20 Ibid, 169. The Tlingit called the interior tribes Gunanaa, meaning "stranger."

21 Willard, location 1374, Kindle edition.

22 Krause, 170.

23 Ibid, 172–173.

24 Willard, location 1471, Kindle edition.

CHAPTER FOUR

1 Krause, 192–194.

2 Martha F. Betts, "Chilkat and Chilkoot Rivers Subsistence Eulachon Fishery," Division of Subsistence Technical Paper No. 213.

3 Willard, Kindle edition, location 1827.

4 Krause, 198.

5 Willard, location 1667.

6 Thornton, 74.

7 Willard, location 1667.

8 Thornton, 74.

9 Cruikshank, *Reading Voices*, 129. The exact birthdate of Shaaw Tláa's daughter is unknown.
10 McClellan, *My Old People Say*, 208.
11 Betts, 15.
12 Betts, 19.
13 *Gutzkakon* is a Germanized spelling used by Aurel Krause, a German naturalist who lived in Chilkoot in 1882–1883.
14 Krause, 197–198.
15 John D. McDermott, "Were They Really Rogues? Desertion in the Nineteenth Century US Army," *Nebraska History 78* (1997), 165–174, accessed Dec. 18, 2012, http://www.nebraskahistory.org/publish/publicat/history/full-text/1978-3-NSHS_100_Years.pdf.
16 Rose Carmack, letter to George W. Carmack, Feb. 27, 1883, George W. Carmack Papers, Special Collections, University of Washington Libraries.
17 George Carmack, letter to Rose Watson, Dec. 5, 1885, George W. Carmack Papers, Special Collections, University of Washington Libraries.
18 Ibid.
19 A risk that George fails to mention in his letter: he was himself at the mercy of the gunboat crew. Alaska was a big territory with few people; you were always crossing paths with someone you knew. As it turned out, there were in fact two men from the *Pinta*'s crew aboard the *Wachusett*. They outted George to their officers, but he was not arrested.
20 George Carmack, letter to Rose Watson, May 9, 1885. Outsiders often confused the Chilkoot and Chilkat Tlingit; George's reference to "chilcat" is mistaken.
21 Thornton, 116.
22 Thornton, 118.
23 Polly and Leon Gordon Miller, *Lost Heritage of Alaska* (New York: Bonanza Books, 1967), 171.
24 Ted C. Hinckley, *The Americanization of Alaska, 1867–1897* (Palo Alto, CA: Pacific Books, 1972), 101.
25 Miller, 172–173.
26 Thornton, 120.
27 Hinckley, 100.
28 Miller, 177–178.
29 Thornton, 117.

30 David Neufeld and Frank Norris, *Chilkoot Trail: Heritage Route to the Klondike* (Whitehorse: Lost Moose Publishing, 1996), 39.
31 Miller, 179.
32 Thornton, 117
33 Thornton, 120–121.
34 Krause, 128. Thornton (123) says these letters belonged to Daanawáak, first chief of the Chilkoot.
35 Nora and Richard Dauenhauer, *Haa Kusteeyi: Our Culture: Tlingit Life Stories* (Seattle: University of Washington Press, 1994), 752–753.
36 Ibid, 753.

CHAPTER FIVE

1 John Muir, *Travels in Alaska* (New York: Houghton Mifflin, 1917), 209.
2 Neufeld, 46.
3 Though the exact date that Shaaw Tláa began packing is unknown, it's likely before 1887, when she was hired, along with Keish and George Carmack, to pack for surveyor William Ogilvie.
4 Thornton, 124.
5 McClellan, *Part of the Land, Part of the Water*, 148–149.
6 Michael Gates, *Gold at Forty Mile Creek* (Vancouver: UBC Press, 1994), 21.
7 Thornton, 129.
8 Thornton, 125.
9 Ibid, 124.
10 William R. Hunt, *Whiskey Peddler: Johnny Healy, Northern Frontier Trader* (Signal Mountain, TN: Mountain Press, 1992), 32.
11 Ibid, 51.
12 Despite killing an Indian several years later, Jack Wade became famous enough for his name to be attached to a gold-bearing creek, dredge, and mining town.
13 Louis Renner, *Alaskana Catholica* (Portland, OR: the Society of Jesus, 2005), 577.
14 Willard, Kindle edition.
15 Thornton, 128.
16 Thornton, 119.
17 Ibid.

18 Neufeld, 48.
19 George Carmack, "My Trip to the Yukon" (unpublished), 4, Alaska State Archives. The first part of this manuscript, in Carmack's handwriting, is a reliable source; the latter, typewritten part (beginning in May 1896) has been highly embellished by George T. Snow, who compiled the memoirs of Yukon pioneers for publication.
20 Gerald Steckler, *John Seghers* (Fairfield: WA, Ye Galleon, 1986), 213 as quoted in Hunt, 109.
21 Carmack, "My Trip," 3.
22 George Carmack, letter to Rose Watson, Aug. 18, 1885, George W. Carmack Papers.
23 George Carmack, letter to Rose Watson, Nov. 16, 1885, George W. Carmack Papers.
24 George Carmack, letter to Rose Watson, Aug. 18, 1885, George W. Carmack Papers.
25 Thornton, 107.

CHAPTER SIX

1 McClellan, *My Old People Say*, 226–227.
2 Hinckley, 171.
3 Had Kult'ús died first, Shaaw Tláa would have understood his need to take the child with him, to help him find his way in the afterlife.
4 McClellan, *My Old People Say*, 372.
5 Ibid, 375–376.
6 Carmack, "My Trip to the Yukon."
7 Henry Davis, "Recollections," in *Sourdough Sagas*, Herbert Heller, ed. (New York: Ballantine Books, 1967), 29.
8 Carmack, "My Trip," 5.
9 Ibid.
10 Ibid.
11 Ida Calmagene, interview August 18, 2013. Ida says that this information about the Tagish finding George Carmack was passed down from Billy Smith and Patsy Henderson, both nephews of Kate.
12 According to Carrie Willard (Kindle edition, location 1135), in 1882, Jim got into a furious argument with L'unáat. The problem began when L'unáat directed an insult at Jim. Though normally mild-tempered, Jim responded with a threat to kill L'unáat. A few

months later, as a Chinook wind blasted warm air up the coast and into the mountain pass, bringing rain, slush, and the danger of avalanche, Jim tried to make amends with a peace offering of white man's food and blankets. But L'unáat would have none of it. Contributing to L'unáat's overall bad temper, or perhaps because of it, his two Sitka wives had gotten angry and left his house. L'unáat blackened his face and refused to eat. He went to the missionaries, who counseled with him for three hours and reported his mind settled. He called for a general peacemaking. His wives returned, and Skookum Jim was made guest of honor at a large feast. Willard describes Skookum Jim as "a powerful man of his [Lunaát's] own tribe." Since the coastal Tlingit and the Tagish were related through both of Jim's parents, and since L'unáat and Skookum Jim were contemporaries, the assumption is that the Skookum Jim described in this incident is indeed Shaaw Tláa's brother, who married on the coast. Though it's possible that there was another "Skookum Jim," no such reference surfaces among the sources, and the Tlingit and Tagish were both careful about distinguishing names.

13 By Tlingit and Tagish reckoning, L'unáat's sister may have been a woman related to him through his mother, such as a niece.

14 Frank Buteau, "My Experiences in the World," in *Sourdough Sagas*, 87.

15 Wright, Allan. *Prelude to Bonanza* (Sidney, British Columbia: Gray's Publishing Ltd, 1976), 186.

16 Ibid, 182.

17 In Tagish oral histories, this sister (or niece) is mentioned but not named, indicating that she may have been much younger than Kate, as those who died in childhood were intentionally not included in family histories. In other records, she is named either Jennie or Kitty, but Carmack in his discussions with Ogilvie called her Kitty, while others called Aagé by the name Jennie.

18 J. Bernard Moore, *Skagway in Days Primeval* (Skagway: Lynn Canal Publishing, reprint 1997), p. 133.

19 William Ogilvie, letter to John Durst, April 4, 1901, George W. Carmack papers. Ogilvie, a highly reputable source, says that George Carmack told him these facts of his two marriages.

20 Johnson, 63.

21 White, *The Middle Ground*, xxv. White quotes James Clifford from *The Predicament of Culture*: "Stories of cultural contact and change

have been structure by a pervasive dichotomy: absorption by the other or resistance to the other . . . Yet what if identity is conceived not as [a]boundary to be maintained but as a nexus of relations and transactions actively engaging a subject? The story or stories of interaction must then be more complex, less linear and teleological."

22 Because it's uncertain as to exactly when Kate left the coast following the deaths of Kult'ús and their daughter, it's impossible to know for certain whether she knew of George Carmack before the Tagish took him in during the fall of 1886.

23 This was a relatively new development, beginning in the mid-nineteenth century; earlier, there was a greater tendency for fur traders to stay with their Indian wives; see Sherill E. Grace, *Canada and the Idea of the North* (Montreal, Queen's University Press, 2001), 96.

24 Moore, 137. Despite his initial devotion, Moore decided in the end that his marriage had been a mistake. "Lifelong unhappiness was brought about for her and for me," he wrote. "And which one's fault was it? Surely not hers, but mine."

25 Davis, 32.

26 A Chinook wind blows from the south.

27 Ibid, 36.

28 Carmack, "My Trip," 6.

29 Gates, *Gold at Fortymile*, 35.

30 Ibid, 32–34.

31 Hunt, 188.

CHAPTER SEVEN

1 Moore, 22–25.

2 Thornton, 126.

3 Moore, 18 and 23.

4 Neufeld, 47.

5 *Alaska Boundary Tribunal, the Case of the United States* (US Government Printing Office, 1903), 393.

6 Another white man, John Wilson, had also been granted this privilege, likely also because he had married a Native woman, but he had a falling out with L'unáat.

7 A note on spellings: the river is Fortymile; Forty Mile is the mining district and also the town that supplied it; see Gates, *Gold at Fortymile*.

8 Ken S. Coates and William R. Morrison, *Land of the Midnight Sun* (McGill-Queens University Press, 2005), 66.

9 William Ogilvie, letter to John Durst, April 1, 1901, George W. Carmack papers. In confidence, Carmack confessed to Ogilvie about deserting from the Marines and marrying Kate three weeks after Kitty's death.

10 Thornton, 127.

11 Thornton, 126.

12 Dawson Dall and William Ogilvie. *The Yukon Territory* (London: Downey, 1898), 374.

13 Moore, 87.

14 Moore, 75. How long the "large house," as Moore describes it, was in this location is unknown. The Tagish people say they did not begin moving to Caribou Crossing until the railroad came through, so the house that was there in 1887 must have been used only seasonally. See also McClellan, *Part of the Land, Part of the Water*, 134 and 182.

15 McClellan, 244.

16 J. S. Newell to the Secretary of the Navy, May 23, 1887, as published in the Alaska Boundary Tribunal proceedings.

17 Neufeld, 45.

18 Neufeld, 47.

19 Whit Grant letter to Commander John Newell, March 1, 1888, published in the proceedings of the Alaska Boundary Tribunal, 395–396.

20 Hunt, 125.

21 Moore, 105–109. There are several conflicting accounts of the Packer War of 1888. Moore arrived on the scene as the schooner carrying Wilson and the women was leaving, and he was well acquainted with those involved.

22 Carmack, "My Trip," 8.

23 Ibid.

24 Paul McKenna, unpublished memoir (San Benito County Historical Society, 1983), 18.

25 There is nothing to indicate that Sed Wilson was related either to Edgar Wilson, trading partner of John Healy, or to John Wilson, who had packed with the Chilkoot until he angered L'unáat.

26 Gates, *Gold at Fortymile*, 11.

27 The river is "Fortymile" (one word), while the district and town are "Forty Mile" (two words).

28 Schwatka, 54.

29 When Carmack later wrote of the years leading up to the Klondike discovery, he omitted Kate and their daughter Graphie completely. But in a deposition in 1901, he said that Kate accompanied him on his travels up and down the Yukon, including the time he spent prospecting at Fortymile and Birch Creek. He also acknowledged the birth of their daughter at Fort Selkirk in January of 1893.

30 Kathryn Morse, *The Nature of Gold* (Seattle: University of Washington Press, 2003), 128.

31 McClellan, *My Old People Say*, 87.

32 Mary Giraudo Beck, *Shamans and Kushtakas: Northwest Tales of the Supernatural* (Alaska Northwest Books, 2003) and McClellan, *My Old People Say*, 142–143.

33 For more on these earlier ruses and exaggerations, see Karamanski's *Fur Exploration and Trade*.

34 McClellan, *Part of the Land, Part of the Water*, 152.

35 Carmack, "My Trip," 8.

36 Ibid, 10.

37 McClellan, *Part of the Land, Part of the Water*, 203. Not understanding this taboo, missionaries and teachers used to scold brothers and sisters for not talking to each other.

38 Ibid, 278. Self-reliance is highly valued among the Tagish people.

CHAPTER EIGHT

1 McClellan. *Part of the Land, Part of the Water*, 227.

2 Schwatka, 57.

3 Gates, *Gold at Fortymile*, 51.

4 Spellings are of the Tr'ondëk Hwëch'in, as the local Hän call themselves, rather than Tagish spellings

5 Craig Mishler and William Simeone, *Hän Hwech'in: People of the River* (University of Alaska Press, 2004), 2.

6 Coates, 51.

7 Schwatka, 69.

8 Mishler, 46–47 and Schwatka, 69. The Russians may have at one time come as far up the Yukon as the Stewart River;Jennifer Voss, *Klondike Trail* (Seattle: The Mountaineers Books, 2001), 143.

9 The Fortymile Hän were called Charlie's Band, although their Chief, Charlie, was not actually Hän but Gwich'in, from a neighboring tribe near Old Crow, on the Canadian side of the border. Genial and well-respected, Charlie was first called *Nootl'et*, from the Hän word for "white man," explained perhaps by some Russian blood in his ancestry.

10 Gates, *Gold at Fortymile*, 43.

11 Karamanski, 192–193. In extreme cases, the traders reported that starving Indians had even murdered each other in order to eat the bodies.

12 McClellan, *My Old People Say*, 434.

13 The only mention George makes of Wilson in his correspondence is to inform Mary Wilson (1900) that her father doesn't seem to care about her, a statement that is contradicted by a subsequent letter from Wilson to Mary.

14 Will Chase, *The Reminiscences of Captain Billie Moore* (Kansas City: Burton Publishing, 1947) 169–170.

15 The Showman's House is associated with a man called the Black Showman (possibly "shaman"), an Indian who dove into in the Fortymile River in an attempt to save his wife and children, who had been carried off in the current.

16 The trading post was also called Rampart House, resulting in some confusion with the thrice-moved Hudson Bay post that began at Fort Yukon, also called Rampart House.

17 Chase, 170.

18 Gates, *Gold at Fortymile*, 48 and Carmack, "My Trip," 11.

19 McClellan, *Part of the Land, Part of the Water*, 129.

20 McClellan, *My Old People Say*, 138.

21 In exchange for $100, Sed Wilson left his claim in July to guide journalist E. Hazard Wells toward the headwaters of the Copper River over a traditional trading route that would later become known as the Eagle-Valdez Trail. After Wilson took Wells the agreed-upon fifty miles, he somehow got turned around. He ended up on the Tanana River, where his boat swamped and all his provisions were carried off by the swirling water. Undaunted, he and his companions repaired their raft and floated back to the Yukon.

22 Save for a crippled finger, Mock's health improved in the West. He pressed north to the Stewart River in 1887, and from there

he followed the general rush to Forty Mile. Along the rivers and streams that crisscrossed the Alaska-Yukon boundary, Mock at last found his home. Over the next four decades, he would watch miners come and go from Forty Mile while resisting himself a miner's greatest temptation, to keep moving in search of fortune.

23 "Nugget Gulch," US Geological Survey, accessed Feb. 15, 2013, http://mrdata.usgs.gov/ardf/show-ardf.php?ardf_num=EA087.

24 Argument in the Matter of the Estate of George W. Carmack, deceased, filed Dec. 7, 1923 in the Superior Court of the State of Washington for King County, George W. Carmack papers. This argument quotes from a deposition taken from George Carmack on Feb. 15, 1901, in which he gives a forthright account of his married life with Kate.

25 McClellan, *Part of the Land, Part of the Water*, 142–147, for the tanning and sewing details in this and the preceding paragraph.

26 Coates, 91.

27 Gates, *Gold at Fortymile*, 79–80.

28 Ken S. Coates, *Best Left as Indians* (Montreal: McGill-Queens University Press, 1991), 87.

29 Anna DeGraf, *Pioneering on the Yukon*, Roger S. Brown, ed. (Hamden, CT: Archon Books, 1992), 22. In 1892, DeGraf's 23-year-old son left their home in Seattle, saying he'd be back in two weeks. When he didn't return, his mother enlisted the help of everyone she could find. On a report that he and some friends had passed through Juneau, she sold her sewing business and went north to find him. She had many adventures among the miners but never found her son.

30 Argument in the Matter of the Estate of George W. Carmack, deceased, filed Dec. 7, 1923 in the Superior Court of the State of Washington for King County, George W. Carmack papers.

31 Mary was Aagé's third daughter; L'unáat's family had insisted she leave her firstborn, Susie George, with them on the coast, and her second, Louise George, was raised by her Tagish relatives.

32 McClellan, *My Old People Say*, 352.

33 McClellan, *My Old People Say*, 371–373.

34 Buteau, 99.

35 Davis (*Sourdough Sagas*, 64) mentions Hank Wright's plans to leave his son Arthur at the Anvik Mission, and a Mr. Walker, a trader, who left his son David with Bishop Canham at Fort Selkirk.

CHAPTER NINE

1 Kerry M. Abel, "COX, CHARLOTTE SELINA," in EN:UNDEF:public_citation_publication, vol. 14, University of Toronto/Université Laval, 2003–, accessed June 18, 2014, http://www.biographi.ca/en/bio/cox_charlotte_selina_14E.html.

2 Ibid.

3 Ibid.

4 Charlotte Selina Bompas, *A Heroine of the North. Memoirs of Charlotte Selina Bompas (1830–1917), Wife of the First Bishop of Selkirk (Yukon), with Extracts from Her Journal and Letters,* compiled by S.A. Archer (London: SPCK, 1929), Project Canterbury, accessed Oct. 7, 2013, http://anglicanhistory.org/women/bompas/.

5 The Forty Mile missionary was J. W. Ellington, who as the result of a nervous breakdown had to be escorted out of the Yukon.

6 Bompas, *A Heroine of the North.*

7 Ibid.

8 For more on these stereotypes, especially as they apply to Indian women, see Rayna Green's "The Pocahontas Perplex: The Image of Indian Women in American Culture," *The Massachusetts Review,* 27, no. 4, 1975.

9 Bompas, *A Heroine of the North.*

10 McClellan, *My Old People Say,* 88.

11 Bompas, *A Heroine of the North,* letter written September 1, 1892, Chapter VIII, "Fortymile Creek,"

12 Thornton, 69.

13 McClellan, *Part of the Land, Part of the Water,* 208.

14 There was also the fact that in battling diseases introduced by outsiders, missionary medicine often worked in cases where the ministrations of Indian doctors failed. For a comprehensive discussion of Native perspectives on missionary and medicine, see Robert Fortune's *Chills and Fever: Health and Disease in the Early History of Alaska*. For more on the maternalistic impulse as manifested in settler colonialism, see *White Mother to a Dark Race,* by Margaret D. Jacobs (Lincoln: University of Nebraska Press, 2009).

15 Bompas, *A Heroine of the North.*

16 Greg Hare and Ruth Gotthardt, *A Look Back in Time: The Archaeology of Fort Selkirk* (Whitehorse: Government of the Yukon, 1996), 2.

17 Ibid, 24.

18 When word reached Fort Selkirk that the AC Company's brand-new steamer, the *Arctic*, had wrecked, Jennie and Arthur Harper and their family, along with Joe LaDue, had loaded the *New Racket* with the provisions they brought to Fort Selkirk and headed for Fortymile, where they picked up eighty passengers, including Kate and George Carmack, for transport downriver.

19 Interview with Ethel Pronesti, descendent of Arthur and Jennie Harper, Feb. 17, 2013. German author Peter Freuchen immortalized Chief Larion in a historical novel published by McGraw-Hill in 1952. Larion may not have been Jennie's biological father; he may have adopted her

20 Jane Haigh and Claire Rudolf Murphy, *Gold Rush Women* (Seattle: Alaska Northwest Books, 1997), 22–25. Four years after Harper married Seentahna, Jack McQuesten married Satejdenalo, also called Katherine (Kate), a Russian-Athabaskan woman he had met in the village of Kokrines, downriver from Tanana, the same summer that his partners married.

21 As early as 1880, there were fifteen to twenty trading posts along the Yukon River between St. Michael and Fort Reliance, most associated with the Alaska Commercial Company, which Harper represented for many years. At the time, the population along this long stretch of the Yukon was estimated at eighteen whites, nineteen "Creoles," 2,557 Athabaskans, and 4,276 Eskimos. From their posts, traders took in an estimated $75,000 to $80,000 in furs per year.

22 When Jennie and Arthur were first married, he ran the Alaska Commercial Company trading post at Nuklakayit, which like Fort Selkirk had been, in the pre-contact era, the site of annual trading fairs among tribes. At times, Harper would recruit McQuesten or Mayo to mind the store so he could prospect for gold along the rivers of Interior Alaska and the Yukon while Jennie stayed behind in Nuklakayit with their growing family. Though he found only a little gold, Harper's letters to miners in British Columbia touted the mineral prospects of Alaska and the Yukon; in part, his correspondence was responsible for the increasing number of outsiders who ventured over the Chilkoot Trail each year.

23 The seasonal rounds of a trader meant buying up furs in the winter and spring, then transporting them downriver to St. Michael in the summer, where they were exchanged for supplies to restock the

trading posts. Eventually, Jennie began to accompany her husband on his travels. Their fourth son, Samuel, was born not in Alaska but in the Yukon Territory, in 1884.

24 At the mouth of the Sixtymile River, Joe LaDue set up trading at a place he called Ogilvie, after surveyor William Ogilvie, honoring a promise made by Harper's former partners to name Canadian posts after Canadian officials.

25 "Early Traders and Steamboats," *Fortymile Interpreters Manual*, Tr'ondëk Heritage, accessed June 18, 2013, http://Tr'ondëkheritage.com/images/pdfs/Early_Traders.pdf,

26 McClellan, *Part of the Land, Part of the Water*, 233.

27 Ibid, 208. It was important that pregnant women kept busy—the old people said that this would make them good mothers. However, birthing practices differed somewhat between Tagish and Koyukon women.

28 The Harper descendants believe that like their sister Marianne, Walter and his sister Margaret, born on January 20, 1891, were born in Tanana, Alaska, thought it seems unlikely that after traveling to Fort Selkirk with Arthur in August of 1892, Jennie could have returned to Tanana to give birth that winter. The Yukon freezes in late September or October, so it would have been risky to try to get in another trip before freeze-up, and an overland journey on winter trails would have been long and hazardous at best.

29 Walter would also be the only Harper child spared from attending boarding school in California, and the only one omitted from Arthur Harper's will when he died.

30 McClellan, *Part of the Land, Part of the Water*, 191. The Selkirk Indians left their temporary homes near trading posts during the winters, so it seems most likely that Jennie and Helen would have been the ones who assisted with Graphie's birth.

31 McClellan, *Part of the Land, Part of the Water*, 207.

32 Ibid, 155.

33 Davis, 65–66.

34 Like Arthur Harper, Henry Davis had covered a good deal of ground in Alaska and the Yukon. Early in his travels, he met and married Helen, a Koyukon woman. Unlike Kate, Helen often stayed with her family in Tanana when her husband was out looking for gold. Helen sometimes got jealous, and they quarreled often. "I told her

if she didn't quit getting mad I was going to quit her and go get me a white woman," Davis wrote. Given the scarcity of white women in the North, this empty threat was received with laughter. "Huh, I wish you would," Helen told him. "That's good enough for you." But when Helen died, Davis was "broken up"; she'd been a "good pardner," he wrote (Davis, 75).

35 Tappan Adney, *The Klondike Stampede* (Vancouver: UBC Press, 1997 reprint of the 1900 edition), 156.

36 Davis, 66, and Ed and Star Jones, *All That Glitters* (Whitehorse: Wolf Creek Press, 2005), 105. Jones attributes John J. Healy with setting Carmack up at the post. But firsthand accounts point to Arthur Harper as the one who made it possible for Carmack to run his own post, however briefly.

37 McClellan, *Part of the Land, Part of the Water*, 157.

38 Davis, 66.

39 Ibid. The original Fort Selkirk schoolhouse, which also served as a church until 1931, still stands. It is the oldest building in the Yukon, built in 1892; the work Carmack did in 1893 would have been after its original construction. A later author, Ella Lung Martinsen, in her book *Trails to the North Star Gold* (Hillsboro, OR: Binford & Mort, 1974), attributes Carmack with later giving a "large stack of gold nuggets" from his Klondike strike to pay for the "little log-church" in Fort Selkirk and a large pipe organ inside. However, the Fort Selkirk Church predates the Klondike, and it was not large enough to house a large pipe organ, so it appears that only bit of truth in this fanciful story was that Carmack did help build the church, pre-Klondike—but like Henry Davis, he was paid for doing so.

40 When the Koyukon men and their wives traded $250 in gold for tobacco, tea, and calico at the Nuklakayit post, three miners followed them to Forty Mile. Their silence was broken when one of them got "blind drunk" at a Forty Mile saloon. A hundred miners followed them back to Birch Creek and spread out from there.

41 Gates, *Gold at Fortymile*, 65–67.

42 Exactly how many from Kate's family lived in Dyea prior to 1896 isn't certain. Two years passed without them seeing her, and Kate's father along with Jim's son are buried in Dyea, where Jim had a cabin. Tagish John and his wife Maria, cousins with whom Kate and Jim were quite close, also had a house in Dyea.

43 Phyllis Fast, descendant of Jennie Harper, interview Jan. 28, 2013.

CHAPTER TEN

1 "The Romance of Indian Kate Who Showed the Gold of the Klondike to George Carmack," *San Francisco Call,* Volume 87, Number 143, October 21, 1900.

2 From a letter in the *San Francisco Chronicle* by W. J. Burke of Eagle City, Alaska, printed Feb, 8, 1926.

3 "Tagish Kate." *The Semi-Weekly Nugget,* Dawson, YT, November 11, 1900.

4 The closest to a firsthand account would have been in a letter he wrote to his sister. Unfortunately, while much of George's correspondence has survived him, this particular letter has been lost.

5 Gates, Michael, *Gold at Fortymile,* 80.

6 George W. Carmack papers. Early in 1900, George Carmack testified under oath in a deposition that he and Kate had lived and traveled together in the Yukon from 1886 to 1898, when they left for Seattle.

7 George T. Snow, attributed to George W. Carmack, "My Experiences in the Yukon," draft obtained from the University of Washington Archives.

8 The accounts of the little yellow-breasted bird and the broken mirror are in an early version of Snow's compilation; they do not appear in later versions, including the account published by Marguerite Carmack in 1931.

9 Snow for Carmack, page 4 of Draft #3. Snow numbers only Draft #4, in which he reverts to a third person point of view; #3 is my numbering for the one that precedes it.

10 Snow for Carmack, page 7 of Draft #3.

11 Ibid, 8.

12 Snow for Carmack, page 13 of Draft #3.

13 Ibid, 14. Snow for Carmack, page 14 of Draft #3.

14 Ibid.

15 Ibid.

16 Ibid.

17 Ogilvie, 134

18 Johnny Johns, "Skookum Jim's Later Life," Yukon Territorial Archives, 88/58 SR Tape 11-3, 11-4, accessed June 19, 2014, www.canadianmysteries.ca/sites/klondike/archives/oralhistoryorinterview/3286en.html.

19 "Johnny Johns recalls Skookum Jim," *The Yukon News*, Dec. 5, 1973.

20 "Johnny Johns recalls Skookum Jim." *The Yukon News*, Dec. 12, 1973. In his telling of the story of Jim and the coffee beans, Jim's nephew Johnny Johns notes that Jim bought the beans from a trader named Mr. Mason, who ran the Dyea post after Healy left, first to Pyramid Harbor and then to Circle City. Jim took "Mason" as his last name; typically, this would be either a sign of his admiration or because he believed Mason owed him something. Maria Johns, also called "Mrs. Dyea John," is also associated with the story, as someone to whom Jim goes for advice.

21 Rab Wilkie and the Skookum Jim Friendship Centre, "Skookum Jim: Native and Non-Native Views," (Heritage Branch, Government of Yukon, 1992), 51–53. See also Cruikshank's *The Social Life of Stories* for more on how Tagish stories contextualize post-contact cultural changes.

22 Sidney, *Life Lived Like a Story*, 62 and McClellan, "Wealth Woman."

23 For a Tlingit version of the Wealth Woman legend, see the Tl'anaxéedakw story as told by Seidayaa Elizabeth Nyman in *Gágiwduł.àt: Brought Forth to Reconfirm: the Legacy of a Taku River Tlingit Clan* (Alaska Native Language Center, 1993). My thanks to Lance Twitchell for directing me to this narrative.

24 The connection between defecation and money (gold in particular) goes well beyond this particular legend: Sigmund Freud wrote, "The connections between the complexes of interest in money and of defecation, which seem so dissimilar, appear to be the most extensive of all," noting that "wherever archaic modes of thought have predominated or persist—in the ancient civilizations, in myths, fairy tales, and superstitions, in unconscious thinking, in dreams and in neuroses—money is brought into the most intimate relationship with dirt." Sigmund Freud, *Character and Anal Eroticism*, excerpted in "Brown Gold," *Latham's Quarterly*, Spring 2008.

25 Catharine McClellan, "Wealth Woman and Frogs among the Tagish Indians," *Anthropos* 58, 1963, Yukon Archives PAM 1963-0005.

26 McClellan, *My Old People Say*, 178–179.

27 Sidney, *Life Lived Like a Story*, 57–59.

28 Ibid. Angela Sidney was the daughter of Maria Johns.

29 At about this same time, Kate and Jim's father, Kaachgaawáa, may have died; a few years later, in Dyea, a photographer took a picture of a fancy Spirit House, white clapboard with a roof and two

double-hung windows, that marked the grave of "Kuck-Shaw, Tagish chief" (Thornton, 267). Jim's son may also have been buried in the Dyea cemetery (Jeff Brady, *Skagway: City of the New Century*, Lynn Canal Publishing, 2013, 10). Eventually, erosion washed from the Taiya River washed away all the gravesites in Dyea, except those at Slide Cemetery.

30 Because of this incident, Crag Lake is to this day considered a special place; in the hills overlook the lake, there is a rock in the shape of a killer whale, the crest of Jim and Kate's clan.

31 Sidney, *Life Lived Like a Story*, 60–61.

32 William Ogilvie, letter to John Durst, April 4, 1901, George W. Carmack papers. Ogilvie affirms that in June of 1887 (which he mistakenly types as 1897), Kate and George were at Dyea, "living together as man and wife; and understood to be so according to Indian custom." Ogilvie hired George for "about six weeks" and "Mrs. Carmack also did considerable work in the way of packing for me."

33 As is evident from the notes that follow, the version of the discovery presented here relies on multiple sources, and especially those that are internally consistent.

34 Sidney, *Life Lived Like a Story*, 63. In recounting Jim's responsibility, Sidney mentions that both Aagé and Kate had been missing for two years, but in fact, Aagé had died four years earlier.

35 Accounts vary; it's likely, though not entirely certain, that both Jim and Charlie's wives were with them. It appears that Jim's son had died.

36 Omer Maris, correspondent for the *Chicago Record*, met Jim's family as they were crossing Lake LaBerge. He commented on the black grease paint and, because Jim's wife wore a dress of bright red calico, he assumed they were making "a holiday excursion." *Chicago Record*, Oct. 23, 1896. My thanks to Mark Kirchhoff for directing me to this source.

37 Ida Calmagene, granddaughter of Maria Johns, interview August 18, 2013; also noted by her mother, Angela Sidney, in *Life Told Like a Story*. About her parents turning back, Sidney says, "Bad luck, eh? But maybe it was just as well . . . All those men who found gold split up with their wives . . . (64)."

38 Charlene Porsild, *Gamblers and Dreamers* (Vancouver: UBC Press, 1998), 50. The Tr'ondëk Hwëch'in, also known as Chief Isaac's band, were the same group that had encouraged Jack McQuesten

to open the trading post at Fort Reliance, near their downriver village of Nuklako. In the 1840s, their population had been estimated at 1,000, but disease and other casualties of contact had substantially diminished their numbers.

39 Karamanski, 251.

40 It was because of Kate that the Carmacks had access to salmon in a region traditionally occupied by the Hän; like all Yukon Indians, they shared resources with neighboring bands. According to Johnny Johns, the Carmacks were away from their camp when Kate's family arrived, so Jim went briefly up the Tr'ondëk River before returning to the fish camp across from Tr'ochëk.

41 "Billy Johnson Tells His Story." Yukon Territorial Archives, YTA, COR 1096 88/58 SR11 (7) Skookum Jim Oral History Project Fonds, accessed June 19, 2014 at www.candianmysteries.ca/sites/klondike/archives/oralhistoryorinterview/3318en.html. Johnson relies on a narrative told to him "dozens of times" by Patsy Henderson.

42 Smith, *Life Lived Like a Story*, 187.

43 McClellan, *Part of the Land, Part of the Water*, 136.

44 Maris, Omer. *The Chicago Record*, Oct. 23, 1896.

45 The post named Ogilvie was at the Sixtymile River, not quite sixty miles upriver from point zero, the old Fort Reliance, which put it about a hundred miles from Forty Mile, which was forty miles downriver from Fort Reliance.

46 Ogilvie, 124.

47 Ogilvie, 131.

48 James R. Little, "Squaw Kate," *Alaska Life*, March, 1943, and *Alaska-Yukon Gold Book* (Sourdough Stampede Association, 1930), 28. Both authors correlate Kate finding a gold nugget with the discovery on Aug. 17, 1896, but based on firsthand accounts, it's unlikely she was at the Klondike River that day, though for the purposes of registering larger claims, George counted her among the discovery group.

49 Ken Shortt, "How gold was discovered in the Klondike." *Klondike '73* publication.

50 Snow for Carmack, page 12 of Draft #3.

51 Sources say Henderson may have accessed Gold Bottom via the Klondike, but that would have required a portage with his large load.

52 Gates, *Gold at Fortymile*, 145.

53 Ogilvie, 126–127.

54 Smith, *Life Lived Like a Story*, 187–188.

55 Ogilvie and also Patsy Henderson, in an oral history recorded by Bonnie Piper during the 1960s and archived in the Tr'ondëk Hwëch'in Archives, 1995.

56 In some versions ("Billy Johnson Tells His Story," Skookum Jim Oral History Project Fonds, Yukon Territorial Archives), Jim is getting water to make tea.

57 Smith, *Life Lived Like a Story*, 188. In Kate's version of the discovery narrative, Charlie shoots the moose, and Patsy is with the other three men at the creek, but in substance, her story as told to her niece (by marriage to Billy Smith, a brother of Charlie and Patsy) is the same as the version Ogilvie reports Jim and Charlie telling him.

58 Ogilvie, 125–134. Personally acquainted with the primary players in the various versions of the Klondike discovery, Commissioner Ogilvie presents a well-researched and objective account of the events, based on interviews. From Charlie and Jim, interviewed independently, he gets the most consistent and reliable information. The account given by Patsy Henderson, who was by his own admission not present when the gold was first found, also agrees in substance with Ogilvie's compilation. In his later years, Carmack told a similar story, though embellished. In an unpublished memoir archived with the San Benito Historical Society, dated July 20, 1983, longtime Tres Pinos resident Paul McKenna talks about spending "a great deal of time listening to the tales of Alaska, which Geo. [Carmack] told us from time to time, including this version of the gold discovery. 'He was a member of a hunting party camped on a small creek that emptied into the Yukon River. His brother-in-law Skookum Jim had killed a very large deer, he wiped the mud off the antlers with his bare hands, and when he opened them there was the gold.'"

59 Henderson, in an oral history recorded by Bonnie Piper during the 1960s and archived in the Tr'ondëk Hwëch'in Archives, 1995.

CHAPTER ELEVEN

1 Johns likely acquired the moose hide from the Pelly band of the Tutchone, near Selkirk, who sold meat and hides to prospectors on their way downriver.

2 William Douglas Johns, "The Early Yukon, Alaska and the Klondike Discovery as They Were Before the Great Klondike Stampede Swept Away the Old Conditions By One Who Was There" Typescript, Coutts Collection, Yukon Archives #78/69 Box F-89 Folder 20 & 21. Whitehorse. My thanks to Michael Gates for directing me to this source.
3 Ogilvie, 129–130.
4 George Carmack, "My Experiences in the Yukon," published by Marguerite Carmack, 1931, 14. Though the language is clearly Snow's, the attribution is to Carmack in this published edition of the narrative.
5 Ibid.
6 Ibid.
7 Ed and Star Jones, *All That Glitters: The Life and Times of Joe LaDue,* Founder of Dawson City (Whitehorse: Wolf Creek Books, 2005), 127.
8 Patsy Henderson, "Early Days at Caribou Crossing and The Discovery of Gold on the Klondike," published by Jennie Mae Moyer, 1950, 13.
9 Ibid, 12.
10 Gates, *Gold at Fortymile Creek,* 139.
11 *Alaska-Yukon Gold Book,* 30.
12 Ogilvie spelled "Carmack" as "Carmac."
13 Snow, Draft #3, 11.
14 Gates, *Gold at Fortymile Creek,* 138.
15 Carmack, "My Experiences in the Yukon," 15.
16 Ibid, 15–16.
17 Gates, *Gold at Fortymile,* 139.
18 Coates, *Land of the Midnight Sun,* 83.
19 William Ogilvie, "Bonanza and Eldorado Creeks, Survey of Placer Mining Claims 1897 (Natural Resources Canada, 1995 reprint).
20 Coates, *Land of the Midnight Sun,* 83–84.
21 When filing a claim, each miner received a free Miner's Certificate that granted him rights to harvest whatever timber was needed from the staked parcel of land.
22 Adney, 197–201.
23 Ibid, 241–243.
24 McClellan, *Part of the Land, Part of the Water,* 55.
25 Morse, 102.

26 Joe LaDue reported the coldest temperature that winter was 54 below; *St. Lawrence Republican,* Aug. 25, 1896, as noted by M. J. Kirchhoff, author of *Clondyke: The First Year of the Rush* (Alaska Cedar Press, 2010).

27 Jones, 140–141.

28 Gates, 127–128.

29 Adney, 310–311.

30 Johnny Johns, Skookum Jim Friendship Center Oral History Project, 1973.

31 It's not know for certain whether Jim and/or Charlie's wives spent the winter in the Klondike; with their children, they may have returned upriver.

32 Frances Backhouse, Women of the Klondike (Vancouver: Whitecap Books, 2010), 40–41.

33 It's not certain exactly when the Cooks arrived in Dawson, but another prospector spoke of Kate's friendship with Jennie Cook, who appears on the 1901 census as a resident of Dawson City.

34 Ogilvie, "Bonanza and Eldorado Creeks, Survey of Placer Mining Claims 1897." Patsy was also called "Paddy." On Ogilvie's survey, No. 1 Above is assigned to "Tagish Jim," meaning Skookum Jim, and the fraction cut from it to "Tagish Paddy," meaning Patsy Henderson.

35 Coates, *Land of the Midnight Sun,* 84.

36 The fact that no claim was filed on Kate's behalf affirms that she did not arrive at Bonanza Creek until after all the nearby claims were taken.

37 Jones, 143.

38 *Alaska Miner,* Juneau, March 31, 1897; cited by Mark Kirchhoff in *Clondyke.*

39 Report of Trip to the Yukon, W.H. Scarth, Yukon Archives, Whitehorse, as reported by Mark Kirchhoff, *Clondyke.*

40 George Carmack to Rose Watson, June 20, 1897, George W. Carmack papers. Though his birth date wasn't a matter of record, Kate's nephew Patsy was likely underage, and with the pressure of newcomers to snatch up wrongly filed claims, his was quickly sold. Patsy reports the sale was at $10,000.

41 Ibid.

42 Ibid.

43 Ibid.

44 Ibid.
45 Ibid.

CHAPTER TWELVE

1 Jones, 146.
2 Ibid.
3 Jones, 144.
4 Chris Clarke and the K'ahacha Group, *Tr'ëhuhch'in Näwtr'udäh'a: Finding Our Way Home* (Dawson City: Tr'ondëk Hwëch'in, 2009), 8–10. In recent years, the songs have been retrieved by the Tr'ondëk Hwëch'in.
5 Clarke, 11.
6 White, 318. "British Indian policy initially feared contact between Indians and whites and hoped to make it as restricted and supervised as possible," writes White of eighteenth century contact in the Upper Midwest.
7 Porsild, 48.
8 Ibid, 48–49.
9 His Lordship the Bishop of Selkirk, dated at Buxton Mission, Upper Yukon River, Oct.28, 1895, Yukon Archives, Gov 1629, f. 4682.
10 C. Constantine Insp. NWM Police and Act. Gov.t Agt., to The Deputy Minister of the Interior Ottawa Ont., Nov. 19, 1896, Yukon Archives, Gov 1629, f. 4682.
11 Ibid.
12 In August of 1897, the Department of Indian Affairs settled the matter with a 160-acre temporary reserve three miles downriver from Dawson, called Moosehide after the distinctive bluff that looked like a skin, tanned and stretched. In exchange for the reserve, the Tr'ondëk Hwëch'in were required to abandon all claims to their former village of Nuklako, across the river from Dawson.
13 Porsild, 49.
14 Ibid, 52.
15 Archer, accessed October 11, 2013, http://anglicanhistory.org/women/bompas/09.html.
16 Jones, 149.
17 Morse, 122–125.

18 *The Klondike News*, Vol. 1, No. 1, April 1, 1898.
19 Johnson, 113–144. The firewood incident was told to Johnson by Ed Conrad, who prospected the creeks in 1897 and 1898.
20 The Klondike News, Vol. 1, No. 1, April 1, 1898. The 1,500 feet owned would have been after the sale of one claim. The article also attributes to Carmack a poem that, judging from the language, seems unlikely to have been penned by him.
21 White, 186, quoting Greg Dening, *Islands and Beaches*.
22 Martinsen, 49–54. The prospector was Ed Lung.
23 Johnny Joe, interviewed by Ye Sa To Communication Society, 1989, 29–33.
24 Hinckley, 218.
25 Thornton, 194–196.
26 Neufeld and Norris, 59–61. Of the candy store, Maria Johns liked to joke that packing ten pounds of candy over the Chilkoot Trail had done nothing good for her teeth. Ida Calmagene, interviewed Aug. 18, 2013.
27 Neufeld and Norris, 64.
28 Neufeld and Norris, 62.
29 Neufeld and Norris, 69.
30 Adney, 105.
31 Neufeld and Norris, 76–69.
32 Neufeld and Norris, 89–91 and 101.
33 The NWMP 1898 report notes fifty-one deaths, as does the Dyea Trail. (M. J. Kirchhoff, email to author, Feb. 16, 2013).
34 Neufeld and Norris, 72–73.
35 Jeff Blystone, email to author, Feb. 1, 2012.
36 Sheila Greer, *Skookum Stories on the Chilkoot/Dyea Trail* (Carcross-Tagish First Nations, 1995), 74–76.
37 It was said that when Jim learned of his sister's death, he poured gold into her coffin (Sidney, *Life Lived Like a Story*, 64). The surviving child, Nadagáat (Susie Joseph), married Tagish Charlie; her daughters Mary Smarch and Lucy Wren are respected Tagish elders.
38 Neufeld and Norris, 103–105.
39 Helene Dobrowolsky, *Law of the Yukon: A History of the Mounted Police in the Yukon* (Madeira Park, BC: Lost Moose Publishing, 2013), 48–49.
40 All of the suspects were Crows, and at least one of the suspects was related by marriage to Kate: Kitty Smith, married to Kate's

nephew Billy, brother to Charlie and Patsy, was the niece of one of the four men.

41 A similar error involving arsenic had been made a decade earlier at Fort Reliance, an early trading post near what became Dawson City.

42 She was the first wife of Kaxootsk'í, called Tagish Jim, brother of Kate's mother.

43 Cruikshank, *The Social Life of Stories: Narrative and Knowledge in the Yukon Territory*, 82–92.

CHAPTER THIRTEEN

1 Hitchcock, 44.

2 Dobrowolsky, 58–59.

3 Hitchcock, 48.

4 Ibid. 45–48.

5 Cruikshank, *The Social Life of Stories*, 85.

6 Ibid, 86–87.

7 Hitchcock, 52.

8 *Klondike Nugget*, Aug. 3, 1898, as quoted in Cruikshank, *The Social Life of Stories*, 86 and 88.

9 Hitchcock and Van Buren traveled in the company of Alex McDonald, who despite being something of a Cheechako himself (he had logged only two years in the North) had amassed a large fortune by acquiring claims from those who failed to adequately work them. From his riches, he gave freely to local causes, including the Catholic Church.

10 "Four Million Dollars: Rich Cargo of Treasure Ship Roanoke from St. Michael" and "Skookum Jim Robbed of a Small Fortune." *Seattle Post-Intelligencer*, Aug. 31, 1898. In their efforts to evade the 10 percent royalty tax on gold taken from Canadian soils, miners were evasive about how much they brought with them in gold when they went Outside.

11 Details of the journey aboard the Cudahy come from the diary of sheepherder Si Dawson, as published in Jeanne Wilkins Wilde, *Tell Me About: A Collection of Memoirs* (iUniverse, 2009). Hoping to make his fortune by selling sheep to the Klondikers, Si Dawson met with disaster when livestock ate some sort of poisonous plants at Caribou Crossing, a Tagish hunting site (later called Carcross). He

lost 115 more when his scow struck rocks at Five Finger Rapids. In Dawson, he sold the remaining sheep for $915 in gold and left on the next steamer out.

12 "Reindeer History in Alaska." School of Natural Resources and Agricultural Science, University of Alaska Fairbanks, accessed Oct. 22, 2013, http://reindeer.salrm.uaf.edu/about_reindeer/history.php.

13 "Skookum Jim Robbed of a Small Fortune." *Seattle Post-Intelligencer*, Aug. 31, 1898. Of note in this brief article is that Jim, not George Carmack, is credited with the discovery of gold at Bonanza Creek.

14 "Selling Seattle." National Park Service, Klondike Gold Rush, Seattle Unit, accessed Oct. 22, 2013, http://www.nps.gov/klse/forteachers/hrs2.htm. Accessed Oct. 22. Confident and assertive and financed by local businesses that received prospective customer lists in return for his services, Brainerd in his role as chief of Seattle's newly formed "Bureau of Information" took out display ads in all the popular magazines to brand his city as the gateway to the north. In October of 1897, he printed 212,000 copies of a special Klondike edition of the *Seattle Post-Intelligencer*, the largest run to date of any paper west of Chicago. These he distributed to post offices, libraries, mayors, and railroads across America. He wrote letter upon letter in which he urged ministers, teachers, and employers to encourage would-be Klondikers to outfit themselves in Seattle. Using a clipping service, he tracked articles on the gold rush and wrote letters to the editors making factual corrections to their stories. He set up an exhibit that displayed $6,000 in Klondike gold, then released it to travel the country aboard the Great Northern Express.

15 Pierre Berton, *The Klondike Fever* (New York: Carroll and Graf, 1958), 128.

16 "From Klondike to Paris," *Seattle Post-Intelligencer*, Sept. 1, 1898.

17 Ibid.

18 Ida Calmagene, interviewed Aug. 18. 2013, says it was Jim and Charlie who used a hatchet to notch landmarks as they navigated the Seattle streets.

19 "Skookum Jim Oral History Project," 81.

20 Ibid.

21 "Throwing Away Money," *Seattle Post-Intelligencer*, Sept. 2, 1898, p. 6. That his relatives were called "native Alaskan" was a common

error. Perhaps because so many of the miners were Americans, most people assumed the Klondike was in Alaska.

22 "WP&YR Facts," accessed Oct. 23, 2013, http://www.wpyr.com/history/facts.html.

23 "Discovered Gold on Bonanza," *San Francisco Call*, Sept. 16, 1898.

24 Ibid.

CHAPTER FOURTEEN

1 Henry D. Barrows and Luther A. Ingersoll, *Memorial and Biographical History of the Coast Counties of Central California* (Chicago: The Lewis Publishing Company, 1893).

2 Marjorie Pierce, *East of the Gabilans* (Santa Cruz, CA: Western Tanager Press), 125.

3 Paicines had been called Tres Pinos before the railroad station went in to the north.

4 Teisha Rowland, "How the Eucalyptus Came to California," *Santa Barbara Independent*, Jan. 15, 2011.

5 Barrows and Ingersoll.

6 "They'll Have a Hot Time in This Old Town," *San Francisco Call*, Jan. 26, 1899.

7 Sherrill Grace, *Canada and the Idea of the North* (Montreal: McGill-Queen's University Press, 2001), 100.

8 James Albert Johnson, interview with Graphie Grace Carmack, undated.

9 "Gold Hunters Go North," *Seattle Post-Intelligencer*, April 4, 1899. Graphie Grace does not appear on the passenger list, but this appears to be an oversight, as she is listed as traveling with her parents on their return to Seattle in July (see note 15).

10 Neufeld and Norris, 111.

11 Klondike Nugget, April 19, 1899. The Berry party was one of the last to travel overland that year. Arriving in Dawson on April 14, they reported the trail in bad shape; they had to leave part of their load at the foot of Lake LaBerge. The earliest Kate would have arrived in Skagway would have been April 9, too late to set out on the twelve-day overland journey.

12 Pierre Berton gives a full account of this fire, which destroyed 117 buildings and resulted in over $1 million in damages (*The Klondike Fever*, 406–409).

13 Terrence Cole, Introduction to Hitchcock, xix.
14 Ibid, xx.
15 Ibid, xix.
16 Cruikshank, *The Social Life of Stories*, 88.
17 Selina Bompas, letter May 29, 1899.
18 The NWMP was only too happy to forward to American authorities in Nome a list of criminals who gained notoriety during their short time in Dawson. As the riffraff stormed the beaches of Nome with shovels, rockers, and wheelbarrows, the US military had its hands full.
19 "Dawson Visited by Another Fire," *Seattle Daily Times*, July 3, 1899.
20 "Badly Beaten by His Indian Wife," *San Francisco Call*, July 7, 1899. The only reference to this incident in the larger Seattle papers was three weeks later, as an aside to the story documenting Kate's arrest (see note 20).
21 Ibid.
22 For more on the difficulties caused by alcohol, see Robert Fortuine's *Chills and Fever: Health and Disease in the Early History of Alaska* (Fairbanks: University of Alaska Press, 1992).
23 Krause, 189.
24 Jim's son appears to have died a few years before, possibly at Dyea.
25 *Seattle Post-Intelligencer*, July 26, 1899.
26 Ibid.
27 *Seattle Post-Intelligencer*, July 27, 1899.
28 *Seattle Times*, July 27, 1899.
29 George Carmack to Mrs. H. R. Watson, July 28, 1899, George W. Carmack Papers.

CHAPTER FIFTEEN

1 For an in-depth discussion of the pressures on Kate as "colonial other" reduced to mimicry as a means of adapting, see Sherill E. Grace, *Canada and the Idea of the North* (Montreal: Queen's University Press, 2001). In her insightful discussion on Kate's "absent" voice and the pressures she faced, Grace relies in part on assumptions drawn by Carmack's biographer James Albert Johnson.
2 Ibid, 495: the 'anyAdi," literally "town child," the noble class.
3 *Seattle Post-Intelligencer*, Sept. 21, 1899.
4 *San Francisco Call*, Jan. 1, 1900.

5 Ibid.

6 McClellan, *My Old People Say*, 101: spring muskrat trapping as part of the yearly round.

7 *Hollister Free Lance*, Feb. 16, 1900, this and the previous paragraph.

8 *Hollister Free Lance*, March 30, 1900.

9 *Hollister Free Lance*, April 13, 1900 and McClellan, *My Old People Say*, 83.

10 *Alaska Dispatch*, Oct. 29, 1900.

11 On the Parks Canada placard at Bonanza Creek, this amount is shown as $4,000,000, but other sources place it at $400,000 ("Came by Topeka," *Seattle Daily Times*, July 16, 1900).

12 George Carmack, letter to Rose Watson, July 25, 1900, George W. Carmack papers.

13 Kate Carmack, letter to "Jim Tigress," Aug. 7, 1900, George W. Carmack papers.

14 George Carmack, letter to Rose Watson, Aug. 18, 1900, George W. Carmack papers; this and the preceding paragraph.

15 Ibid.

16 In January, Mary wrote to her father in care of Mrs. Bompas, and in April he sent a reply from Eagle Creek, in the Circle City District of Alaska, addressing her as "My Dear little Mary." He asked many questions about her life in California and wondered whether she might ever want to return to Alaska and live with Mrs. Bompas again. He promised to write often and sent his best regards to Mrs. Carmack (George W. Carmack papers).

17 Elizabeth Lands, letter to George Carmack, Nov. 16, 1900, George W. Carmack papers.

18 Pathological lying is not so much a moral flaw as a genuine disorder associated with abnormalities in the brain's frontal cortex.

19 Elsie Lee, heir to the estate of Marguerite Carmack, interviewed by James Albert Johnson, George Carmack papers.

20 George W. Carmack papers.

21 Porsild, 113–118.

22 Ibid, 118.

23 Ibid. Porsild reports the location of Marguerite's storefront as Second and Lane, but there was no "Lane" street in Dawson. The source of the error is either transcription or Marguerite's faulty memory in Washington State Supreme Court case 18829. The actual cross street was "Queen."

24 Porsild, 102.

25 Stan B. Cohen, *Queen City of the North* (Pictorial Histories Publishing, 1990), 14.

26 Lael Morgan, *Good Time Girls* (Fairbanks: Epicenter Press, 1998), 106.

27 Ibid, 104.

28 Ibid, 166.

29 1901 Canadian census records indexed at http://automatedgenealogy.com/census/DisplayHousehold.jsp?sdid=9235&household=17 show a Mr. and Mrs. J.A. Collins at Bonanza Creek. J. A. Collins was the owner of claims 1, 2, and 3 at American Gulch, Bonanza Creek. Customs records show that they passed through Lake Bennett on their way to the Klondike in June 1899. No other married Collins appears in the census data.

CHAPTER SIXTEEN

1 McClellan, *My Old People Say*, 228.

2 Robert Fortuine, *Chills and Fevers: Health and Disease in Early Alaska* (University of Alaska Press: 1989), 255 and 263.

3 "Tuberculosis in Europe and North America 1800–1922," Contagion: Historical Views of Diseases and Epidemics, accessed Nov. 4, 2013, http://ocp.hul.harvard.edu/contagion/tuberculosis.html.

4 MB Cooperman, "Chronic Tuberculosis Polyarthritis," *Ann Surg.*, 1932 Dec; 96(6):1065–1077.

5 Fortuine, 75. Trachoma was another eye disease that was common among indigenous populations, but the trajectory of trachoma led inevitably to blindness; since Kate did eventually recover, that affliction seems unlikely.

6 Whether or not they were related to tuberculosis, eye diseases were prevalent among the Yukon Indians during this era. When William Bompas visited England on the occasion of his consecration as bishop, he attended lectures at London eye hospitals in hopes of discovering some means of treatment (Wright, 130).

7 Initially, Mesmer treated a patient by having her drink water infused with iron and then passing magnets over her. But he determined her positive response was not from the work of the magnets but as a result of his own "animal magneticism" being transferred to her.

8 L.A. Steward, letter to John Durst, Jan. 9, 1901. George W. Carmack papers.

9 McClellan, *My Old People Say,* 530–543.

10 Rose's husband James Watson wanted the girls returned to Kate, but Rose wouldn't hear of it.

11 L. A. Steward, letter to John Durst, Oct. 15, 1900.

12 Receipts of deposit and letters from George Carmack, Nov., 1900, George W. Carmack papers.

13 *Hollister Free Lance,* Oct. 5, 1900.

14 Elizabeth Lands, letter to George Carmack, Nov. 16, 1900. George W. Carmack papers.

15 "The Romance of Indian Kate," *San Francisco Call,* Oct. 21, 1900.

16 The figure offered several months later, through Frank Curtis, was $2,500.

17 George Carmack, letter to Rose Watson, Oct. 15, 1900, George W. Carmack papers.

18 *San Jose Evening News,* Oct. 3, 1900.

19 *Hollister Free Lance,* Oct. 12, 1900.

20 George Carmack, letter to Rose Watson, Oct. 15, 1900, George W. Carmack papers.

21 John Durst, letter to Kate Carmack, Oct. 19, 1900, George W. Carmack papers.

22 L. A. Steward, letter to John Durst, Oct. 15, 1900, and John Durst, letter to Kate Carmack, Oct. 19, 1900, George W. Carmack papers.

23 A respected attorney and leader within the city's Republican Party, Durst knew John Healy, and he also knew Clarence Berry, whose wife was one of the few white women who had wintered on the creeks in 1896. Durst's wife and Kate also shared a mutual friend in Sophie Bettles, Koyukon wife of Gordon C. Bettles, who ran the trading post near Showman's House, where Kate and George had spent Starvation Winter. Daughter of a Koyukon woman and a Finnish trader, Sophie was raised in a village on the lower Yukon River. One of the first traders along the Yukon, Sophie's father distilled his own hooch and shared it liberally; on one occasion, he wound up three music boxes and played them simultaneously while demonstrating Russian dances for his fellow revelers. Sophie's husband was from San Francisco, and the two of them were friends with Jack London, who had spent only a year in the Yukon before returning to the city to write his widely read stories

about the North, one of which featured a heroine purported to have been fashioned after Sophie.

24 John Durst, letter to Kate Carmack, Oct. 19, 1900, George W. Carmack papers.

25 A. D. Shaw, letter to John Durst, Oct. 22, 1900, George W. Carmack papers.

26 The Romance of Indian Kate," *San Francisco Call*, Oct. 21, 1900.

27 Multiple sources include interviews with Kate's descendants Annie Auston (July 28, 2011) and Ida Calmagene (Aug. 18, 2013), as well as the documentary *Keish: A Man Standing in Two Worlds* (produced by Delores Smith for Northern Native Broadcasting, 1999). Carmack's account of the time he ran out of food while trying to get back to Dyea late in the season places the event during the fall of 1886, after Bishop Charles Seghers shared his food with Carmack and his companions.

28 "The Romance of Indian Kate," *San Francisco Call*, Oct. 21, 1900.

29 Ibid.

30 Ibid.

31 Ibid.

32 Ibid.

33 Ibid.

34 Ibid.

35 Ibid.

36 George Carmack to Rose Watson, Nov. 3, 1900.

37 The first wife of George Mankins was a sister of James Watson; she died when she was only twenty years old. His second wife, Elizabeth, was also a friend to Kate.

38 George Carmack, letter to Rose Watson, Nov. 17, 1900, George W. Carmack papers.

39 George Carmack, letter to Rose Watson, Nov. 25, 1900, George W. Carmack papers.

40 Ibid.

41 George Carmack, letter to Rose Watson, Nov. 27, 1900, George W. Carmack papers.

42 George Carmack, letter to Rose Watson, Nov. 30, 1900, George W. Carmack papers.

43 George Carmack to Rose Watson, letter to Rose Watson, Nov. 25, 1900, George W. Carmack papers.

44 Ibid.

45 *Hollister Free Lance*, Nov. 9, 1900.

46 George Carmack, letter to Rose Watson, Nov. 25, 1900, George W. Carmack papers.

47 A. D. Shaw, publisher of the *San Benito Advance*, disapproved of Dr. Steward and her maneuvers on Kate's behalf. So did Mary Land (sister of Elizabeth Mankins), a neighbor from Tres Pinos who claimed some Indian heritage. Like Shaw, she believed that Kate had been manipulated by Mary St. Clair and that she was now being manipulated by Dr. Steward.

48 M. S. Land, letter to George Carmack, Nov. 23, 1900, George W. Carmack papers.

49 T. S. Hawkins, letter to John Durst, Feb. 6, 1901, George W. Carmack papers.

50 A. D. Shaw, letter to John Durst, Nov. 28, 1900, George W. Carmack papers.

51 George Carmack, letter to Rose Watson, Dec. 5, 1900, George W. Carmack papers.

52 George Carmack, letter to Rose Watson, Dec. 7, 1900, George W. Carmack papers.

53 George Carmack, letter to Rose Watson, Dec. 8, 1900, George W. Carmack papers.

54 George Carmack, letter to Rose Watson, Dec. 14, 1900, George W. Carmack papers.

55 George Carmack, letter to Rose Watson, Dec. 9, 1900, George W. Carmack papers. One of these letters was not from a neighbor but from Miss Moore, who did little to disguise her self-interest in Kate's situation. As if Kate were dictating, she wrote to George, "I want to learn to read and write, so people cannot cheat me so. If I could play on the piano, and talk good English, you would like me better. Rosa told me you got a divorce from me, in Seattle, and that you would never see me again. She tells Mary and Graphie I am an old Indian, and no good." Through Miss Moore, Kate says she feels jailed among George's family, and that she needs an eye doctor and money for the girls. She tells George she wants a big house in Los Angeles, "a good city," where "some nice Christian lady live with me and teach us," adding that as it happened, Miss Moore was a missionary and a teacher and a music teacher—in short, the perfect person to share a comfortable allowance with Kate. Mary Land, sister-in-law of George Mankins, wrote more

magnanimously. "She [Kate] has the respect and love of the whole community. It is a great curse for a man to be rich. I would advise you to come amediatly & look after you wife. Why should those woman keep you prisoner there? Let them know that they cant come between you & your wife. I hear they give you Absinthe. Do not drink it. Ask a doctor the effects of it, & take Kates part because she is good & pure & she is swindled by designing treacherous people who want to keep you two a part."

CHAPTER SEVENTEEN

1 At Kate's request, the Bank of Hollister confirmed that her gold nugget necklace was still being held there; Rose had set it aside for Kate when George asked her to empty the safe deposit box and send the contents to him. Mrs. Nielson made sure that Miss Moore (the "poor creature," Mrs. Nielson called her) was turned out of Kate's house, and that she took with her nothing that belonged to Kate.

2 Kate Carmack via Miss Moore, letter to John Durst, Dec. 9, 1900, George W. Carmack papers. Miss Moore's concern—later events would prove it unfounded—was that Rose was conspiring with George to ensure that Graphie was declared illegitimate, so that George's inheritance would go to Rose instead of his daughter.

3 George Carmack, letter to Rose Watson, Jan. 29, 1901, George W. Carmack papers.

4 "Carmack Denies Charges." *Daily Klondike Nugget*, Feb. 23, 1901.

5 Ibid.

6 Argument submitted Dec. 7, 1923 to the Superior Court of the State of Washington for King County, in the matter of the estate of George W. Carmack, deceased, George W. Carmack papers.

7 Mrs. Durst, letter to Mrs. Kate Carmack c/o John Nielsen, Feb. 10, 1901, George W. Carmack papers.

8 A.D. Shaw, letter to John H. Durst, March 6, 1901, George W. Carmack papers.

9 George Carmack, letter to Rose Watson, May 3, 1901, George W. Carmack papers.

10 McClellan, *My Old People Say*, 369–370.

11 Pursuant to this question, Durst contacted William Ogilvie, the Canadian surveyor who had been appointed Commissioner of Dawson City. Ogilvie affirmed that both George and Kate Carmack had worked for him in 1887, packing over the Chilkoot Trail, and that they had lived together as husband and wife, "understood to be so according to Indian custom." In addition to the packing they did for him, Ogilvie said he had seen Kate and George at Fort Selkirk, at Fortymile, and many times when he was surveying claims along Bonanza and Eldorado creeks. "They appeared to get along very well together," he wrote, "but I will say this from my knowledge of them both that neither one can afford to throw many stones at the other."

12 Coates, *Best Left as Indians*, 88. The question of whether such marriages were legitimate arose in connection with Native women gaining—by virtue of their marriages to white men—exemption under the Indian Act, which allowed them to drink legally. According to Coates, "The government argued—but did not enforce the point—that marriages conducted under Native rites were legally binding."

13 Mrs. C. S. Danks, letter to John Durst, June 8, 1901, George W. Carmack papers.

14 Mrs. C. S. Danks, letter to John Durst, July 11, 1901, George W. Carmack papers.

15 Mrs. Danks begged Durst to send some word of how the case was progressing. She also wrote to George Carmack directly, following up on a suggestion by Bishop Bompas that George surely had money to help Mary Wilson return to "her friends in the Klondike." But solely on the basis of the Hollister postmark, George refused the letter

16 The attorney was L. W. Jefferson, who had the respect of the business community. He offered to assist Durst if it would be helpful, adding that he had no definite contract with Kate. "In fact she understands so little," he wrote to Durst, "I do not like to have her sign anything."

17 *Hollister Free Lance*, July 19, 1900.

18 R. H. Lindsay, letter to John Durst. July 31, 1901, George W. Carmack papers. While she waited in Seattle, Kate retained yet another attorney, even as Durst, unbeknownst to her, was also seeking the help of R. H. Lindsay, whose work on a recent divorce case promised to be helpful in the Carmack affair.

19 R. H. Lindsay, letter to John Durst. Sept. 2, 1901, George W. Carmack papers.

20 *Klondike Nugget*, April 1, 1900.

21 Johnny Johns, SJFC Oral History Project.

22 H. A. Cody, An Apostle of the North: Memoirs of the Right Reverend William Carpenter Bompas, D.D. (London: Seeley, 1908), accessed Nov. 15, 2013, Project Canterbury http://anglicanhistory.org/canada/bompas/cody1908/17.html.

23 Ibid.

24 Caribou Crossing was a town name that lasted only a few years; when Bishop Bompas became frustrated with mail that got misdirected to two other Canadian communities named Caribou, he shortened it to Carcross.

25 Archer, *A Heroine of the North*.

26 Ibid.

27 *The Daily Alaskan*, Feb. 6, 1900. Shotridge says the potlatch was planned for August, but according to Hinckley it did not take place until October, with Jim and Kate likely in attendance.

28 Hinckley, 280–281.

CHAPTER EIGHTEEN

1 Mrs. George Carmack by H. M. Wooldridge, letter to John Durst, Nov. 7, 1901.

2 Sidney, *Life Lived Like a Story*, 44–48. Animal Mother is also called "Game Mother."

3 Angela Sidney, *Place Names of the Tagish Region: Southern Yukon* (Whitehorse, Yukon: Yukon Native Languages Project and Council for Yukon Indians, 1980).

4 Archer, 28.

5 Anglican Church records, Carcross Baptisms, 1902, Yukon Archives. In the baptismal records, Kate's birth year is given as 1954, and her father's name is given as "Tagish John"; he was actually a cousin.

6 Thornton, 70–71.

7 Henry T. Cook, letter to Jim Mason, undated, Yukon Archives. Jim and Henry referred to each other as "brothers-in-law"; the connection appears to have been through Jim's Tlingit wife, not on the Tagish side. The Tagish say the sum lost was $50,000, but in this letter, the figure $7,000 is given.

8 Charlie filed the discovery claim. At this point, if not before, Jim and Charlie would have discovered that, contrary to what George Carmack told them, Indians could indeed file discovery claims.

9 Johnny Johns, SJFC Oral History, 1973.

10 An Englishman made an even larger investment than Jim, sinking $300,000 into the Bullion Mining Company, and a Vancouver company made plans to invest $1 million in building a railway from Whitehorse to Kluane.

11 "The Gold Rush That Never Was," *Yukon News*, accessed Nov. 14, 2013, http://www.yukon-news.com/letters-opinions/the-gold-rush-that-never-was.

12 Somehow this robe ended up with the Peele family in Vancouver in 1908. Peele's granddaughter Vivian later returned it to the MacBride Museum in Whitehorse.

13 Mary (Minnie) Wilson, letter to Rose Watson Curtis, Feb. 17, 1906, George W. Carmack papers. When George first left Kate, Jake Watson asked George for a loan to pay off a mortgage, but George refused. The nature of the correspondence between Jake and Kate is unknown.

14 Ida Calmagene, interviewed August 18, 2013.

15 Cody, accessed 11/15/2013 at http://anglicanhistory.org/canada/bompas/cody1908/17.html.

16 Ibid.

17 Coates, *Best Left as Indians*, 147.

18 W. L Phelps papers, Yukon Archives, Box I, folder 1, 2–4.

19 Archer, Project Canterbury.

20 I.O. Stringer, letter to Sadie Stringer, June 16, 1906, Yukon Archives. My thanks to lian goodall for her assistance with the Stringer files.

21 Ibid.

22 Clarke, 19–22.

23 McClellan, *My Old People Say*, 360.

24 Coates, *Land of the Midnight Sun*, 155.

25 P. R. Peele, letter to W. L. Phelps, Feb. 7, 1916, Yukon Archives.

26 W. L. Phelps, letter to P. R. Peele, March 30, 1916, Yukon Archives.

27 W. L. Phelps, letter to P. R. Peele, May 19, 1916, Yukon Archives.

28 James Mason Last Will and Testament, January 11, 1904. Yukon Archives, W.L. Phelps Papers, Box 1, Folder 1, 2–4.

29 As noted by Julie Cruikshank (email Feb. 6, 2013): "The name 'Dawson' Charlie was given to him because he went to Dawson

City with his uncle . . . whereas Tagish Charlie stayed closer to home. People used to sometimes joke with me about how 'white people name places after people, but Indians name people after places.'"

30 In their writings, many continue to refer to Kate's nephew as "Tagish Charlie."

31 *Whitehorse Daily Evening News*, July 12, 1904.

32 Ibid.

33 Fred Boss, interviewed by James Albert Johnson. However, a search of the police reports in Dawson newspapers between Oct. 1899 and Jan. 1901 turned up no arrest records for Jim.

34 "It wasn't that he wanted liquor that much," said Johnny Johns, Jim's cousin once removed. "He was a joker and just wanted to have some fun. The Police were breaking up all those bottles, and Jim was trying to get closer to the liquor being poured off the bridge, taking one drink after another. They couldn't put him in jail for drinking [the] Carcross River."

35 Reported among the Tagish people to have been standoffish (interview, Ida Calmagene, Aug. 18, 2013), Jim's wife returned to the coast to live among her own people.

36 William Bompas, letter to I. O. Stringer, March 13, 1905. In a taped interview (Smith, *Keish*), Johnny Johns concurred: "He [Jim] got talked out of a lot of money."

37 In *Beneath the Surface: Thirty Years of Historical Archaeology in Skagway, Alaska* (National Park Service, 2011), Becky M. Saleeby discusses the large number of medicine bottles discarded in the privy belonging to Minnie and Ben Moore, speculating that either Ben or Minnie, his Tlingit wife, may have been addicted to either the alcohol or opiates in the medicinals.

38 "Booze His Enemy," *Weekly Star*, Whitehorse, Yukon Territory, Jan. 1, 1909.

39 Ibid.

40 Coates, *Best Left as Indians*, 94.

41 Following the success of the 1893 Columbian World Exposition in Chicago, world's fairs had become increasingly popular. In 1905, Portland had hosted a huge exposition to commemorate the centennial of the Lewis and Clark Exposition, which had opened Native lands to white occupation, ultimately resulting in the resettlement of American tribes on reservations. In attendance at the Portland fair was Louis Shotridge, grandson of the Chilkat chief, Koh'klux.

Born at Klukwan in 1882, he was educated at the Haines Mission School, where like Susie George, he became fluent in English, as did his wife Kaatkwaaxsnéi, called Florence. He was eventually hired by a museum to collect Tlingit artifacts and died under mysterious circumstances.

42 Smith, *Life Lived Like a Story*, 189.

43 I. O. Stringer, letter to Sadie Stringer, May 9, 1909, I.O. Stringer letters, General Synod Archives, Anglican Church of Canada. My thanks to lian goodall for directing me to this source.

44 Ibid.

45 "Carmack's Old Story," *Dawson Daily News*, July 2, 1909.

46 "Northern Indians and Scenes at the Seattle Fair, *Los Angeles Herald*, May 31, 1909; also Shauna O'Heilly and Bennan O'Reilly, *Alaska Yukon Pacific Exposition* (San Francisco: Arcadia Publishing, 2009), 69 and 76.

47 Ibid.

48 Ibid.

CHAPTER NINETEEN

1 *Seattle Daily Times*, July 11, 1910.

2 Grace, 94.

3 Minnie (Mary) Wilson, letter to Rose Carmack, Feb. 19, 1906, George W. Carmack papers.

4 Smith, Keish documentary.

5 Kitty Smith, *Life Lived Like a Story*, 246.

6 For years Marguerite had been corresponding with the town's tax collector over taxes in the amount of $4.50 per year, on which interest kept accruing because she failed to pay on time. Eager to sell the property, she told the tax collector that if he found a buyer, he could keep anything he got for it over $125.

7 Patsy Henderson and Aubrey Simmons, interviewed by James Albert Johnson for *George Carmack*.

8 Sidney, *Life Lived Like a Story*, 93.

9 Ibid.

10 Stan B. Cohen, *The White Pass and Yukon Route* (Pictorial Histories, 1980), 64.

11 McClellan, *Part of the Land, Part of the Water,* 128. At the MacBride museum, the cape is identified as being made of squirrel pelts, but this appears to be a reference to ground squirrels, or gophers.
12 McClellan, *My Old People Say,* 264.
13 "The Woman behind the Cape," *Yukon News,* July 28, 2008.
14 Van Kempen, Ukjese. History of Yukon First Nations Art. Unpublished doctoral thesis, 50, 161, and 233. My thanks to Lian Goodall for locating this source.
15 Wilkie, "Potlatches."
16 McClellan, *Part of the Land, Part of the Water,* 216–219 and Sidney, *Life Lived Like a Story,* 91–93, for this and preceding paragraphs on the 1912 potlatch in Carcross.
17 "Skookum Jim's Find Declared by Miner to Be Indian Bunco." *Seattle Daily Times,* May 8, 1913.
18 George Carmack, letter to Rose Watson, Oct. 15, 1900, George W. Carmack papers.
19 Johnny Johns, SJFC Oral History Project, 1973.
20 Ibid.
21 P. R. Peele, letter to W. R. Phelps, Feb. 7, 1916, Phelps papers, Yukon Archives. According to the terms of Jim's final will, funds from Daisy's trust were to be invested upon her death, with the income to be devoted to "assisting needy and deserving Indians in the said Territory in any way or manner said trustees [the Anglican bishop and Commissioner] may deem best."
22 Released from the hospital, Jim visited to Tenakee Hot Springs, where the mineral waters were said to have a healing effect. His intent was to go from there to Teslin, where he had cached his furs and rifles along a trail. But he was too ill.
23 Coates, *Best Left as Indians,* 95.
24 P. R. Peele, letter to W. L. Phelps, May 26, 1916. Yukon Archives.
25 "The Discoverer of the Klondike Died a Pauper," *Kansas City Star.* Sept. 10, 1916.
26 Sidney, *Life Lived Like a Story,* 101.
27 Kate Carmack, letter to I. O. Stringer, April 18, 1917, Smith, *Keish* (documentary).
28 I. O. Stringer, letter to Daisy Mason, Nov. 14, 1917, Yukon Archives.
29 Many archival photos purporting to be of Kate Carmack are clearly not of her at all. Ida Calmagene, granddaughter of Maria Johns, married to Tagish John, Kate's cousin, affirmed that this image is authentic. Having portrayed Kate as a shrewish drunk, George

Carmack's biographer said this about her as she appears in this photo, taken in 1919, when Kate was likely in her fifties: "A beautiful girl just out of her teens when she met Carmack, she retained her good looks well into her 30s but uncontrolled drinking caused that beauty to fade. By the time she was 40 she had gained weight, become slovenly in appearance, and aged rapidly."

30 Charlotte Cameron, *A Cheechako in Alaska* (Nabu Press, 2011 reprint), Kindle edition. Cameron describes the pictures of the Native men as "two ferocious-looking Indian chiefs."

31 Coates, *Best Left as Indians*, 173.

32 Cameron.

33 Ibid.

34 Ibid.

35 John Hartman, letter to Ethel Becker, University of Washington Libraries, Biography file: George Carmack.

36 After the publication of Cameron's book, this "most romantic version" of the Klondike discovery appeared in a New York Post article on Cameron's Alaska travels. In the newspaper piece, Kate is said to have claimed credit for discovering gold at the Klondike (*New York Post*, Dec. 12, 1920). In the same article, Cameron describes Kate as wearing a dress in which the entire bodice is made of gold. She also spoke of Jim and Charlie as "half-breeds."

37 McClellan, *Part of the Land, Part of the Water*, 209.

38 Gina Kolata, *Flu: The Story of the Great Influenza Epidemic of 1918 and the Search for the Virus That Caused It* (New York: Touchstone, 2001), 9.

39 Ibid, 12.

40 Ibid, 7.

41 McClellan, *Part of the Land, Part of the Water*, 212.

42 Ida Calmagene, interview Aug. 18, 2013.

43 "Kate Carmack, Woman Discoverer of Bonanza, and Her Strange Career," *Dawson Daily News*, April 15, 1920.

44 Ida Calmagene, interview Aug. 18, 2013.

EPILOGUE

1 McClellan, *Part of the Land, Part of the Water*, 213. In *Life Lived Like a Story*, Angela Sidney recalls only six people (including Kate) living in Carcross one year before Kate's death.

2 Johnny Johns—Our Stories, Carcross-Tagish First Nations, accessed Nov. 26, 2013, http://www.ctfn.ca/video-4-valleys-a-look-at-the-carcross-tagish-first-nation-2.

3 Ibid.

4 John Hartman, letter to Ethel Becker, University of Washington Libraries, Biography file: George Carmack.

5 James Albert Johnson interview with Graphie Grace Carmack.

6 Yukon Order of Pioneers, accessed June 19, 2013, http://www.yukon-seniors-and-elders.org/yukonorder/yukonorder.home.htm. Under the original charter, only men who had arrived in the Yukon prior to 1889 were allowed to join.

7 "The Sinking of the Steamship Islander," *New York Times*, Aug. 19, 1901.

8 "Alaska Miners Attend Banquet," *San Francisco Call*, March 2, 1911.

9 *Dawson Daily News*, May 21, 1904.

10 "George Carmack Passes Away in City Hospital," *Vancouver Sun*, June 6, 1922. Pneumonia has many causes, one of which is tuberculosis.

11 Graphie Grace Carmack, interviewed by James Johnson. After receiving the telegram, Rose promptly removed from her will a clause that left her gold nugget necklace to Graphie's daughter, also named Marguerite.

12 Supreme Court of the State of Washington, In the Matter of the estate of George Washington Carmack, Brief of Respondent, Hermon S. Frye, Administrator, George W. Carmack papers.

13 Superior Court of the State of Washington for King County, Graphie Grace Saftig and Rose Curtis vs. Marguerite Carmack, filed Sept. 22, 1922, George W. Carmack papers.

14 Supreme Court of the State of Washington, In the Matter of the estate of George Washington Carmack, Brief of Respondent, Hermon S. Frye, Administrator, George W. Carmack papers.

15 When questioned as to where she got the cigars, Marguerite testified that she bought them on the streets of Dawson and resold them in her store, netting $55,000 in profits.

16 Superior Court of the State of Washington in and for King County in Probate in the Matter of the Estate of George Washington Carmack, No. 31527, Findings of Fact and Conclusion of Law, Jan. 19, 1924, George W. Carmack papers.

17 Supreme Court of the State of Washington, In the Matter of the Estate of George Washington Carmack, Hermon S. Frye as

Administrator with the Will Annexed of George Washington Carmack, deceased, et al, Respondents, vs. Marguerite Carmack, Appellant, Case 18829, Appellant's Abstract of Record, George W. Carmack papers.

18 Ibid.

19 Supreme Court of the State of Washington, In the Matter of the Estate of George Washington Carmack, Hermon S. Frye as Administrator with the Will Annexed of George Washington Carmack, deceased, et al, Respondents, vs. Marguerite Carmack, Appellant, Case 18829, Supplemental Abstract of Respondents, George W. Carmack papers.

20 Graphie Grace Saftig interviewed by James Johnson, undated.

21 Johnson, 178.

22 Graphie Grace interviewed by James Johnson.

23 Haines, Jan Harper. "Triumph to Tragedy: The Short Life of Walter Harper." Sealaska, accessed Nov. 18, 2014, http://www.sealaska.com/docs/IO/1903/walter-harper.pdf.

24 Johnny Johns—Our Stories. Carcross-Tagish First Nations, accessed Nov. 26, 2013, http://www.ctfn.ca/video-4-valleys-a-look-at-the-carcross-tagish-first-nation-2

25 Ibid.

26 Thomas Martindale, *Hunting in the Upper Yukon* (Philadelphia: G. W. Jacobs and Company, 1913), 286–289

27 Ibid.

28 "A Family Remembers Louise Davis." *Whitehorse Star*, Sept. 2, 1971.

29 *Whitehorse Star*, Oct. 2, 1990.

30 Sarah Davison, "George Carmack's grandson going strong at 80," *The Whitehorse Star*, Sept. 21, 1900.

31 Justin Ferbey. "Arrival, Survival, and Revival." Tedx, Whitehorse. Feb. 5, 2013; this and previous paragraphs about the Carcross-Tagish First Nation.

32 Ibid.

33 Carcross-Tagish First Nation Elders Statement, accessed Dec. 4, 2013, http://www.ctfn.ca/index.php/elders.

BIBLIOGRAPHY

BIBLIOGRAPHICAL NOTE

Anyone reads more than a book or two on the Klondike becomes quickly aware of how difficult it is to sort through contradictory accounts—and flat-out lies—to piece together what actually happened. The lies were told mostly out of eagerness and greed (or as some would say, opportunity)—guides to the Klondike written by those who had never been there; "news" articles written during the "anything goes" era of Yellow Journalism. The contradictions come not only from the usual differences in perspective but also from the way accounts were passed along, person to person, in a vast and sparsely populated region.

In researching this book, I poured through newspapers and archival files as the Yukon Archives in Whitehorse, the Dawson Museum Archives in Dawson City, the University of Washington Special Collections, and the San Benito County Historical Society. I also met with Kate Carmack's descendants, including her great-grandson, Tom Saftig, and Carcross-Tagish First Nations elders Annie Auston and Ida Calmagene. In San Benito County, where George abandoned Kate, I visited a restored ranch from the era and walked the streets of Hollister. Using nineteenth century plat maps, I located the portion of Cottonwood Road where Kate spent two winters, a place that feels little changed since the end of the nineteenth century.

For an understanding of what it means to live off the land and adapt to the demands of a harsh climate, I've drawn on thirty-six years of living in Alaska, especially the years I spent in Yup'ik villages in the Kuskokwim River delta, where I learned about the impact of change on indigenous cultures and also what it means to be an outsider. I've also visited the places Kate lived in the North—Tagish, Marsh Lake, Haines, Dyea, the Chilkoot Trail, Carcross, the Forty Mile district, Fort Selkirk, Carmacks, Dawson City, and Bonanza Creek—places carved from a swath of wilderness so vast and beautiful that it's nearly impossible to put into words.

ARTICLES

"About Athabaskan." Research Institute for Languages and Cultures of Asia and Africa, Tokyo University of Foreign Studies, accessed September 25, 2012, http://www.aa.tufs.ac.jp/Athabaskan/about_e.html.

"Alaska Miners Attend Banquet," *San Francisco Call*, March 2, 1911.

"Badly Beaten by His Indian Wife," *San Francisco Call*, July 7, 1899.

"Booze His Enemy," *Weekly Star*, Whitehorse, Yukon Territory, Jan. 1, 1909.

"Came by Topeka," *Seattle Daily Times*, July 16, 1900.

"Carmack's Old Story," *Dawson Daily News*, July 2, 1909.

"Dawson Visited by Another Fire," *Seattle Times*, July 3, 1899.

"Discovered Gold on Bonanza," *San Francisco Call*, Sept. 16, 1898.

"Early Traders and Steamboats," *Fortymile Interpreters Manual*, Tr'ondëk Heritage, accessed June 18, 2013, http://Tr'ondëkheritage.com/images/pdfs/Early_Traders.pdf.

"Four Million Dollars: Rich Cargo of Treasure Ship Roanoke from St. Michael," *Seattle Post-Intelligencer*, Aug. 31, 1898.

"From Klondike to Paris," *Seattle Post-Intelligencer*, Sept. 1, 1898.

"George Carmack Passes Away in City Hospital," *Vancouver Sun*, June 6, 1922.

"How the Klondike Was Discovered," *Omaha World Herald*, September 11, 1898.

"Indian Bunco." *Seattle Daily Times*, July 11, 1910.

"Johnny Johns Recalls Skookum Jim," *The Yukon News*, Dec. 5 and Dec. 12, 1973.

"Kate Carmack, Woman Discoverer of Bonanza, and Her Strange Career," *Dawson Daily News*, April 15, 1920.

"Lowell Glacier." Yukon Geological Survey, accessed September 26, 2012, http://www.geology.gov.yk.ca/821.html.

"Million and a Half," *The San Juan Islander*, September 8, 1898.

"Mr. and Mrs. Geo. Carmack," *Alaska Dispatch*, Oct. 29, 1900.

"Northern Indians and Scenes at the Seattle Fair," *Los Angeles Herald*, May 31, 1909.

"Nugget Gulch." US Geological Survey, accessed Feb. 15, 2013, http://mrdata.usgs.gov/ardf/show-ardf.php?ardf_num=EA087.

"Reindeer History in Alaska." School of Natural Resources and Agricultural Science, University of Alaska Fairbanks, accessed Oct. 22, 2013, http://reindeer.salrm.uaf.edu/about_reindeer/history.php.

"Returning Adventurers," *New York Times*, August 31, 1898.

"Selling Seattle." National Park Service, Klondike Gold Rush, Seattle Unit, accessed Oct. 22, 2013, http://www.nps.gov/klse/forteachers/hrs2.htm. Accessed Oct. 22.

"Sensational Suit: Klondike Miner Millionaire Opposes Divorce," *San Jose Evening News*, Oct. 3, 1900.

"Skookum Jim Robbed of a Small Fortune," *Seattle Post-Intelligencer*, Aug. 31, 1898.

"Skookum Jim's Find Declared by Miner to Be Indian Bunco," *Seattle Daily Times*, May 8, 1913.

"Tagish Charlie's Troubles," *Seattle Post-Intelligencer*, July 27, 1899.

"Tagish Kate," *The Semi-Weekly Nugget*, Dawson, YT, November 11, 1900.

"Telegraphic Ticks," *The Saginaw Evening News*, July 8, 1899.

"Ten Tons of Gold from the Frozen North," *Tacoma Daily News*, August 31, 1898.

"The Gold Rush That Never Was," *Yukon News*, accessed Nov. 14, 2013, http://www.yukon-news.com/letters-opinions/the-gold-rush-that-never-was.

"The Romance of Indian Kate Who Showed the Gold of the Klondike to George Carmack," *San Francisco Call*, Volume 87, Number 143, October 21, 1900.

"The Sinking of the Steamship Islander," *New York Times*, Aug. 19, 1901.

"The Woman behind the Cape," *Yukon News*, July 28, 2008.

"They'll Have a Hot Time in This Old Town," *San Francisco Call*, Jan. 26, 1899.

"Threw Money at the Crowd: Returned Klondiker and His Alaska Wife Amuse the People of Seattle," *The Reading Eagle*, November 30, 1898.

"Throwing Away Money," *Seattle Post-Intelligencer*, Sept. 2, 1898.

"Tuberculosis in Europe and North America 1800–1922," Contagion: Historical Views of Diseases and Epidemics, accessed Nov. 4, 2013, http://ocp.hul.harvard.edu/contagion/tuberculosis.html.

"Wife of a Discoverer of the Klondike and her Indian Brother Create a Disturbance," *Seattle Post-Intelligencer*, July 26, 1899.

"WP&YR Facts," accessed Oct. 23, 2013, http://www.wpyr.com/history/facts.html.

"Yukon Order of Pioneers," accessed June 19, 2013, http://www.yukon-seniors-and-elders.org/yukonorder/yukonorder.home.htm.

1901 Canadian census records, accessed June 25, 2014, http://automatedgenealogy.com/census/DisplayHousehold.jsp?sdid=9235&household=17.

Abel, Kerry M. "COX, CHARLOTTE SELINA," in EN:UNDEF:public_citation_publication, vol. 14, University of Toronto/Université Laval, 2003–, accessed June 18, 2014, http://www.biographi.ca/en/bio/cox_charlotte_selina_14E.html.

Betts, Martha F. "Chilkat and Chilkoot Rivers Subsistence Eulachon Fishery," Division of Subsistence Technical Paper No. 213.

Burke, W. J. Letter in the *San Francisco Chronicle*, Feb. 8, 1926.

Cooperman M. B. "Chronic Tuberculosis Polyarthritis." *Ann Surg.*, 1932 Dec; 96(6):1065–1077.

Dawson Daily News, May 21, 1904.

Davison, Sarah. "George Carmack's grandson going strong at 80," *The Whitehorse Star*, Sept. 21, 1900.

Green, Rayna. "The Pocahontas Perplex: The Image of Indian Women in American Culture," *Massachusetts Review* 27, no. 4 (1975).

Hollister Free Lance, April 13, 1900.

Hollister Free Lance, Feb. 16, 1900.

Hollister Free Lance, March 30, 1900.

Hollister Free Lance, Nov. 9, 1900.

Hollister Free Lance, Oct. 12, 1900.

Hollister Free Lance, Oct. 5, 1900.

Klondike Nugget, April 1, 1900.

Little, James R. "Squaw Kate," *Alaska Life*, March, 1943.

McClellan, Catharine. "Wealth Woman and Frogs among the Tagish Indians." *Anthropos 58* (1963), Yukon Archives PAM 1963-0005.

McDermott, John D. "Were They Really Rogues? Desertion in the Nineteenth Century US Army," *Nebraska History 78* (1997), 165–174, accessed Dec. 18, 2012, http://www.nebraskahistory.org/publish/publicat/history/full-text/1978-3-NSHS_100_Years.pdf.

Moore, Virgil. "George W. Carmack," *The Klondike News*, April 1, 1898.

San Francisco Call, Jan. 1, 1900.

Seattle Post-Intelligencer, Sept. 21, 1899.

Shortt, Ken. "How Gold was discovered in the Klondike," *Klondike '73* publication.
Smith, Karan. "Gold in the Veins," *The Yukon News*, August 26, 1998.
The Daily Alaskan, Feb. 6, 1900.
The Klondike News, Vol. 1, No. 1, April 1, 1898.
Whitehorse Daily Evening News, July 12, 1904.
Whitehorse Star, Oct. 2, 1990.

BOOKS AND PAMPHLETS

Adney, Tappan. *The Klondike Stampede*. Vancouver: UBC Press, 1997.
Alaska Boundary Tribunal, the Case of the United States. US Government Printing Office, 1903.
Alaska-Yukon Gold Book: A Roster of the Progressive Men And Women Who Were the Argonauts of the Klondike Gold Stampede and Those Who Are Identified with the Pioneer Days and Subsequent Development of Alaska and the Yukon Territory. Seattle: Sourdough Stampede Association, 1930.
Backhouse, Frances. *Women of the Klondike*. Vancouver: Whitecap Books, 2010.
Barrows, Henry D., and Luther A. Ingersoll. *Memorial and Biographical History of the Coast Counties of Central California*. Chicago: The Lewis Publishing Company, 1893.
Beck, Mary Giraudo. *Shamans and Kushtakas: Northwest Tales of the Supernatural*. Anchorage: Alaska Northwest Books, 2003.
Berton, Pierre. *The Klondike Fever*. New York: Carroll and Graf, 1958.
Bompas, Charlotte Selina. *A Heroine of the North. Memoirs of Charlotte Selina Bompas (1830–1917), Wife of the First Bishop of Selkirk (Yukon), With Extracts from Her Journal and Letters*, compiled by S.A. Archer. London: SPCK, 1929, Project Canterbury, accessed Oct. 7, 2013, http://anglicanhistory.org/women/bompas/.
Brands, H. W. *The Reckless Decade*. Chicago: University of Chicago Press, 1995.
Cameron, Charlotte. *A Cheechako in Alaska*. Nabu Press, 2011 reprint, Kindle edition.
Chase, Will. *The Reminiscences of Captain Billie Moore*. Kansas City: Burton Publishing, 1947.
Clarke, Chris, and the K'ahacha Group, *Tr'ëhuhch'in Näwtr'udäh'a: Finding Our Way Home*. Dawson City: Tr'ondëk Hwëch'in, 2009.

Coates, Ken S. *Best Left as Indians*. Montreal: McGill-Queen's University Press, 1991.

Coates, Ken S., and William R. Morrison. *Land of the Midnight Sun*. Montreal: McGill-Queen's University Press, 2005.

Cody, H. A. *An Apostle of the North: Memoirs of the Right Reverend William Carpenter Bompas, D.D.* (London: Seeley, 1908), accessed Nov. 15, 2013, Project Canterbury http://anglicanhistory.org/canada/bompas/cody1908/17.html.

Cohen, Stan B. *The White Pass and Yukon Route*. Missoula, MT: Pictorial Histories, 1980.

Cohen, Stan B. *Queen City of the North*. Missoula, MT: Pictorial Histories Publishing, 1990.

Cruikshank, Julie, in collaboration with Angela Sidney, Kitty Smith, and Annie Ned. *Life Lived Like a Story*. Lincoln: University of Nebraska Press, 1995.

Cruikshank, Julie. *Dan Dha Ts'edenintth'e: Reading Voices*. Vancouver: Douglas and McIntyre, 1991.

Cruikshank, Julie. *The Social Life of Stories: Narrative and Knowledge in the Yukon Territory*. Lincoln: University of Nebraska Press, 1998.

Dauenhauer, Nora, and Richard. *Haa Kusteeyi: Our Culture: Tlingit Life Stories*. Seattle: University of Washington Press, 1994.

Dobrowolsky, Helene. *Law of the Yukon: A History of the Mounted Police in the Yukon*. Madeira Park, BC: Lost Moose Publishing, 2013.

Edwards, Keri. *Dictionary of Tlingit*. Juneau, Alaska: Sealaska Heritage Institute, 2009.

Fortuine, Robert. *Chills and Fevers: Health and Disease in Early Alaska*. Fairbanks: University of Alaska Press: 1989.

Gates, Michael. *Gold at Forty Mile Creek*. Vancouver: UBC Press, 1994.

Gates, Michael. *History Hunting in the Yukon*. British Columbia: Harbour Publishing, 2010.

Grace, Sherill E. *Canada and the Idea of the North*. Montreal: Queen's University Press, 2001.

Greer, Sheila. *Skookum Stories on the Chilkoot/Dyea Trail*. Carcross: Carcross-Tagish First Nation, 1995.

Hare, Greg, and Ruth Gotthardt. *A Look Back in Time: The Archaeology of Fort Selkirk*. Whitehorse: Government of the Yukon, 1996.

Heller, Herbert, ed. *Sourdough Sagas*. New York: Ballantine Books, 1967.

Henderson, Patsy. *Early Days at Caribou Crossing and The Discovery of Gold on the Klondike*, published by Jennie Mae Moyer, 1950.

Hinckley, Ted C. *The Americanization of Alaska, 1867–1897*. Palo Alto, CA: Pacific Books, 1972.

Hitchcock, Mary E. *Two Women in the Klondike*. Fairbanks: University of Alaska Press, 2005.

Hunt, William R. *Whiskey Peddler: Johnny Healy, Northern Frontier Trader*. Mountain Press, 1992.

Jacobs, Margaret D. *White Mother to a Dark Race*. Lincoln: University of Nebraska Press, 2009.

Johnson, James Albert. *George Carmack*. Vancouver: Whitecap Books, 2001.

Jones, Ed, and Star. *All That Glitters*. Whitehorse: Wolf Creek Press, 2005.

Karamanski, Theodore. *Fur Trade and Exploration*. Norman, OK: University of Oklahoma Press, 2010.

Kirchhoff, M. J. *Clondyke: The First Year of the Rush*. Juneau: Alaska Cedar Press, 2010.

Kirchhoff, M. J. *Dyea, Alaska: The Rise and Fall of a Klondike Gold Rush Town*. Juneau: Alaska Cedar Press, 2012.

Kolata, Gina. *Flu: The Story of the Great Influenza Epidemic of 1918 and the Search for the Virus That Caused It*. New York: Touchstone, 2001.

Krause, Aurel. *To the Chukchi Peninsula and to the Tlingit Indians, 1881/82*. University of Alaska Press, 1993.

Martindale, Thomas. *Hunting in the Upper Yukon*. Philadelphia: G. W. Jacobs and Company, 1913.

McClellan, Catharine. *My Old People Say: An Ethnographic Survey of Southern Yukon Territory*. Ottawa: National Museums of Canada, 1975.

McClellan, Catharine. *Part of the Land, Part of the Water*. Toronto: Douglas & McIntyre, 1987.

Mighetto, Lisa, and Marcia Montgomery. *Hard Drive to the Klondike*. Seattle: University of Washington Press, 2002.

Miller, Polly, and Leon Gordon. *Lost Heritage of Alaska*. New York: Bonanza Books, 1967.

Mishler, Craig, and William E. Simeone. *Hän Hwëch'in: People of the River*. Fairbanks: University of Alaska Press, 2004.

Moore, J. Bernard. *Skagway in Days Primeval*. Skagway: Lynn Canal Publishing, reprint 1997.

Morgan, Lael. *Good Time Girls*. Fairbanks, AK: Epicenter Press, 1998.

Morse, Kathryn. *The Nature of Gold*. Seattle: University of Washington Press, 2003.

Muir, John. *Travels in Alaska*. New York: Houghton Mifflin, 1917.

Neufeld, David, and Frank Norris. *Chilkoot Trail: Heritage Route to the Klondike*. Whitehorse: Lost Moose Publishing, 1996.

Nyman, Seidayaa Elizabeth. *Gágiwduł.àt: Brought Forth to Reconfirm: the Legacy of a Taku River Tlingit Clan*. Fairbanks: Alaska Native Language Center, 1993.

Ogilvie, William. *Early Days on the Yukon*. New York: Arno Press, 1974.

Pierce, Marjorie. *East of the Gabilans*. Santa Cruz: Western Tanager Press.

Porsild, Charlotte. *Gamblers and Dreamers*. Vancouver: UBC Press, 1998.

Renner, Louis. *Alaskana Catholica*. Society of Jesus, 2005.

Saleeby, Becky M. *Beneath the Surface: Thirty Years of Historical Archaeology in Skagway, Alaska*. Alaska Regional Office: National Park Service, US Department of the Interior, 2011.

Schwatka, Frederick. *Along Alaska's Great River*. Anchorage: Alaska Northwest Publishing, 1983 (reprint).

Scidmore, Eliza. *Alaska: Its Southern Coast and Sitkan Archipelago*. Boston: D. Lothrop, 1885.

Sidney, Angela. *Place Names of the Tagish Region: Southern Yukon*. Whitehorse, Yukon: Yukon Native Languages Project and Council for Yukon Indians, 1980.

Sidney, Angela. *Haa Shagóon*. Whitehorse, Yukon: Council for Yukon Indians and the Government of Yukon, 1983.

Thornton, Thomas F. *Klondike Gold Rush National Historical Park Ethnographic Overview and Assessment, Final Report*, 2004.

Thornton, Thomas F. *Being and Place among the Tlingit*. Seattle: University of Washington Press, 2008.

Thornton, Thomas F., ed. *Haa Léelk'w Hás Aaní Saax'ú: Our Grandparents' Names on the Land*. Seattle: University of Washington Press, 2012.

White, Richard. *The Middle Ground*. Cambridge, UK: Cambridge University Press, 2011.

Wilde, Jeanne Wilkins. *Tell Me About: A Collection of Memoirs*. Bloomington, IN: iUniverse, 2009.

Wilkie, Rab, and the Skookum Jim Friendship Centre. *Skookum Jim: Native and Non-Native Stories and Views*. Whitehorse, YT: Heritage Branch, Government of Yukon, 1992.

Willard, Carrie, and Mrs. Eva McClintock, ed. *Life in Alaska: Letters of Mrs. Eugene S. Willard*. Philadelphia: Presbyterian Board of Publication, 1884.

Wright, Allan. *Prelude to Bonanza*. Sidney, British Columbia: Gray's Publishing Ltd, 1976.

ARCHIVAL SOURCES

"Billy Johnson Tells His Story." Yukon Territorial Archives, YTA, COR 1096 88/58 SR11 (7) Skookum Jim Oral History Project Fonds, accessed June 19, 2014, www.candianmysteries.ca/sites/klondike/archives/oralhistoryorinterview/3318en.html.

C. Constantine Insp. NWM Police and Act. Gov.t Agt., to The Deputy Minister of the Interior, Ottawa Ont., Nov. 19, 1896, Yukon Archives, Gov 1629, f. 4682.

George W. Carmack papers, Special Collections, University of Washington Libraries.

Hartman, John, letter to Ethel Becker, University of Washington Libraries, Biography file: George Carmack.

His Lordship the Bishop of Selkirk, dated at Buxton Mission, Upper Yukon River, Oct.28, 1895, Yukon Archives, Gov 1629, f. 4682.

I.O. Stringer papers. General Synod Archives, Anglican Church of Canada.

Johns, Johnny. "Skookum Jim's Later Life." Yukon Territorial Archives, 88/58 SR Tape 11-3, 11-4, accessed June 19, 2014, www.canadianmysteries.ca/sites/klondike/archives/oralhistoryorinterview/3286en.html.

Johns, William Douglas. "The Early Yukon, Alaska and the Klondike Discovery as They Were Before the Great Klondike Stampede Swept Away the Old Conditions By One Who Was There," Typescript, Coutts Collection, Yukon Archives #78/69 Box F-89 Folders 20 & 21.

Paul McKenna, unpublished memoir. San Benito County Historical Society, 1983.

Snow, George T., and George Carmack, "My Trip to the Yukon" (unpublished), Alaska State Archives, Snow Family Papers, MS 38.

W.L. Phelps Papers, Yukon Archives.

OTHER SOURCES

Auston, Annie. Interviewed July 28, 2011.

Calmagene, Ida. Interviewed Aug. 18. 2013.

Carcross-Tagish First Nation Elders Statement, accessed Dec. 4, 2013, http://www.ctfn.ca/index.php/elders.

Ferbey, Justin. "Arrival, Survival, and Revival." Tedx, Whitehorse. Feb. 5, 2013.

Johns, Johnny. "Johnny Johns—Our Stories, Carcross-Tagish First Nations," accessed Nov. 26, 2013, http://www.ctfn.ca/video-4-valleys-a-look-at-the-carcross-tagish-first-nation-2.

Murray, T. J. Email Nov. 6, 2013.

Ogilvie, William. "Bonanza and Eldorado Creeks, Survey of Placer Mining Claims 1897. Natural Resources Canada, 1995 reprint.

Smith, Delores, producer. *Keish: A Man Standing in Two Worlds*. Northern Native Broadcasting, 1999.

Van Kempen, Ukjese. *History of Yukon First Nations Art*. Unpublished doctoral thesis.

INDEX

K

L

M